CONTESTING THE MORAL HIGH GROUND

SERIES TWO   IN MEMORY OF GEORGE RAWLYK
DONALD HARMAN AKENSON, EDITOR

Contesting the Moral High Ground

Popular Moralists in Mid-Twentieth-Century Britain

PAUL T. PHILLIPS

McGill-Queen's University Press
Montreal & Kingston • London • Ithaca

© McGill-Queen's University Press 2013

ISBN 978-0-7735-4111-5 (cloth)
ISBN 978-0-7735-4112-2 (paper)

Legal deposit second quarter 2013
Bibliothèque nationale du Québec

Printed in Canada on acid-free paper that is 100% ancient forest free
(100% post-consumer recycled), processed chlorine free

This book has been published with the help of a grant from the Canadian
Federation for the Humanities and Social Sciences, through the Awards to
Scholarly Publications Program, using funds provided by the Social Sciences
and Humanities Research Council of Canada.

McGill-Queen's University Press acknowledges the support of the Canada
Council for the Arts for our publishing program. We also acknowledge the
financial support of the Government of Canada through the Canada Book
Fund for our publishing activities.

Library and Archives Canada Cataloguing in Publication

Phillips, Paul T., 1942–
    Contesting the moral high ground : popular moralists in
mid-twentieth-century Britain / Paul T. Phillips.

(McGill-Queen's studies in the history of religion, ISSN 1181-7445)
Includes bibliographical references and index.
ISBN 978-0-7735-4111-5 (bound). – ISBN 978-0-7735-4112-2 (pbk.)

1. Huxley, Julian, 1887–1975 – Ethics. 2. Russell, Bertrand, 1872–1970 –
Ethics. 3. Muggeridge, Malcolm, 1903–1990 – Ethics. 4. Ward, Barbara,
1914–1981 – Ethics. 5. Ethics – Great Britain – History – 20th century.
6. Ethicists – Great Britain – Intellectual life – 20th century. 7. Great
Britain – Moral conditions – History – 20th century. I. Title. II. Series:
McGill-Queen's studies in the history of religion

BJ1012.P45 2013   170.92'2   C2012-908074-8

This book was typeset by Interscript in 10.5/13 Sabon.

To my grandchildren,
Paul, Maria, Jacqueline, Joseph, Callum,
Thomas, Owen, and Connor

Contents

Acknowledgments

I would like to thank the following libraries for access to sources that made this study possible: The Wellcome Library, London; the Lambeth Palace Library, London; the Houghton Library of Harvard University, Cambridge, Massachusetts; the Westminster Diocesan Archives, London; the Buswell Memorial Library Archives and Special Collections of Wheaton College, Wheaton, Illinois; Georgetown University Library Special Collections, Washington, DC; and the Angus L. Macdonald Library University Archives of St Francis Xavier University, Antigonish, Nova Scotia. For permission to quote from materials in their possession, I thank the Woodson Research Center, Fondren Library, Rice University, Houston, Texas (Julian Sorel Huxley papers); the Bertrand Russell Centre; Mills Memorial Library; McMaster University, Hamilton, Ontario (Bertrand Russell Archives); and the BBC Written Archives Centre, Caversham Park, Reading (BBC copyright documents pertaining to Julian Huxley, Malcolm Muggeridge, and Barbara Ward). I also acknowledge permission to quote from the papers of Julian Huxley from Francis Huxley, Malcolm Muggeridge from Leonard Muggeridge, Barbara Ward from Robert Jackson, and Bertrand Russell from Carl Spadoni, Director, William Ready Division of Archives and Special Collections, McMaster University.

The *Journal of the History of Ideas* (*JHI*) and the University of Pennsylvania Press allowed me to reproduce my article, "One World, One Faith: The Quest for Unity in Julian Huxley's Religion of Evolutionary Humanism," *JHI* 68, number 4 (October 2007), 613–33, as a major portion of my chapter on Julian Huxley. I wish to thank the University Council for Research and the Gatto Chair of

Christian Studies of St Francis Xavier University, and acknowledge the SSHRC Small Institutional Grant (received through my university), for funding my research. This book has been published with the help of a grant from the Canadian Federation for the Humanities and Social Sciences, through the Awards to Scholarly Publications Program, using funds provided by the Social Sciences and Humanities Research Council of Canada.

·Special thanks are owed to Trevor O. Lloyd, professor emeritus of history at the University of Toronto, for his very thorough reading and comments on the first draft of this book. The readers of the manuscript for McGill-Queen's University Press also deserve my thanks. Professor Donald Harman Akenson, senior editor, supplied the initial interest in the manuscript on behalf of the press. I was greatly assisted and guided by editors, Mary-Lynne Ascough and Joan Harcourt. Kathryn Simpson did an excellent job of copyediting. Ryan Van Huijstee, managing editor, provided expert supervision in seeing the book through the later stages of production. In preparing the original manuscript, I thank the very efficient administrative assistant of the St Francis Xavier University History Department, Mary Teasdale Porter.

Lastly, I am always grateful for the steady support of a group of colleagues at St Francis Xavier University – John Blackwell, director of the Research Grants Office; Laurie Stanley-Blackwell; Pat Hogan; Steve Baldner; Jim Cameron and Mary McGillivray, academic vice-president and provost. As always, from first to last, through every step, I thank my wife, Barbara.

Preface

I began my interest in this subject through my personal reactions to life during two decades of recent history. Working backwards, the first was the decade of the twenty-first century, just completed. In that period we witnessed 9/11 and all that unfolded on the international scene, including wars and Western reactions to Islamic fundamentalism. What was ultimately revealed was a considerable degree of religious fanaticism on all sides, as well as the not unrelated wave of New Atheism, with its own possible links to scientific fundamentalism, as some would term it. New, fast-moving developments in genetics and the anatomy of the brain, as well as other scientific discoveries, also raised new questions about the actual physical basis of our thought processes – including belief systems. And everything seemed framed in an aura of heightened fears over a variety of other concerns including the state of the environment, energy shortages, the health of the economy, and even the scandals of the Catholic Church. I also experienced, on a number of occasions, a certain déjà vu having lived in Britain, principally in London, in the late 1960s, when a similar sense of impending societal breakdown generated daily thoughts midst speculation over the outcome of civil strife and international conflict. My apprehension then as today rested on the ambiguity concerning an outcome that could be for good or ill.

It is too early to speak as a historian on the decade just passed. But it would seem, as many good historians have demonstrated, that one can reflect with some authority on the 1960s in the way that impressed some of my students when looking at the 1920s in my first year of teaching in 1969–1970. Some of those students excitedly drew parallels between the 1920s and their experience of the 1960s. I recall my hesitation to place those two decades in juxtaposition. I initially was reluctant to do so again with our own times and the 1960s though I have had first-hand experience of both – one of the blessings of a longer life. I now see all of this as a continuum from times before the 1960s, through the 1960s, to our present situation having completed the first decade of the twenty-first century.

Therefore, in the belief that something could be learned of value for our own times about the contest between belief and unbelief in the mid-twentieth century, I began this study some years ago. More recently, I also returned from formal retirement to take up a bout of teaching, connected with this topic, as Gatto Chair of Christian Studies, for the fall term of 2009 at St Francis Xavier University. A cross-disciplinary course on Belief and Unbelief in Modern Britain, which I taught, proved to be valuable to me in testing some of my theories and I hope for the students involved. Likewise, I found the feedback from the audience during a public lecture in the same period to be extremely useful. What follows here is a book somewhat in the same area but on slightly redefined lines.

Paul T. Phillips
Antigonish, Nova Scotia, Canada

CONTESTING THE MORAL HIGH GROUND

Introduction

It is almost a cliché to trace many of the social attitudes and mores of the early twenty-first century in the Western world, whether in condemnation or exaltation, to the turbulent 1960s. One could even speculate about forty year cycles moving backward to the 1920s, 1880s, and 1840s. Yet there is much truth in that assertion concerning the 1960s, especially if one were to expand the time frame to roughly what the late Arthur Marwick has called the "long sixties,"[1] from the late 1950s to the mid-1970s, keeping the actual 1960s at the core. I follow Marwick's time designation in this book.

This book, however, is not intended to provide a full account of why we are the way we are at the present time in the history of the Western world. Nor can it explore with any authority the entire life of the mind in the mid- to late decades of the twentieth century. Rather it is an historical analysis of the moral philosophies and agendas of a quartet of prominent figures who reached the apogee of their careers during the long sixties in Britain: Julian Huxley (1887–1975), Bertrand Russell (1872–1970), Malcolm Muggeridge (1903–90), and Barbara Ward (1914–81). It is also about the context of these ideas, how they were transmitted to the public, and their impact, in so far as this can be determined. The formulation of their philosophies is also obviously relevant to this study and in all four cases takes us back considerably before the long sixties.

Moral philosophies are about ethics, and through the writings of figures such as Richard Dawkins (*The God Delusion*, 2006), it is currently being claimed in Britain that an ethical system, and a superior one at that, can be produced without the sanction of theism, theism being essentially a lie. Needless to say, this claim has been rigorously challenged by theists in Britain and elsewhere. There is nothing especially new about this situation, going back as it does to the mid-Victorian period, if not the Enlightenment and the Scientific Revolution. But the immediate contours of the present battleground may well have been laid in the period from the 1950s to 1970s, and through the individuals considered here, at least in part. In that period much of the work of the figures chosen for this study either focused directly on the place of ethical systems and religion in society or, more often than not, accomplished the same by discussing a range of issues – from world peace to ecology – that revealed the basis of their various moral visions.

In a sense, Britain had been a bellwether for all modern societies for quite some time. It was noted especially for its status as the cradle of the industrial revolution and for its practical advances of science. But there were additional considerations in the realm of moral philosophy and religion (or irreligion). The themes of the decline of religion, and Christianity in particular; secularization; and related questions have constituted a major cottage industry in the historiography of modern Britain. Originally historians emphasized the shortcomings of the Victorian churches in reaching the working classes, as well as the Crisis of Faith among intellectuals in the mid- to late nineteenth century. To these factors was added the growing disaffection of the middle classes toward institutional churches by the First World War. Questions surrounding the more accurate charting of these developments, the validity of secularization theory, the interpretation of those quantifiable sources of evidence that have been uncovered, and so forth, have led many to argue that the decline of the churches and the so-called advance of secularism, whatever the latter entails, happened much later in the twentieth century. And there is the persistent problem of the links between the decline of Christianity and the advance of organized unbelief which are not at all clear.[2]

Thus it is understandable that moral philosophies derived from religion or irreligion would be particularly relevant in the eyes of historians studying British life of the mid-twentieth century. The consequences of this approach are great, as moral views could affect a variety of decisions by both the state and the general populace. Christine Davies has written of the shift from moralism to "causalism," which influenced lawmakers (legislators and judges) in their determinations of what was good or bad for society at that time.[3] In that sense, postmodernists could certainly argue that the meanings and values were seen more as constructions based upon social utility, having no intrinsic value in themselves.

Issues abounded in Britain perhaps even more than in some of the troubled centres of America or Western Europe as a whole. To the questions arising from post-colonialist responsibilities; Britain's redefined role in the world; its further directions for the welfare state; the growing threat of atomic warfare; the early environmentalism, multiculturalism, and the continuance of class division; the impact of the post-war baby boomers; the drugs; and the state of the economy, liberation movements – working on behalf of women, sexual freedom, as well as racial, ethnic and, in the case of Northern Ireland, religious equality – added new uncertainties. The place of institutional religion itself was hotly contested both in relation to the state and in a variety of other areas of national life where the impact of these new issues would be felt. Frank exchanges of opinion on all of these questions abounded, as did the articulation of underlying values which would inform opinions.

Facing such diversity of opinion, this book is organized around what has been conceived as significant schools of thought, and focuses on high profile representatives of each. Not all schools of thought or ideas have been represented in detail, though some of their exponents do surface. These other groups, not at the centre of this book, include: Socialist Humanists (Ethical Socialists) such as E.P. Thompson and Raymond Williams; communists; Catholic writers such as Evelyn Waugh and Graham Greene; and outspoken individuals for conservatism, liberalism, or pragmatism.

The term which I chose to use in describing the individuals in this book was "popular moralist." I did so after some sharp challenges from colleagues regarding other terms that I had attempted to use. I use the term moralist in the sense in which Stefan Collini used it in his book *Public Moralists* (1995), which focuses upon figures engaged largely in the dissemination of provocative thought for the improvement of society in an earlier period. While the moralists in my study do engage in a didactic role, they should not be confused with the commonly used, more negative idea of a busybody seeking to impose very personal standards upon others. Indeed an assessment of moral behaviour in their private lives has not been an important concern in this book except when something of greater significance was revealed thereby. For example, it is ironic that the two individuals (Russell, Muggeridge) in this book whose moral philosophies most related to the behaviour of individuals, were themselves the least exemplary in their marital relations. While I generally refrain from testing the consistency of their moral philosophies in relation to their personal lives, I am nevertheless conscious of the fact that my writing may reveal my own attitudes and values. I confess that Russell's courage and Ward's perseverance are more appealing than the repentant sinner image Muggeridge created, or the generally more restrained diplomacy of Huxley.

"Intellectual" is certainly another possible descriptor, and is in fact used in this book from time to time, interchangeably with moralist. In his recent book *Absent Minds: Intellectuals in Britain* (2006), Collini also entered into an old debate about the very existence of an English intelligentsia. Collini comes down in favour of using the term, overcoming the peculiarly indigenous aversion to the term – even in its ostensible exemplars. I support Collini's position but I have nevertheless encountered opposition to including some of my figures in this category, even with the loose usage which I am proposing.

And then there are the problems encountered in the more recent use of the term "public intellectual," for example, as described in America by Richard Posner.[4] There, the term has been used to describe the academic who frequently, usually too frequently, expounds in the media either in his or her narrow area of expertise, or at times goes recklessly beyond this domain to satisfy the "sound bite" requirements of broadcast news. In my study, which is rooted in a particular time and place, only some of the figures studied were in fact attached to universities – and even then, not in any consistent way. Encounters in public discourse, through print and broadcast, were of a more prolonged and reflective nature, then, than they are today. It was perhaps the last era of the generalist whose worth was measured by one's erudition, though most of my figures did have specialist training. But the era of intellectuals appealing to an educated elite was already over, replaced by the demand, which Marshall McLuhan describes, to reach a mass audience.

Popularity, even by 1960, became a prerequisite for any thinker who sought to be a public intellectual. No longer could any person who wished, or indeed was driven, to change the course of history rely upon reaching only the more influential. This was the effect of the proliferation of radio and television sets and changes in print media, as well as the sheer democratization of society and the demands of a fuller, more open national life in Britain since the Second World War. Thus "celebrity" is also a word which is applicable in such circumstances. So much more than public intellectuals in the past, success inevitably would lead to being a household name. Whether we like it or not, celebrity is now part of the apparel of the public intellectual. In the case of moral philosophies there has usually been the desire to share its truths with others and thereby build a better world. I argue here that celebrity status was not necessarily the goal of these figures, but still in the service of something more important celebrity could not be shunned completely. While having its enjoyable aspect, it is *not* primarily the desire to be famous for the sake of being famous that drove these popular moralists.

While the main figures discussed in this book were all British, they also became international, or at least transatlantic, in their impact. While it is perhaps more the fashion to see trends in this period flowing west to east, especially from California, and to limit the British invasion of North America to rock stars, this was clearly not the cases. Again much of Britain's international influence can be ascribed to vastly improved communications.

In *A Shrinking Island: Modernism and National Culture in England*[5] Jed Esty contends that the decline of empire contributed to a growing insularity of views among British writers between the wars. If so, this was not evident, nor would it be expected, in the case of the individuals selected for this study. As moralists, while perhaps addressing initially a British audience, their lessons were obviously intended for humanity as a whole, even in some cases going against the immediate interest of their homeland. Their audience was also not intended to be limited to any socio-economic group, though perhaps their style of discourse could lend itself to such categorization by others. I believe that they expressed their ideas in an intended, meaningful, and straightforward way that would reveal some essential truths. It is ironic that it was this very period under study that gave birth to the post-structuralist and ultimately postmodernist discourses that could challenge my assumptions to some degree.

This is not to say that the figures studied here were unaware of the huge cultural changes occurring at this time, or of the manipulations of modern media, especially television. Like some others at the time, they displayed much communications savvy including, in one case, a figure (Muggeridge) who, while seeing much potential evil in the functioning of modern media, nonetheless fully exploited its possibilities. In this study the key individuals who have been selected were major figures in society, enjoying a near celebrity status in their time. Two, Malcolm Muggeridge and Barbara Ward, are associated with Christian moral principles, but differed significantly in their interpretation and application of those principles. They have received less consideration in historical literature than they deserve. The other two figures, Julian Huxley and Bertrand Russell, held non-theistic ethical philosophies, again with some diversity in their elaboration and implementation. Huxley is now being studied beyond scientific circles. Russell has always received attention but not usually from the point of view of his ethical motivations in interacting with others in the various causes of his later years.

At stake for all these individuals was the future direction of society, as well as more immediate decisions about a host of important issues facing society. In garnering support each hoped to mold public opinion. These figures were moral teachers, not merely moral perceivers. But was there some sort of existing consensus or at least majority view on many of the issues that they raised – or did they in fact largely build them?

Statements made since the mid-1970s by contemporaries, and even one survey conducted at the end of the 1960s, reveal very polarized views of the situation by the public at the time. Since then both the best hopes and worse nightmares that were born of this period seem to have taken place, depending on who you consult. This question of legacy and influence within and beyond the confines of Britain will be taken up in the conclusion. Otherwise each moralist chapter will be devoted to one figure in the context of the times.

One final descriptor may appear from time to time in this book – that of "prophet." It is used in the sense of someone displaying considerable insight into a situation, not readily apparent to others. As prophets, or popular moralists, the reputation of these four individuals has risen and fallen in the eyes of many since they died. But let us not forget that even at the time there were many who never held their opinions in high regard. So, in that sense, this book is not intended as, nor could it probably ever be, the last word on these figures.

There is substantial literature on most of these figures. Ronald W. Clark produced a "living biography" of some value fifteen years before Julian Huxley's death. Clark also dealt with Julian Huxley in parts of his later work *The Huxleys* (1968). J.R. Baker produced a biographical memoir three years after Huxley's death which makes interesting points, but is by its very nature incomplete.[6] Krishna R. Dronamraju's life and selected correspondence of Huxley, *If I Am to be Remembered* (1993) is also illuminating in places. It is, however, too brief and focuses in large measure on scientific activities, as befits a work published by World Scientific. Vassiliki Smocovitis successfully places Huxley's scientific endeavours in the broader context of the general scientific community, especially in attempting to unify biology.[7]

Beyond Smocovitis, works connecting Huxley's scientific thought and research to broader intellectual, social, and political considerations include articles by Roger Smith, Michael Freeden, Diane Paul, John R. Durant, Peter J. Bowler, and Paul T. Phillips, as well as the PhD Thesis by Marc Swetlitz.[8] The excellent collection of conference papers entitled *Julian Huxley: Biologist and Statesman of Science* (1992), edited by C. Kenneth Waters and Albert Van Helden, is filled with insights and suggestions for further work, but obviously forms no integrated overall study of the man's life. There are also other works dealing with T.H. Huxley, such as "From Huxley to Huxley: Transformations in the Darwinian Credo," by John C. Greene in his essay collection entitled *Science Ideology and World View* (1981), which raise some interesting perspectives that carry over to his grandson. Broader issues raised in general studies such as those of Ernst Mayr and William Provine and, more recently, Michael Ruse and Bowler, provide useful context for the culture in which popularisers of science operate.[9] Jose Harris's article on "Political Thought and the Welfare State" (1992)[10] has interesting reflections on the continued influence of Idealism[11] in the twentieth century that have applications to Huxley's social philosophy.

Bertrand Russell has, of course, been the focus of a cottage industry of academic productions. Biographies by Ronald Clark, Caroline Moorehead, Anthony Grayling, and Ray Monk are all useful.[12] Studies have begun to link the various areas of his thought and activities to his liberalism, as in Philip Ironside's recent book on his social and political thought.[13] But there is still much to do relating these positions to his moral philosophy. A good exploration of aspects of this question can be found in the two parts of the collection of essays entitled "The Social and Political Philosophy of Bertrand Russell," edited by Bart Schultz for the journal *Philosophy of the Social Sciences* (1996).[14] While his moral activism is obvious, Russell's theoretical ethics has received little attention. Charles Pigden has recently challenged what he calls this "consensus of error."[15] The profitability of this new debate is yet to be determined.

Malcolm Muggeridge has yet to be fully analysed in biographical studies. His comparatively recent death and the deposit of his papers for research should yield much more. The most thorough contributions to date have been those written by Gregory Wolfe, Richard Ingrams, and Ian Hunter.[16]

There is no authoritative biography of Barbara Ward, though one seems to be underway.[17] This parallels the absence of an autobiography – whereas the other figures all published autobiographies. The most complete study to date is a political science PhD Thesis by Kenneth LeRoy Gladish.[18]

Julian Huxley, Bertrand Russell, Barbara Ward, and Malcolm Muggeridge all shared a strong aversion to materialism. The first three subscribed to a liberal, progressive view of the unfolding of history and of the future with a strong emphasis upon the use of reason. Muggeridge believed that the assumptions of liberalism were a destructive force contributing to the disintegration of Western civilization. Muggeridge also stood out as one who ultimately identified emotionally with the aspirations of the dispossessed, but in a different way than, for example, Ward. His final, uncompromising, traditional Christianity was at odds with many in the intelligentsia. In this he shared something in common with the socialist humanists. Even earlier, during the 1950s, Muggeridge also defied the establishment in other ways, and continued to do so. Was his fearlessness not something that Russell, an archenemy, could admire?

In the grouping of the agnostic/atheists here there was less division within their ranks than in those of the Christians. In the latter case, Ward's vision of the "Kingdom on Earth" was in sharp contrast to Muggeridge's view of Christ's Kingdom as not being of this world. This disagreement reflected a general and fundamental cleavage within the message of Christians. Differences between Russell and Huxley, on the other hand, appeared to be much less important and their legacies often seem to overlap each other. The impact of each of these figures in their own time was also diverse, often involving the question of how effectively the media could be exploited. Of all the figures, seemingly the least likely to succeed in reaching the masses, given his age and the rigour of his mind, not to mention his frankness, was Bertrand Russell. And yet he clearly was the most successful.

Following this introduction is a chapter entitled "The Setting" which deals with the question of the decline of British Christianity, the legacy of unbelief, and the mixing of these traditions and other influences during the crucial long 60s. This is the context for the chapters which then follow on Huxley, Russell, Muggeridge, and Ward, each with their own themes, and finally for a conclusion that also considers the effects of all of this, in Britain and abroad, on the present. In that sense the four figures and the long sixties were part of a continuum linking intellectual and cultural currents of previous generations at one end to similar trends that are part of our lives at this very moment. How pivotal our figures and the long sixties were to this wider picture will have to be judged more definitively in the future.

1

The Setting

While Huxley, Russell, Muggeridge, and Ward had individual stories to tell, they did not operate in isolation from each other, no matter how much they might have wished that this was the case. To some degree their portraits are interlocking, as they were all popular figures at their peak within roughly the same time frame, and occasionally they were in open dialogue and even conflict with each other. It is probably true that each would have claimed a unique contribution. The uniqueness of their contributions, however, must be measured against certain trodden paths or traditions within which they can be roughly fitted. And all of these figures had developed their moral vision and worldviews prior to the long sixties. Hence, what follows is a more detailed examination of the traditions which helped to mold their worldviews and style of presentations to audiences in the key periods of their careers. These traditions of belief and unbelief were also not sealed off from each other through history, before the contests of the long sixties. With that caveat in mind, these compartments will now be presented with intermixing where significant.

THE DECLINE OF CHRISTIANITY

What brought Christianity in Britain to its reduced status by the mid-twentieth century is no easy matter to determine with certitude. Arguments abound, many involving the supporters and opponents of the sociological theory of secularization. Region is also significant, some preferring to confine discussion to England alone, which I mainly do. And then there is the question of time frame, especially given Callum Brown's recent contention that British

Christianity's collapse was sudden, and specific to the 1960s. I will deal with this latter question, involving the 1960s, mainly in the last section of this chapter.

As this is a historical study, it is fitting that we begin with the time frame. Though it would appear that Britain, from the end of the eighteenth century to the First World War, "was immersed in the greatest exercise in Christian proselytism this country has ever seen,"[1] nevertheless many staunch Christians living in that period, especially from the mid-Victorian decades onward, were already expressing doubts concerning the continued hegemony of Christianity in their homeland. A century later, E.R. Wickham, an Anglican clergyman in charge of the Sheffield Industrial Mission, undertook a dissection of what he saw as the declining health of the church over the past century or so, with much the same alarmist view. It was from the publication of his *Church and People in an Industrial City*[2] in 1957 that much of the modern wave of historical investigation on the question of the decline of British Christianity can be dated. His view, of course, was not shared by historians such as G. Kitson Clark, Owen Chadwick, or Desmond Bowen,[3] all of whom optimistically stressed the positive achievements of the churches. We shall return to this.

Recently Charles Taylor in *A Secular Age* has, in tracing the answer to why adherence to Christianity is now but one option facing people in our times, even widened the relevant time frame for Britain and Western Europe (Latin Christendom) back through the Renaissance and Reformation, to the late Middle Ages. The question is "why was it virtually impossible not to believe in God in, say, 1500 in our Western society, while in 2000 many of us find this not only easy, but even inescapable?"[4] Obviously it is related in part to the story of the growth of unbelief dealt with in the next section of this chapter. It is about transformations in the status of unbelief but also, in this symbiotic relationship, it is about the changes that weakened Christianity in the Western world or, as Taylor puts it, a belief in God "isn't quite the same thing in 1500 and 2000."[5]

The world which Taylor paints in 1500 was, for most people, an enchanted one. He describes the border between the observed, physical world and the world of the mystical as "porous," guided by a feeling of transcendence, infused by agape. This guided people's moral sense, which was embedded deeply within the fabric of the traditional community. The movements for reform since 1000, however, had begun to erode this situation, which demanded a more general and explicit religious commitment and the leveling up of intensity to as many as possible. Through the Reformation and Counter-Reformation there was a shift away from practices of popular piety to new ways of religious thinking and practice. By advocating the renunciation of evil ways more generally in society, religiousness was being made into something which demanded an intense personal commitment. According to Charles Taylor disenchantment, reform, and personal piety went together.[6] Religion also began to be more anthropocentric and immanent.

The challenge of new ways of knowing (or perhaps the conclusion that inductive reasoning was the only way) later took direction from the Scientific Revolution and the Enlightenment as it first affected elites in the eighteenth century. But the trickle-down effect would affect other people in due course given the demolition of the enchanted cosmos which had already popularly occurred through the Reformation. For Taylor, deism – theism without an intervening God – supplied a bridge to further, more significant changes in the eighteenth century. What he has also termed "Providential Deism"[7] furthered the anthropocentric shift, making humankind the central focus. As Taylor sees it through the benevolent gift of reason, coupled with the concept of grace vanishing, humankind could determine its own destiny and morality. Through this sense of will, moral power was immanentized. A clear line to unbelief in "exclusive humanism"[8] was the next phase that Taylor observed. But Deism, even of the providential sort, was certainly enough in itself to limit or eliminate the active role of God in human affairs.

This brings one back to the more immediate studies of the decline of British Christianity in the last two centuries, which also widens the picture to a consideration of the masses in relation to religion. In his well-known *Churches and the Working Classes in Victorian England* (1963), K.S. Inglis makes the point that Wickham, in his pioneering study of Sheffield some six years earlier, had entered into "sociological history"[9] when exploring the effects of demographic change, industrialization, and urbanization upon the place of the church in society from the previous century to the present one. Inglis, like Wickham, was particularly concerned about the alienation of the working classes from the church in the nineteenth century. Inglis, Wickham, and some more recent historians have largely taken the line that through exclusionary practices such as pew rents the churches kept large numbers of less well-to-do from attending services. These mistakes accounted, at least in part, for the poor attendances in predominantly working-class areas as recorded on Census Sunday, 1851.[10] Though massive campaigns were launched to reclaim people for the churches in the decades that followed, many of these actions were the product of narrow middle-class, biased concerns such as instilling habits of thrift, temperance, and even cleanliness. They have been viewed as an attempted process of embourgeoisement.

Denominational rivalry, particularly in Church versus chapel disputes, and anti-Catholicism did not help to strengthen Christianity in the long run, though they may have increased group loyalties in the short run.[11] The partial crumbling of the Church-State connection in the early decades of the nineteenth century initiated some momentum for these disputes. This crumbling had to do with constitutional issues related to reform, in combination with the growing strength of religious dissent within England.

Protestant Nonconformity had benefited from the industrial revolution by bolstering the economic power of some Congregationalist, Baptist, Unitarian, Quaker, and Methodist entrepreneurs, factory owners and managers, as well as those in related businesses, who were especially strong in the provinces, the growing cities of the Midlands, and Northern England. This is not to say that there were not Anglican industrialists in many parts of the country. But the presence of Nonconformist elites was very noticeable in many of the rapidly expanding cities. The Evangelical Revival had also added greatly to the rank-and-file members and attendees of these chapels, though it did not directly impact the Unitarians or some of the small sects such as the membership of the New Church (Swedenborgians). Economic power and numbers had serious political consequences in driving demands for the ending of their religious disabilities.

Similarly, the influx of Irish immigrants driven to find work in England by the economic and demographic disasters in Ireland helped to add both a significant element to the labour force of areas like Lancashire and a noticeable presence of Roman Catholicism. Catholicism was reinforced by Irish ethnicity in such urban ghettos. It also helped fuel anti-Catholicism, which became another significant political factor by the middle decades of the nineteenth century in England. Thus in the first third of the nineteenth century both Catholics and Protestant Nonconformists gained strength within a society that was facing philosophical challenges to the old order of Church and State.

The momentum for modernization in the short run favoured the opponents of the established church, the Anglican Church, which seemed to be embedded in the old order. Building upon Whig and radical political criticism demanding constitutional reform, the repeal of the Test and Corporation Acts in 1828 and Catholic Emancipation in 1829 encouraged an atmosphere leading to the Great Reform Act of 1832, Municipal Reform in 1835, and the establishment of the civil registry of births, marriages, and deaths in 1837. One further step would lead to Jewish Emancipation in the 1850s and to the admissions of non-believers to parliamentary seats in the 1880s. Another path was the possible disestablishment of the Church, seen later in Ireland in the 1860s, and in Wales in the next century – but not in England itself. Nevertheless campaigns to disestablish the Church and to formally end privileges, such as the church rate and religious tests at the ancient universities, were important political issues keeping nonconformity united and furthering concepts of liberal democracy. With such developments the foundations were laid for a more egalitarian society in which rights would be enshrined. However, as A.D. Gilbert has also observed: "The Church-Chapel confrontation, in short, succeeded in delaying for more than half a century the most obvious manifestations of secularization. It ensured for Victorian religion an undiminished public role and social significance throughout a period in which all the Churches were experiencing mounting difficulties in the task of mobilizing the wider society for religious ends."[12]

Though these divisions patterned much of the role of religion in politics both at the parliamentary and local government level, it did not preclude advances in the general thinking on the place of religion in public life. Prime Minister Gladstone's speech supporting the atheist Bradlaugh's admission to parliament in the 1880s kept British politics firmly on a course of expanding tolerance.[13] Gladstone argued that unbelief should pose no real threat to believers, as well as keeping faith with his definition of liberalism as the removal of privilege. The British Gladstonian notion that belief and liberalism could freely mix also contrasted with Continental liberalism which seemed to be perpetually in battle with the Catholic Church, if not all churches.

The Conservative party did play more of a reactionary role with its line of "Church in danger," and the Church of England was seen by many as the Conservative party at prayer. But under Disraeli the party showed a creative side in its Romantic vision of a more organically united society making practical inroads into gaining support among urban dwellers, from its traditional base in the countryside. It assumed Nonconformists were in league with the Liberals. Under Disraeli's successors, the Conservative party's appeal to anti-Catholicism also strengthened the Conservative position in urban areas, and it later played the Orange card (the Orange lodges) against Home Rulers and the Gladstonian Liberals in England and Northern Ireland in the last years of the nineteenth century.

The Church of England itself proved to be creative on the ecclesiological front with clerical figures like Abraham Hume of Liverpool, Vicar Hook of Leeds, and Bishop Fraser of Manchester. They often displayed good social insights in adapting the parish system to the new realities of urban life, also pointing to the fact that the national church, like the minority Roman church, did not abandon the inner city churches – as did some Nonconformist denominations which lost local cadres of wealthy members (who migrated away from the industrial cores of cities) who had sustained them.

Perhaps the most creative element which sprang out of Anglicanism, ultimately influencing all of the other churches, was Christian socialism. Begun by the Reverend F.D. Maurice and the lawyer J.M. Ludlow in the 1840s, the movement stressed co-operation and a return to a sense of community and brotherhood fractured by industrialization. Maurice, a convert from Unitarianism, also espoused a liberal theology open to areas of new learning (and away from doctrines like eternal damnation) as well as a concept of a national church encompassing all denominations. He was a leader within the so-called Broad Church group that espoused these liberal doctrinal ideas within the Church of England. Maurice's work on comparative religion was what E.R. Norman has called a "precursor of the sociology of religion."[14] Theologically Maurice also stressed the Incarnation, placing God in fatherhood over society, linked to the Brotherhood of Humanity, infusing "Christ in every man." Social compassion and social unity would thus follow.

The Christian socialist movement under Maurice and Ludlow lasted scarcely ten years, and translated itself into action mainly in aid of the cooperative movement (which was inspired by Owenite socialists and Secularists) and the appeal to brotherhood against the waves of class division and political strife during the 1840s. Maurice's ideas resurfaced later in another wave of Christian socialism by the 1880s through Anglican figures like the Reverend Scott Holland, Bishop Brooke Foss Westcott, and the Christian Social Union. In this period Christian socialism, in concert with other social reformers of the period, developed a more specific social critique as well as links to political socialism through figures like the Reverend Stewart Headlam.

The movement was also referred to more broadly at the time as "social Christianity," and embraced many clergy and some laity in other denominations. Even more than in Anglican circles, the advance of social Christianity into the ranks of Nonconformists represented the retreat of individualism and the old virtues emphasized at mid-century, for the view of the merciful Fatherhood of God and the need for social action. Gone were the days of the great preacher, C.H. Spurgeon, in the heyday of Evangelical Nonconformity; he was replaced by figures such as Hugh Price Hughes, leader of the Methodist Forward Movement.

As Hughes stated in a sermon entitled "Jesus Christ and Social Distress" from his sermon collection, *Social Christianity: Sermons Delivered in St. James's Hall, London* (1890): "I have long been persuaded that the reason why the masses of the people have to so great an extent failed to realize that their best friend is Jesus Christ, is the fact that we ministers of religion have taken the very course which my excellent correspondent urged upon me last Monday. We have dealt too exclusively with the individual aspect of the Christian faith. We have constantly acted as if Christianity had nothing to do with business, with pleasure, and with politics; as if it were simply a question of private life and of prayer meetings."[15] The correspondent Hughes referred to was a member who the previous Sunday afternoon was "very much grieved" that Hughes did not preach the Gospel, Spurgeon-style, but talked about "unsanitary dwellings" and the duty of citizens to elect Christian vestrymen who would close them. Undoubtedly this "excellent Christian gentleman" was an affluent financial backer of the chapel. Such men would now be exposed to many more social justice sermons from the pulpits of many denominations in the years to come.[16]

A constant concern from such religious leaders was also the challenge posed by secular socialists of the continental type often linked to godlessness. In that way it was an imperative that the churches act as a counterpoise to potential class warfare. A criticism of social Christianity which developed into the twentieth century was that it simply reflected secular thinking; in the words attributed to Sir William Harcourt, "we are all socialists now." In that sense, social Christianity was argued to be merely a conduit for secular thought into the churches. This, of course, overlooked theological principles such as Incarnationism which had provided so much of a foundation for the new thinking on social matters.

Within Roman Catholic circles, the cadence of social concern ran at a different pace. While many clergy were individually committed to help the plight of the dispossessed, it took direction from the top in figures like Cardinal Manning to elevate their concerns to the level of policy. Leo XIII and *Rerum Novarum* gave social Catholicism a huge leap forward in the 1890s. But, for the most part, social Catholics maintained their distance from their social Christian counterparts until a later generation.

While social Christianity and social Catholicism earned the praise of some secular reformers, as well as the wrath of some followers of Marx, there is no evidence that it greatly strengthened the churches in relation to the unchurched or indeed the position of the mainline churches *qua* churches. New groups such as the Salvation Army, which embraced elements of social Christianity with an added feeling for evangelicalism, made a dent in their very specific mission. Other fusions such as the Labour Church and the Brotherhood movement in the long run were less successful in reaching the working classes.

Arguments and forms of evidence have been put forward by historians that church membership and attendance generally began to wane in the last decades of Queen Victoria's reign in relation to the steady growth in population. Thus whether church leaders were evangelicals or social Christians, the results of their efforts seemed to be similar overall. Building on groundwork laid by pessimistic views of religious historians such as E.R. Wickham and K.S. Inglis, advocates of the sociological theory of secularization have concluded that it all fits into a pattern of inevitable decline, with secularization as the "long-term concomitant of industrialization."[17] This school of thought has supplied additional statistical evidence such as in R. Currie, A.D. Gilbert, and L. Horsley, *Churches and Churchgoers: Patterns of Church growth in the British Isles since 1700* (1977). Though strict adherents to this theory have dwindled and critics abound within the ranks of academe, as one opponent has admitted, it remains a master narrative and the "most influential general account of religion in modern Europe" to date.[18]

The sociological theory rests upon a concept of modernization in which industrialization, urbanization, and accompanying population surges obliterate tradition patterns rooted in the old rhythms of life in agriculture and the village. In the process people are exposed to more modern science-based explanations of the world and nature about them, diminishing the role of traditional folkways and religion. As the magical and the mystical erode away in people's perceptions, religion shrinks into occupying less and less territory within their minds, lurking only in a few "gap" areas, such as for the purposes of consolation at the time of death. It is like the contraction of a balloon with more and more air escaping.

Certainly in the transformations of industrialization and urbanization, the nature of community was altered – in fact it is fair to say that there were now *communities* of work, of leisure, and of worship involving the mixing together of different sorts of people in each instance. It became more of a free market of options – ideas, choices, rather than what was always done and sanctioned by the traditional community. In most cases, therefore, what emerged were more complex attitudes and behaviour patterns in religion than there had been in village life. That the pessimist case, or the modernization or secularization thesis can be firmly established, is questionable. The optimistic school has not collapsed.

Jeffrey Cox's landmark book, *The English Churches in a Secular Society* (1982), attacks the inevitability aspect of the modernization argument for the decline. Cox's work on Lambeth was followed by other local studies which raised additional questions concerning the statistics of decline issued by pessimists. S.J.D. Green's *Religion in the Age of Decline* (1996) discusses the associational ideal, which encompassed a host of church-connected organizations and approaches that operated with reasonable success in industrial Yorkshire until as late as the 1920s, when they were pushed aside by rival secular organizations. Certainly the argument of viability extends well beyond the beginning of the twentieth century when

Gilbert and other pessimists argued that the slide was under way, that the die was cast.

Gilbert, of course, emphasized the decline of the Nonconformist Chapel which in his view sank significantly after 1885, with the exception of 1902 and 1906 when "Nonconformist density indices"[19] held. He conceded that the Church of England actually experienced increases in communicant participation which were "more rapid than population growth" between 1885 and 1914.[20] However, Jeremy Morris has pointed out that in the very statistics supplied in *Churches and Churchgoers*, other and later surges in Nonconformist membership present "such a curious pattern of ups and downs" that the statistics do not naturally support the 'modernization' thesis."[21] The later dating of decline moves the focus of discussion significantly into early decades of the twentieth century, far from the period when historians such as W.R. Ward once saw the earlier divisions and class tensions within denominations as indicative of religious decline.[22]

Other studies, such as that of Sarah Williams's *Religion and Popular Culture in Southwark, 1870–1920* (1999), have taken the debate to new areas of evidence beyond the rhetoric of church leaders and the narrow records of churches. Instead she views religiosity from the working-class perspective, in terms of popular beliefs and practices. Her interpretation also corresponds with many historians' dissatisfaction with crunching numbers, a process which mimics the Victorian middle-class statistical obsessions, as in the religious census of 1851, which make so many assumptions in measuring religious strength. It is the quandary of understanding believing without belonging, of diffusive Christianity, which Jeffrey Cox discusses. As Hugh McLeod concluded in his *Class and Religion in the Late Victorian City* (1974), "The obvious implications of these facts is that however local patterns were moulded by social and political circumstance, the primary source of the religious changes of the period must be sought in the flow of ideas rather than in situations peculiar to particular regions and countries."[23] This is not to pursue E.R. Wickham's metaphysical observation that goes beyond the realm of the historian, "That is to say that the Church is properly subject to historical and sociological analysis, even though the essence of her reality must elude an empirical sociology."[24]

Charles Taylor, who dwells mainly in the realm of ideas, has observed the complexity of Evangelicalism during the Victorian era in terms of both its long and short-term effects. W.R. Ward years ago observed the deleterious effects of the deterioration of the Evangelical Revival's broad spirit into a process of schism within the Methodist fold, which heralded a religious decline in the early decades of the nineteenth century. Similarly A.D. Gilbert argued that the growth of Evangelical Nonconformity, and then its precipitous decline through the length of the Victorian period, contributed to the overall retreat of Christianity. In the short run, Taylor has seen Evangelical Christianity powerfully contributing to the Victorian British code of respect for law, decency, freedom, and benevolence. Following God meant disciplining the self, thereby instilling a sense of both duty and altruism.[25] But it was also personal and immanent. As he states concerning its ultimate effects into later generations: "But just as the earlier form of piety I've called 'Providential Deism,' prepared the ground for an exclusive humanism, so this strenuous Evangelicalism opened the road to an unbelieving philosophy of self-control. The very success in self-remaking encouraged, as the creation of a disciplined, buffered agent invited a reinterpretation in purely human terms."[26]

How this process took place is intriguing. Much of it depends on how you view the strength of diffusive Christianity after 1900. John Wolffe argues, using Cox's concept, that in 1900 British people were closer to the essence of Christianity than ever before but "in a diffuse and passive sense."[27] This requires some definitional generosity unless, as Charles Taylor has pointed out, one thinks back to something analogous to the old magical world of folk religion, which was itself assailed by that very evangelical fervor which demanded, unrealistically, a "100 percent commitment."[28] There perhaps a "penumbra" had been acceptable. Perhaps E.R. Wickham was always conscious of this situation, but still pessimistic concerning a creeping "secular mode of thought, that almost total preoccupation with immediate and temporal affairs – always a characteristic of the bulk of the working classes – became more and more widespread in the second half of the century, and deeply pervaded the traditionally religious middle classes, even where their religious practice was maintained."[29]

Wickham originally had gone much further in his considerations than looking only at those with tenuous links to institutional religion. Like others, even Horace Mann, the census taker, reflecting on the Religious Census of 1851, Wickham believed that the squads of atheists and secularists should not be held responsible for "the fact is that England has been singularly unfavourable ground for dogmatic atheism, as also perhaps for dogmatic religion."[30] Thus perhaps Taylor's point about the slide from Evangelicalism to respectable unbelief is, in the long run, more relevant. As Wickham further stated: "Sharp lines between fidelity and infidelity cannot be drawn in English society, and one way of stating this is to say that the secular-minded outside the churches have a Christian colouration, and that the practicing Christians inside have marked secular characteristics. It still persists, a baffling feature of English life."[31]

In explaining the rise and fall of modern Christianity into the twentieth century, historians such as A.D. Gilbert and Callum Brown have supplied more elaborate and specific mechanisms than those found in Taylor's marching anthropocentrism. Gilbert, together with Robert Currie and Lee Horsley, presented a model of decline in *Churches and Churchgoers*, recapitulated in Gilbert's *The Making of Post-Christian Britain*,[32] consisting of the following stages relating to the wider society:

I   The *progressive* phase, which involved the expansion of religious organizations into wider society (from the Evangelical Revival into the early Victorian era).

II The *marginal* phase, in which religious organizations struggled to maintain their position through innovations in membership retention (from the early Victorian era to about 1914).

III The *recessive* phase, in which the religious organization faltered in recruiting outsiders and the ranks of adherents began to deplete (from the First World War to about 1960).

IV The *residual* phase, which involved a serious downward direction within the religious organization that suggested a future of even greater losses or even disappearance, with no strength in the wider society (from about 1960 to 1980 in the case of Gilbert's book).

Key factors in this process seem to be the growing failure to recruit from the wider society, or the lack of allogenous growth, and the fracturing of the old, complete sense of community into different community functions involving new cultural pluralism, no longer with a specific sense of place. After Nonconformity, this eventually even brought down the Church of England, which was initially "more progressive than its rivals in adapting to the new situation."[33] Once again, however, problems seem to persistently appear in the statistical basis for the conclusions in these and other studies – problems which, as Jeremy Morris points out, have forced the generally accepted narrative of decline to move to later periods, first from the early nineteenth century to the 1880s, then to the beginning of the twentieth century, and finally to the interwar period.[34] He has also noted that the core evidence for many historians has shifted to popular beliefs and practices, away from church institutional statistics as well as broader, more comprehensive attempts to redefine "religion" away from biases rooted in the thought processes of the Victorian middle-class, including the clergy.[35] In his recent work *The Death of Christian Britain* (first edition, 2001, second edition, 2009) Callum Brown has taken the focus of the discussion into the 1960s; this work is extremely important, and will be examined in the last section of this chapter. But in the sections of his book setting up the context for his arguments concerning the 1960s he has much to say about the overall period after 1800.

Brown uses another term similar to Cox's use of "diffusive" for believing in, but not belonging to, churches. In this case it is "discursive Christianity," meaning the manifestations of personal identification with Christianity which infused media of all sorts as well as designated organizations in a "salvation economy." This salvation economy was responsible for making the public culture of Britain that of a strongly religious nation in its heyday during the nineteenth, and much of the twentieth, centuries. As Jeremy Morris has critically noted, Brown's discursive Christian world was not synonymous with popular belief, nor with the teachings of the churches, but was "somewhere in the middle, between church and people, as a sort of free-floating structure of ideas."[36] According to Brown, it was also linked to the feminization of religion when women formed the backbone of the churches and upheld the conventions of family values, so much the image of respectable society.

With the erosion of many of these values by the 1950s, and with the radical redefinition of women's roles into the 1960s, discursive Christianity rapidly crashed and Christian Britain died. For Morris there are a host of problems in Brown's picture. These include the omission of assaults upon Christian theology, rifts within churches, sectarian conflict, the relation of churches to politics and social issues, and regional variations involved with institutional marginalization and attenuation. Some of these criticisms can also be applied to Green and others.[37] Again a return to the time sequence may also be called for in this case. Was there overall a more gradual pattern to be observed here? If so, Callum Brown's extreme emphasis upon the 1960s may well be too revisionist.

THE HERITAGE OF UNBELIEF

Unbelief has a tradition woven of many strands. There were atheists, people later known as agnostics, freethinkers, skeptics, or simply those who suffered from doubt, sustained or periodic, concerning the central beliefs of Christianity. Just as Christians were divided by denominational loyalties, differing approaches to the application of principles, and social class, so too were unbelievers. Throughout their history, unbelievers, like believers, faced challenges from fellow adherents, especially if they took unusual positions, as well as from the multitudes who were hostile or altogether indifferent to their call in an analogous way to what the apologists for Christianity faced.

It is reasonable to assume that unbelief in its various forms has been around for a long time. It certainly had its visible exponents during the Scientific Revolution and Enlightenment, as well as many less visible exponents who feared repression by church and state, and often even by local society, if their freethinking was exposed. By the end of the eighteenth century, intellectuals such as British agnostic philosopher David Hume had laid the groundwork for later assaults upon the basic beliefs of Christianity. But the path of unbelief beyond individual thought was not at all clear if it in fact mandated the conversion of others. How exactly was it to replace theism; what would be its impact upon social behaviour in the face of God's disappearance; and would pure reason be the societal guide or rather reason, with due reference to human emotion?

Soon another route of unbelief was established, much of it a function of political impulses unleashed by the American and French Revolutions. As Keith Robbins has stated, "If we may take the French Revolution as the beginning of modern history, then these years also saw the first systemic attempt to replace organized Christianity."[38] It focused in particular on the issue of repression. Here the deism of more elite groups poured downward into popular radicalism through figures such as Thomas Paine. By the early nineteenth century a host of plebeian figures had appeared attacking the established Church as part of the repressive apparatus of the Ancien Regime of Britain. This had implications for the place of Christianity as a whole. Distrust of the Church from local clergymen magistrates to the bishops in the House of Lords inspired much political ill will against the institutional church, which sometimes paved the way to unbelief. By the mid-nineteenth century, the proscribed press activities of Richard Carlile, the freethinking disciples of Robert Owen, and the Secularists under G.J. Holyoake all laid the foundations for a working-class, unbelieving presence. This is not to say that we can assume that these so-called infidels were numerous. The steady growth of the Church and Nonconformity in the early Victorian age, as well as new sects, confirmed that Christianity in all its forms continued to be an important element in society, and in the lives of many in the labouring masses. There were concerns, of course, about the increasing number of people, especially in the industrial areas after the Religious Census of 1851, who did not attend church or chapel. But then, as now, it was not widely concluded that Secularist societies and other freethinkers had much to do with their behaviour.

By that time unbelievers of various persuasions from the middle classes had also made their appearance to bolster the efforts of radical plebeian infidels. The culture of the labouring masses by the 1830s could include the services of a deist preacher like Robert Taylor, who was Cambridge-educated and had been trained both as an Anglican clergyman and a surgeon. The audience attracted to his London infidel theatre, with its "irreligious melodrama and burlesque," as I.D. McCalman has described it, was mostly of the prosperous artisan and lower middle class.[39]

Some disseminators also used another stage – the courts as a place to liberate the voice of unbelief among the masses. A number were charged under the blasphemy laws. Charles Southwell (who had also been an actor), bookseller and orator, was an Owenite socialist and atheist. In 1841 he edited and published the first issue of *The Oracle of Reason*, which was professedly atheist, and was soon indicted. Attacking religion for purveying the falsehoods of Jesus, and for the "odious Jewish" production of the Bible, his trial again witnessed these slurs from Southwell as well as a much longer list of attacks upon the Judeo-Christian heritage. Southwell's conviction resulted in a fine and imprisonment.

Southwell's successor as editor was George Jacob Holyoake, a former tinsmith who was also an Owenite and Chartist. Holyoake, however, was far more circumspect and careful with his words in print. He was undoubtedly more in the nature of an agnostic – a term that would come into usage later in the century. However, in 1842 he too was charged with blasphemy; the *Cheltenham Chronicle* stated that he was a blasphemer, citing a speech Holyoake had given on another subject which strayed into religion in response to a question from the audience. Subsequently he was tried in Gloucester, where he demonstrated both the weakness of the prosecutor's case and of the Blasphemy Statute in general. Holyoake's conviction succeeded in emboldening freethinkers who claimed to be persecuted for their beliefs and politics. Holyoake had always maintained that his speech was on socialism.[40] Later trials for blasphemy, including the acquittal of the clearly atheistic Charles Bradlaugh, demonstrated by the late 1880s that the law had assisted the cause of unbelief and free speech by publicizing the ideas of unbelievers. The prosecutions then ceased.

Science would also have a more significant impact, generally negative, upon traditional religious belief in the nineteenth century than it had during the Scientific Revolution of the seventeenth and eighteenth centuries. It began with advances in geology where geologists, a surprising number of them clergymen, began to establish facts about the age of the earth. These facts undermined many well-trodden arguments and views of the devout. The seventeenth-century calculation of Archbishop Ussher, that creation took place in 4004 BC, was easily disproven; grave doubts were also registered concerning the truth of the Biblical great flood. Robert Chambers' journalistic *Vestiges of Creation*, which appeared in 1841, created no general outcry except from the most conservative believers, though it was of the same genre. By the 1850s for many educated Christians Chambers' idea of a series of developmental stages in the chronology of nature, linked to divine superintendence, seemed a better explanation of the history of the world than a sequence of miracles.[41]

The outcry had to wait for the publication of Charles Darwin's *On the Origin of Species* (1859). Now, with the theory of evolution through natural selection clashing directly with the Bible's version of creation, the battlelines between science and religion grew sharper. The theory of natural selection provided a mechanism of change without the intervention of God. If any uncertainty remained about the place of man in Darwin's account, or the role of God, this was clarified in *The Descent of Man* published in 1871. By this time Darwin himself had joined the company of unbelievers and the cause of agnosticism, which as a concept was increasingly linked with adherence to science, and as a cause was advanced powerfully by Darwin's friend Thomas Huxley. Huxley, "Darwin's bulldog," had distinguished himself for his work in comparative anatomy. But he is remembered principally for his famous triumph over Bishop Samuel Wilberforce in defence of the theory of evolution at the Oxford meeting of the British Association for the Advancement of Science in 1860. Indeed for Huxley a new avenue of hope for British society, and for the world, lay in science. Along with J.D. Hooker and Alfred R. Wallace, Darwin and Huxley presented a new way of looking at ourselves. Huxley, himself, had some doubts about Darwin's idea of natural selection.

John Tyndall, among others, became a strong backer of Darwinism among eminent, practicing scientists. John Galton also envisaged a leadership role for humanity in nature by taking charge of the evolutionary process as a consequence of the dethroning of God. He gave birth to eugenics in his *Human Faculty and Its Development* (1883). Herbert Spencer saw possibilities in the social sciences for Darwinian applications captured in the phrase "survival of the fittest." Social Darwinism was thus born.

As Bowler has pointed out, "Darwinism triumphed only because the open-ended character of evolution in Darwin's original theory was ignored or misrepresented. The majority of late-Victorian evolutionists did not believe in random variation."[42] This therefore led many to appreciate Lamarck's work anew, and to derive from Ernst Haeckel's later publications "the popular assumption that evolutionism is principally concerned with the detailed reconstruction of the history of the earth."[43] But this Victorian "progressionism," as Bowler has called it, received further challenges as the underlying trend of Darwin's thinking re-emerged.[44] Even before the First World War, belief in the inevitable progress of science in society was in question.

For Christians, of course, consequences of various sorts arose. It was obvious that Christians, seeing the immediate inadequacy of standard approaches by Christian authorities like William Paley in *Natural Theology*, would have to rethink defences of Christianity – though the arguments from design still persist to this day. Edmund Gosse later presented readers with the touching account of his father's failed attempts to reconcile his Plymouth Brethren fundamentalist faith with science in *Father and Son* (1907).

In *The Post Darwinian Controversies* (1979) James R. Moore cautioned us not to overstress the warfare aspects of the encounters between religion and science in this period. Christian Darwinists did appear, as well as others who thought reconciliation was not out of the question. This reconciliatory strand of thinking is still going strong. Nevertheless those who already opposed Christianity were emboldened. It also affected those outside academic and intellectual circles. As G.J. Holyoake, the Secularist leader, concluded: "The salutary forces of the world are secular. Christianity is receding. Science is advancing: Christianity is being explained away, Science is being explained into potent existence."[45]

A.D. Gilbert has argued for the importance of the impact of science upon popular consciousness in the advance of secularization in the form of what he terms "scientism," "the kind of worldview derived, not from the scientific method as such, but from popular conceptions – and misconceptions – about the nature and efficacy of science."[46] Gilbert also states that scientism rests epistemologically upon the assumption that all knowing is amenable to scientific proof and anything which is not is irrelevant. The popular form of scientism also "seems an ineradicable cultural feature of an advanced technological society,"[47] as it was emerging at the end of the Victorian period. Its impact on the public has been hard to measure and Gilbert has made the point that scientism does not consciously move against religion by contradicting beliefs but rather "by fashioning a type of consciousness which leaves little place for religiosity."[48] The public clashes of theists and unbelieving scientists, on many occasions, seem to corroborate Gilbert's theory. But Charles Taylor has warned us not to overstress the causal role of science in our general irreligious outlook today. He notes, as an example, that "the disciplines of our modern civilized order" have led us to precise timekeeping as part of a framework of modernity, rather than the need for scientific measurement per se. In so doing, it "occludes all higher times" so linked with the eternal.[49]

There were other areas of investigation that began to undo traditional beliefs in the Victorian age. They often coalesced with Darwinian science in progressionism (Bowler's term). The intention of German Higher Criticism to scrutinize the Bible no differently from any other ancient document was in accord with growing historical professionalism. The appearance in 1846 of an English translation of Strauss's

Life of Jesus had an impact, in Christian circles, similar to the English translation of Marx's *Das Kapital* in socialist circles forty years later. It stimulated not only more Biblical scholarship but also a retreat from the interpretive literalism seen in the production of *Essays and Reviews* in 1860. The immediate effect of all of this was not encouraging to the Broad Church movement in the censorious reactions of church authorities, but in the long run liberals in the Church of England, and Nonconformity had considerable influence in the theological training of younger clergy by the First World War. By that time there were more publications, such as R.J. Campbell's best-selling *The New Theology* (1907), which refuted many traditional beliefs – calling them not merely misleading but even "unethical."[50] Through the interwar period, however, the fears of theological conservatives seemed to bear some fruit in further developments on the international scene, which also impinged on Britain. These consisted not only in the thoughts of figures like Karl Barth but others who even questioned existentially the essential Christian assumptions of liberals. All of this set the stage for works such as John A.T. Robinson's *Honest to God* in the 1960s.

In the late nineteenth century within the ranks of learned clergy doubt spread concerning traditional beliefs. This made it difficult for church leaders to maintain some semblance of order and agreement about core beliefs at times of ordination, and later, to maintain positions as functioning, salaried ministers of religion. The novel *Robert Elsmere* (1888) by Mrs. Humphry Ward brought this problem to the public attention of many clergy who privately faced such difficulties, and many laity who were now made more aware. It raised the additional problems of the importance of living lives of truth and moral good without a traditional set of religious beliefs, as Robert Elsmere did after abandoning his life as a vicar. Many academic figures at the ancient universities of Oxford and Cambridge who were linked with the established church also faced these dilemmas. The gamut ran from T.H. Green, a neo-Christian who inspired much altruism in a generation of young Oxford undergraduates (and was also a figure in *Robert Elsmere*), to Henry Sidgwick at Cambridge, who, as Owen Chadwick said, was thought by some to be "a sort of agnostic saint" but nonetheless also worried that in the present culture too sharp a decline in religion might have moral repercussions.[51]

Since the early Victorian years the wider ranks of public intellectuals and writers beyond universities had seen a steady increase in the number of unbelievers. These included figures such as the philosophers John Stuart Mill and Herbert Spencer, the historians Lecky and J.B. Bury, the poet Algernon Charles Swinburne, the literary critic John Morley, the editor Leslie Stephen, and the novelist, George Eliot (who had also translated Strauss's *Life of Jesus* under her own name, Mary Ann Evans). Owen Chadwick has noted the quality of "bitterness" associated with some figures who wrote fiercely against Christianity, such as Viscount Amberley (Bertrand Russell's father), in his *An Analysis of Religious Belief* (1876). But Chadwick also noted that "the atmosphere of the nineties was more mellow" compared with the 1870s and 1880s.[52] As Chadwick suggests, this undoubtedly had something to do with the greater public freedom which existed by that time. Again, the turning point could well have been the support given to Bradlaugh for admission into Parliament by Gladstone. This action negated the argument that Christianity maintained itself in public life through political repression, and likewise diminished the influence of unbelief in English liberalism, present from John Stuart Mill to John Morley.

However the Victorian Crisis of Faith continued, especially for younger, thinking people in the late Victorian years. The continued outpouring of novels of doubt or clerical failure, such as *The Autobiography of Mark Rutherford, Dissenting Minister* (1881), and the general feeling of religion being in distress can be seen as evidence. And with every public utterance of this sort there were undoubtedly many more moments of quiet unease. Those who early and permanently made up their minds that they did not believe were really not part of this. The final destination of those experiencing the crisis of faith was never certain or inevitable.

Frank Turner has noted that loss of faith usually was experienced in one's late adolescence or early adulthood, frequently as a product of the disruption of family expectations for the person, or as an expression of personal adult autonomy. This could be a generational rebellion. For those who entered the realm of higher education, added to this the new environment of university life was, frequently, exposure to unfamiliar but attractive intellectual influences. In turn this was often accompanied by emotional pain or angst, as it entailed the rejection of one's religious upbringing or later on, the even greater complication of tension with the views of one's wife or husband.[53] In this last matter, one can think of many instances in which prominent unbelievers had religious parents and, in the case of Charles

Darwin or the fictitious Robert Elsmere, a devoutly religious wife. Occasionally the passage to doubt could be made easier, as it was for Annie Besant by having a tyrannical vicar for a husband.

As we have seen, Victorians worried and debated about whether one could have a moral system without religion. Established authority, or course, had long believed that irreligion and social instability went hand in hand, and proselytizing infidels were indeed as much persecuted for their politics, if they had any, as for their views on religion. Owenites were associated with 'godless' socialism. This association resulted from their gatherings, which were often linked to the halls of science that proliferated in the mid-nineteenth century in industrial towns. In turn Owenites were linked to the Secularist movement led by Holyoake, a freethinker who, in spite of his conviction for blasphemy, had clashed with the outright atheist Bradlaugh, and was willing to work with Christians, in cooperatives, for the advancement of the public good. Holyoake pursued the idea of improvement, believing that we could pursue moral lives through the guidance of science. However, as Edward Royle has pointed out, "in the late nineteenth century both secularism and religion were in decline. Religious aspirations were being translated into social action and secularization had made Secularism unnecessary."[54] Their numbers were never great. Soon broad belief in socialism would find new expression with the Social Democratic Federation, the Fabians, and the early Labour Party, with unbelievers and believers (especially rebounded Christian Socialists) of whatever social background mixing together. As such individuals sometimes exhibited influences both from Christianity and unbelief, as with Keir Hardie, and in curiously associated hybrids, such as John Trevor's Labour Church.

Among public intellectuals similar mixing could occur as with the Ethical Movement when it appeared in the mid-1880s. For some naturalists it was necessary to formally replace existing religion with new science-based ideas but also, for the sake of order, to exercise new power and authority through their own type of priestly leadership. James R. Moore has pointed to the attempts to secularize religion by constructing a "naturalistic theodicy."[55] The most ambitious of these attempts in nineteenth-century Europe was Positivism, led by the French philosopher Auguste Comte, which took on many organizational aspects of Catholicism inspired by science (sociology) in the cause of order and progress. In Britain Positivism had a number of disciples, perhaps the best known being

Frederic Harrison. Yet other intellectuals were sympathetic to different ideas of a new science-based creed, including Leslie Stephen, George Henry Lewes (who published his 5 volume *Problems of Life and Mind* from 1875 to 1879), and John Morley (who published *On Compromise* in 1874).

Certainly they tried to adhere to T.H. Huxley's dictum that the enemy of knowledge was the old belief system and the future lay in science. But George Levine believes that there was little hope for success. They could not believe in progress with full confidence because Darwin had only proven that change was inevitable, not progress. True scientific naturalism could only refute lies but had no prior assumptions, and declined to speculate on ontological questions.[56] The positivists would have to live with the tentative, the changing, and always with the lack of conclusive evidence on many questions – as they still do.[57] In the view of Goldwin Smith in 1884, the critics of Christianity were in much disarray as "Mr. Harrison pours scorn on Mr. Spencer's Religion of the Unknowable; Mr. Spencer pours scorn on Mr. Harrison's Religion of Humanity; Sir Fitzjames Stephens pours scorn on both."[58]

Put in a better light, all of this produced a richness of viewpoints, though quite divisive, among the ranks of unbelieving public intellectuals by 1900. As Charles Taylor has stated: "In the nineteenth century, one might say, unbelief comes of age. It develops a solidity and a depth, but also and perhaps above all, a variety, a complex of internal differences."[59] Moving beyond into the twentieth century many of these influences and disagreements persisted into the age of Sigmund Freud and Albert Einstein. As Taylor has also said "The deeper more anchored forms of unbelief arising in the nineteenth century are basically the same as those which are held today. We can see the Victorians as our contemporaries in a way which we cannot easily extend to the men of the Enlightenment."[60]

Beatrice Webb, who was the aunt of Kitty Muggeridge, lived until 1943. Webb is best remembered as a Fabian intellectual who helped found the London School of Economics with her husband, Sidney. The Webbs also founded the *New Statesman* and much of the policy of the early Labour Party. She also had a vivid memory, especially of evolving cultural life. Her book *My Apprenticeship* (1926) captures many of the important links between the late Victorian years and the interwar period. As she looked back on the mid-Victorian trend of thought and feeling, the two outstanding tenets, as she saw them, were belief in the scientific method of synthesizing observation and verification, and a new motive which transferred "the emotion of self-sacrificing service from God to man."[61]

In the late Victorian and Edwardian era she believed the scientific method affected the working classes through Halls of Science and Bradlaugh "the fearless exponent of scientific materialism."[62] Among the intellectual elite, she saw the effective attack upon metaphysics and theology by George Henry Lewes's *History of Philosophy* and others culminating in Comte's union of the religion of humanity with the glorification of science. His English disciple, Frederic Harrison, "a brilliant publicist," and his wife, were able to socialize as "full-fledged members of political society … at the social functions of the Gladstonian Administration of 1880 to 1886" and were on terms of "intimate comradeship with the rising group of Radical statesmen and journalists."[63]

Webb was never a member of the Church of Humanity. However, she did believe by the 1880s that social questions "took the place of religion," that "a higher standard of motive" was asked for in social action,[64] and thus she saw the importance of the social investigator as a sort of religious vocation. But Webb's idealism was tempered by the realistic appraisal that the special attention to social conditions was the result of "a panic fear of the newly enfranchised democracy."[65]

Webb did acknowledge the deep disillusionment experienced in the Great War with the illustrations of "what vile uses the methods and results of science may be put."[66] The naïve belief, pushed on by the earlier "hero-worship" of men of science as the leading British intellectuals, that science would end all human misery was now gone.[67] But she nevertheless concluded in 1926 that science, though not an end in itself, still remained "the only way in which the chosen purpose" of efforts to establish the Kingdom of Man could be attained.[68] Bowler has pointed out that the late Victorian tradition of linking rationalism, unbelief, social reform, and the call for a scientifically literate meritocracy was carried through into the twentieth century by figures like Sir Edwin Ray Lankester (1847–1929) and the Rational Press Association.[69] Through its publications it both reprinted the works of Darwin, T.H. Huxley, Ernst Haeckel, and introduced new authors such as Julian Huxley.

The First World War brought complications to the paths of both Christianity and secularization. In the former case patriotism first gripped the churches, followed by disillusionment as this first episode of total war went on. In the long run, it may have helped to discredit the church in the eyes of many. Callum Brown has discussed the effects of trench religion, as well as standard Christianity, on male piety in this period.[70] Certainly after 1918 there was a more intense interest in modernism in religion, as in so many other areas. But J.M. Winter has also called attention to the upsurge, into the 1920s, of spiritualism, a pre-war combination of science and emotion that was obviously called upon as a coping mechanism for the alarming number of sudden deaths in the Great War.[71] The surge was gone by the 1930s, perhaps the last reviving glimpse of a long-departed, traditional, enchanted world, a slightly mixed version of the transcendent.

Even before the end of the Great War it was obvious that the social creed of the churches, a religious version of the social concerns Beatrice Webb talked about, would be the order of the day in the Church of England and the Free Churches (the new term for Nonconformity). Was this merely a reflection of the secular world? Or was it a natural continuation of the renewed social Christianity since the 1880s? Perspective would affect the answer here.

The power of the state had been greatly augmented through the interventions of the war. The moral dilemmas posed in the creation of a great killing machine seemed as much or even more the concern of secular figures like Bertrand Russell than of religious figures. Such dilemmas included concern about the overall, unchecked power of the state over freedom. However, there were also all the positive possibilities regarding how state intervention could assist in dealing with social problems. Here New Liberals, socialists in and out of the Labour Party, and social Christians could be in agreement. In the latter group the Archbishops' enquiry into social issues was led by a committee composed of Christian Social Union bishops as well as R.H. Tawney and the politician George Lansbury. This led quickly into the Industrial Christian Fellowship and the Conference on Christian Politics, Economics, and Citizenship (COPEC) in the 1920s.

The involvement of some of the church leadership in political issues of the 1920s such as the 1926 General Strike was also clear, as was its ineffectuality. So too was the negative reaction of some politicians, including devout Christians. Just as clergy were sometimes urged to stay out of politics politicians were criticized by clerical groups, such as the Anglo-Catholic Life and Liberty Movement, for Parliamentary interference with the Prayer Book. Some in the

Church of England then sought autonomy or separation from the state as in the case of the Life and Liberty Movement. Some upheld the connection, or thought it useful, like William Temple, then Archbishop of York.

In terms of numbers, A.D. Gilbert has noted that all the churches lost ground "substantially" during the First World War. However, the decline was arrested in the 1920s when most churches held their own "even in proportion to the still-growing British population." This ceased in the 1930s with a resumed decline, continuing into the Second World War and 1950s with a brief upturn in the late 1940s and early 1950s.[72]

To what degree was the increased attrition rate of the 1930s simply part of the renewed modernization process? Certainly the disruption of the recreational functions of churches was well under way. The cinema and sports took much attention away from church-sponsored activities. Improved public transit and the motor car increased mobility and undermined Pleasant Sunday Afternoons.

Again there is little evidence that any of this was the result of growing unbelief, though these developments may have sustained it. It is true that unbelief continued to weave its place into the fabric of national culture. The long-term effects of Providential Deism in the earlier centuries, as Charles Taylor defined it, had firmly given birth to exclusive humanism. Through figures like H.G. Wells (*The Science of Life*, 1929–30), science remained one compass of direction for perfecting society. This contributed powerfully to "Middle Opinion in the 1930s,"[73] as Arthur Marwick has called it. The hostility between unbelief and belief had been renewed in the 1920s and 1930s in the arena of science. In *The World of Life* (1911), published shortly before his death, Alfred Russel Wallace illustrated how a former collaborator with Darwin could firmly join the ranks of Christian evolutionists. This was a good harbinger for things to come on the Christian side. Similarly, after authenticating Einstein's theory of relativity in 1919, Sir Arthur Eddington embarked upon a series of writings, as did other popularizers of science like James Jeans, which presented a case for a universe governed by God to the public.

Countering these initially encouraging developments for theism with general readers, however, was the ongoing success of the writings of H.G. Wells, in spite of anti-materialist attacks by Christian writers such as Hilaire Belloc. Ultimately, it was a group of rationalists within the actual scientific community who made successful advances in their view of the universe in this period. Among the best known was J.B.S. Haldane, an associate of Julian Huxley, who helped to renew the cause of natural selection among biologists. For Haldane "no truce" with religion was possible.[74] As Bowler has pointed out, while surveys into the early 1930s indicated that a large number of scientists held religious beliefs, a growing number among the younger ranks did not.[75] Adrian Hastings has also noted how the legacy of unbelief of Hume, Mill, and Darwin appeared progressively less radical and through transitions from Thomas Hardy, C.P. Snow, A.J.P. Taylor, and finally A.J. Ayer, such beliefs came to be viewed as a subsection of so-called 'establishment thought' by the 1950s.[76]

Even though the 1950s broadcasts of Mrs Margaret Knight extolling a morality without religion could evoke stern criticism, it seemed much less out of the mainstream than the agnostic secularism of the 1920s, especially after the 1947 decision that the BBC not act as an ally of Christianity any longer.[77] While the twentieth century produced its share of great Christian writers, many of these – like G.K. Chesterton, Waugh, and Greene – were Roman Catholic and therefore not quite mainstream in the national culture. They were very often converts who saw wisdom in the ancient ways of a church that was not under the sway of liberalism before the Great War and was confirmed in its belief in original sin by the horrors of that war. Communism was another faith in the 1920s and 1930s for younger people in Barbara Ward's generation. It is instructive that while C.S. Lewis and T.S. Eliot, being Anglican, were more central to the national culture, according to Adrian Hastings they were also both former agnostics.[78] The converted Lewis spoke of being in "enemy territory" as a Christian intellectual in *Mere Christianity* (1952). Eliot, the Anglican, doubted that the concept of blasphemy could be profitably maintained in a society generally so indifferent to God. It was now more of "a breach of good taste."[79]

Social Christianity, together with a related Social Catholicism, seemed to reach a peak of influence in the 1920s but then began to experience internal division and doubts. Within the Free Churches there was some retreat to Evangelicalism within an overall atmosphere of institutional decline. In the Established Church the extreme Left, represented by the English Church Struggle and Christian Democrats, was eventually at loggerheads with Anglican public figures such as T.S. Eliot and the Reverend V.A. Demant. The Church Left ultimately became a fringe, and by the 1950s was represented by eccentric figures such as Hewlett Johnson, the "Red" Dean of Canterbury. The Left was effectively marginalized by public opinion not to mention the long-serving post-Second World War conservative Archbishop of Canterbury, Geoffrey Fisher.

Had the extreme Left of social Christianity become pawns of the Marxists? On the lesser and more general charge of the issue of non- or anti-Christian influences upon the many well-intentioned clergy within the Peace Movement there too were problems. Anglicans such as Charles Raven and Nonconformists such as Donald Soper could mingle with predominantly secular groups in founding the Peace Pledge Movement in the 1930s. Gerald Heard, citing Aldous Huxley, could hope in 1936 that though the Christian will go "the Christian way" and "the secularist the psychological way," nevertheless "there need be no conflict here but only the best emulation as to which can best deliver the goods."[80] But perhaps Archbishop William Temple, writing to the popular priest Dick Sheppard, knew better when he stated "Do you hold that you are called at this time to put pacifism first, in respect of the question whether those whom you persuade become Christian or not? Or do you put Christianity in its total content first, and urge pacifism chiefly as a corollary of Christianity?"[81] As Keith Robbins has observed in the later 1930s, the "prophets" who renounced war in their obsession for peace were also often seen as ignoring other political and ethical concerns in the era of appeasement and the approaching war. In that sense, to many observers they threatened the future of the very democracy they claimed to admire, and thus "were not merely tiresome" but in fact "anachronistically dangerous."[82]

Temple, of course, best exemplified a centrist social Christianity as a national figure, and his death in 1942 was an enormous blow to the future of that movement. Ultimately there were going to be many more Robert Elsmeres who subordinated or abandoned their faith or, more commonly, redirected their labour to secular purposes. The welfare state, as we know it, loomed on the horizon – paradoxically encouraged by many social Christians, now made redundant in their social mission. The Labour Government of 1945 saw Stafford Cripps as the only staunch representative of social Christianity on its front bench of cabinet ministers. Well before that, the Christian churches no longer set social agendas or had significant influence in politics.

Early in the century they moved more to the periphery and governments addressed issues of health, housing, pensions, and unemployment as tax matters. The churches were entitled to consultation on education, but in a less public, quiet way – as evident in the 1944 Education Act. Perhaps for some with a social Christian bent, throwing themselves into their activities in the company of many unbelievers may have concealed doubts about their traditional belief system. These doubts would no longer be given a rest.

Adrian Hastings makes an interesting observation about the period just preceding the crucial long 60s. As he states "the odd thing about the 1950s is the cohabiting of these two intellectual in-worlds, the religious and the agnostic, each self-assured, each apparently thriving, each rather sneeringly dismissive of the other."[83] Hastings also indicates that there were "frontier areas" where allegiance to one or the other world would be sought among the undecided. These frontier areas included schools of historical interpretation, social anthropology, and philosophy, where the debate was taking place on "the very middle of the ground."[84] This cohabitation by intellectuals and the general public was about to be placed in a much more fluid condition.

SECULARISM AND THE SIXTIES

In *The Religious Crisis of the 1960s* (2007) Hugh McLeod has identified four major themes that came to fruition in the long sixties in Western countries, including a huge leap in the range of theistic belief systems (some non-Christian), divisions within churches as they moved to greater ecumenical dialogue, a weakening of religious upbringing, and the end of the assumption that one was living in a Christian country.[85] All of the above themes apply to Britain, especially the last one. This last theme shares something in common with one of the meanings of secularity Charles Taylor uses in *A Secular Age* (2007), namely the situation in which religious belief is merely one option, and a frequently challenged one, in today's Western world. By being one option, religious belief was demoted as a result of the visible decline of belief and practice discussed above (another of Taylor's meanings of secularity), and of the detachment and privatizations of religion from public institutions, which was yet another of Taylor's meanings of secularity, and has been discussed in part already, but is completed in this section.[86]

In the late 1950s there was actually no general anticipation of religious belief becoming merely one option in a market place of ideas. Richard Weight has noted the relative popularity of Anglicanism through such figures as John Betjeman and C.S. Lewis in the 1950s.[87] Indeed, agnostics and atheists were not triumphalist in spirit, and often feared a religious revival. No generally aggressive spirit existed in the fashion of late Victorians, as exhibited by a Charles Bradlaugh, or, in our own times, by the New Atheists. As Professor Stephen Toulmin, a prominent atheist, put it at the time: "Unbelief has always had a bad press. Though often widespread, it has less often been vocal. Discretion and lack of opportunity to declare itself have kept it mostly silent. This has especially been so at times like the present, when a religious revival has been – officially at any rate – in progress."[88] Certainly there still was a perception that figures like Margaret Knight, who tried to advance the cause of freethinking, were savaged by the press. The best hope of E.M. Forster, among other prominent agnostic intellectuals, was that an unbeliever might hope for a fairer share of media time without necessarily being coupled with a mandatory and immediate believer's response.[89]

Yet very soon public figures and movements energized opinion to move public bodies toward "causalism," as Christine Davies had called it, in which laws and regulatory norms would be informed by social consequences rather than the fixed set of Christian ideals. As Callum Brown, among others, has pointed out, the ending of moral censorship over theatre (1968), and the legalization of abortion (1967) and homosexuality (1968), were responses in part to pressures from youth culture, women's groups, and rebellious students in the period. In Brown's view Christianity was "the immediate victim."[90] Science had not enjoyed any particular theoretical breakthroughs such as those of Darwin in the mid-nineteenth century that sparked this, save in practical areas such as the production of the birth control pill.

Ironically the pressure for change also came from some within Christian churches. The trial of Penguin Books in 1960 for publishing *Lady Chatterley's Lover*, a novel by D.H. Lawrence which had long been suppressed for alleged obscenity, highlighted the testimony of the Rt Reverend John A.T. Robinson and other clergy who defended the novel. Together with secular humanists such as Richard Hoggart, they helped make this a landmark legal decision in favour of ending moral censorship. It signaled the beginning of the end of an older oppressive order of general thought control, and the comments of the lead prosecutor, Mervyn Griffith-Jones, that heads of households would not wish their wives or servants to read it have specific socio-political connotations as well.[91] But as Mark Roodhouse has observed, it also exposed the public to the ideas of radicals within the Church as well as fostering a response by conservatives who also now used the media. The ensuing in-house debates may have undermined the moral authority of the church in general.[92] Certainly Hugh McLeod's theme, of divisions within churches as the churches themselves moved closer together in ecumenical dialogue, is born out. Rifts between the liberal, more secular-minded elements and conservatives, rigidly evangelical and individualistic in the case of many Protestant churches (more complicated in classification for Roman Catholics and Anglicans) was evident in virtually all churches. As Bryan Wilson has also argued, ecumenism itself may have been a symptom of an embattled and weakened Christianity.[93]

Internal division, of course had been going on for some time in each of the major churches. The earlier era of advancing social Christianity had also seen many Protestant Christians who opposed its concept of a Kingdom on Earth. This concept went against the emphasis upon individual salvation found in C.H. Spurgeon and the like, and was often linked to unacceptably liberal theological positions. Social Catholicism similarly had some difficulties in spite of the views of Leo XIII and some of his successors. But, modernism was more the issue there with early, stiff opposition from above within the Roman Catholic Church hierarchy. In Britain the huge investment made by the churches on behalf of the Kingdom on Earth in the proliferation of expensive agencies bore meager returns for the churches *qua* churches – which was obvious by the 1960s. Ultimately much of the apparatus of social mission was replaced by the welfare state. In the meantime, the thrust and content of so many sermons on Social Gospel themes were made redundant. The concomitant neglect of the more traditional themes of preparation for the next life in many pulpits over a generation was equally obvious. This was duly noted by the conservative minded within the Anglican and Nonconformist churches.

While by the 1960s it was clear that evangelicalism would not be a very distinctive feature of English religious life in the way it was and is in the United States (especially after the failed hopes for a general revival in the late 1950s), there were some notable exceptions. An outstanding example was the career of the Reverend John R. Stott, Rector of All Souls, Langham Place, London. Through his evangelism Stott's parish maintained a high number of active members throughout the long sixties, and the parish also served as a base for Stott's national and worldwide efforts as an evangelical leader. *Basic Christianity* (1958), a compilation of his university mission sermons of the 1950s, was an attempt to place Christian beliefs back into the realm of national intellectual discussion. As with the success of his subsequent publications and public appearances the robust sales of *Basic Christianity* had an even broader impact, and were especially important in revitalizing the evangelical wing of the Church of England and evangelicalism in general. What is also interesting, as Alister Chapman noted, was Stott's early awareness of the secularization thesis, as seen in the writings of Bryan Wilson, and thereby an increased concern over the general direction of society by the late 1960s.[94]

Throughout the 60s, from John A.T. Robinson's *Honest to God* to the meetings of Vatican II, the urgent call for liberal change in thought and practice within the churches was met with equal defiance from those who urged that things remain as they were or even return to older ways, before the advent of social Christianity. In both camps there was an implicit assumption that their own position must necessarily prevail. Thus, divisiveness within the fold escalated, marginalizing the overall influence of the institutional churches in society in the process. It seemed a price worth paying, either in the name of revitalization by liberals or in defence of core beliefs and another type of revitalization.

In such circumstances there are also those who will go elsewhere. In seeking a sense of "awe," as Julian Huxley would put it, the religions of the East were a possibility – another theme McLeod cites. Often repackaged for the West, specific examples could be seen in the public attachment of the Beatles to the maharishi Yogi. Generally the traditions of Western Christian mysticism were completely ignored. Ostensibly drugs also supplied a means toward a higher level of transcendental meditation.

Permeating all of this was a sense of experimentation that led in some cases to the idea of a new morality, and which for others was merely promiscuous behaviour. This latter view provoked figures such as Mary Whitehouse to lash out against these trends by focusing upon the media, which was seen as promoting such developments. For those who abandoned old religious behavioural norms, a life of hedonism was actually a logical possibility. Certainly Michael Onfray, in his book *In Defense of Atheism* (2007), would argue that a positive libertarianism and hedonism was superior to the irrationality of religion based upon fear of death. But agnostics and atheists in fact tended to encourage a secular version of a Judeo-Christian behavioural code, at least for the sake of an orderly society, and with the belief, in some cases, that a degree of altruism and service to the community were innate. At root, however was a deeper consideration. As Austin Dacey has said, "If one's practice of a religion is to be authentic, it must be based on one's own honest assessment of what makes sense. The difference between believers and unbelievers, then, is not that the latter lack a conscience, but rather that their conscience inclines them away from belief."[95]

John A.T. Robinson's ideas (or Harvey Cox's, with his *Secular City* in the United States) on the new morality also had the further effect of subdividing the ranks of liberal Christians. The condemnation of conservative Archbishop Fisher was predictable. But even Michael Ramsey, his liberal, social Christian successor, also had sharp disagreements with Bishop Robinson's theological views. Doing away with the idea of a God "out there" also went too far for many on the Christian Left. The transcendent seemed to disappear altogether. Involvement with causes such as aid-to-liberation forces in the developing world through the World Council of Churches caused similar rifts, especially for Christians in the centre. It brought back the question posed to the Reverend Dick Sheppard, "the radio priest," by Archbishop William Temple in the 1930s regarding Sheppard's involvement with the secular leaders of the peace movement. Were the objectives of Christianity being fulfilled, or was the Churchman being exploited by others for secular purposes? Of Bishop Robinson's *Honest to God*, Alasdair MacIntyre of Oxford noted at the time that "what is striking about Dr. Robinson's book is first and foremost that he is an atheist."[96] This statement was not that unique, but he later expanded his observation to note that Robinson "is a very conservative atheist. He wants an atheist Christology, he wishes to retain and to revise the notion of worship, and his moral attitudes are in fact intensely conservative."[97] He sounded like an Anglican Comte.

Robinson defended himself by saying that he wrote the book in order to move the majority of people whose lives seem "to have nothing to do with 'God'" and that he was therefore glad to touch so many, even if criticism did bring some pain to him.[98] MacIntyre understood this in part by asserting that "between the 10 percent or so of clear and convinced Christians at one end of the scale and the 10 percent or so of convinced skeptics at the other there is the vast mass of the population, mostly superstitious to some degree."[99] Clearly that great middle group was Robinson's target but did he understand them? Was this manner of approach really appropriate for an Anglican bishop? Robinson risked satisfying no one.

At this time the theme of Christianity in trouble was part of a general view of a society in trouble. As G.I.T. Machin has stated, "Within a century in which the churches had to face and adapt to an unprecedented amount of social change, the 1960s provided the most intense concentration of innovation and challenge."[100] Even though recent historians like Brown have highlighted the 1960s as a period of rapid decline for the churches, there is no general agreement about the pivotal nature of the 1960s in this respect. Some have stuck to older views of the decline as more gradual over a very much longer period. There was certainly a contemporary consciousness of decline in the 1960s among the church leaders and engaged members of congregations, which compelled a sense of urgency in restructuring a packaging of Christianity in a more modern and seemingly relevant way. Brown's emphasis upon the disaffection of women with attendance and membership could be linked to the rising issue of the need to ordain women in all the churches at the time. George Berstein has pointed to another "paradox" that "while people in the middle class were more likely to attend church, those in the working class actually had a more positive attitude towards Christianity."[101]

Richard Hoggart in *The Uses of Literacy* (1957) described the working-class world of "primary religion" of the early 1950s. He acknowledged that Christianity was weakening, with most people not attending church or chapel except for "special family occasions"[102] and being "along with other classes ... affected by ideas which seemed to have disposed of the claims of religion."[103] Yet, as Hoggart pointed out the working classes "still believe underneath in certain ways."[104] For Hoggart they still believed in "the purposiveness of life," some sort of afterlife that they constantly were reminded of, and a basic, unanalysed Christianity held as "the best form of ethics," or "morals not metaphysics."[105] In summary, "doing your best to be an 'ordinary decent' person – that is what Christianity means,"[106] not being fanatic or idealistic. For Hoggart they were "confirmed pragmatists" in a real world of difficult circumstances.[107] It could also consist of an old hymn or sentimental song displaying "a feeling heart," "not to be derided,"[108] when respectfully performed at gatherings.

In his book *The Need for Certainty* (1984) Robert Towler uses the term 'exemplarism' to describe a moral type of religiousness, not associated with the formal church, in the fashion of Hoggart.[109] At a more formally intellectual level that appealed to other social classes, exemplarism was seen in Ernest Renan, author of *The Life of Christ* (1863), who left the Catholic Church twenty years earlier but remained a religious follower of the exemplary Christ.[110] As Towler pointed out, exemplarism was compatible with science and individualism, was certainly one part of the general practical message of the Christian churches, and lived in many organizations associated with the churches, such as the Samaritans.[111] Berstein would also see considerable evidence of confidence in Christianity not only among the traditionally, non-attending working class but in the recently disaffected middle class who continued to support a network of charitable organizations largely for religious reasons.[112] Diffusive Christianity remained as difficult a thing to measure as it had been decades earlier.

In spite of contemporary writers who dwelt on the theme of decline, such as Arthur Koestler, Berstein generally questions its validity. On the moral side the Conservative Norman Tebbit referred to the 1960s as the "third rate decade."[113] Malcolm Muggeridge enlarged the period under review to 1951–64, which he then categorized as "political, economic and moral free wheeling."[114] This image of "self-indulgence" of course played heavily into the need for a reintroduction of old Victorian virtues which was part of Margaret Thatcher's reforms in the 1980s, although the Conservatives had also been in power in the period Muggeridge discusses.[115]

Divorce rates rose enormously, as seemingly did abortions after their legalization, and so, too, did the prominence of homosexuality when it was legalized. After the *Lady Chatterley's Lover* case, the stage, film, and books were all more explicit about sexual issues than ever before. As Philip Larkin said, "sexual intercourse began in 1963." But the period of greatest advance for these things was also one of affluence: "You never had it so good," was the phrase popularly associated Conservative Prime Minister Harold Macmillan stated. The stagflation years of the 1970s had as much to do with the emergence of Thatcherism in the next decade as a reaction to the moral evils of the 1960s.

In *Family Newspapers? Sex, Private Life and the British Popular Press, 1918–1978* (2009) Adrian Bingham describes the role of the popular press in moving society forward through more public acceptance of discussions of sex during the era of democratizing sex from the Second World War to the late 1960s. Here the 1950s are cited as the period in which many earlier influences were integrated, which lessened the emphasis upon the "permissive 1960s." This affected religion, of course, and set a wider context for the behaviour of women and other excluded groups once one reached the 1960s. Indeed the Lady Chatterley case was also just into the 1960s, and John A.T. Robinson was known as the "Lady Chatterley Bishop" by the late 1960s because of his frank statements in defence of Lawrence, years before the publication of *Honest to God*.[116]

In the *New Society* survey at the end of the decade there was in fact a 77 per cent objection to "the publicity given to sex."[117] Though over half the sample felt that one of the things that people like was the "freedom of the individual," nevertheless a surprisingly high number objected to student unrest and supported capital punishment (70 per cent were in favour of retaining hanging). The editors concluded that one could as easily call it "the Cautious Sixties" as the "Swinging Sixties." This has not been part of the collective memory-image since the 1960s. However, there was also evidence in the survey that people "overwhelmingly" believed in higher old-age pensions. This is supported by John Benson who saw in the increased care of the vulnerable, elderly, and children a refutation of any argument for an increase in "self-absorption" by those of wage-earning age.[118] As the survey also indicated, "the continuing change which people plumped for, after pensions, was a 'rising standard of living.'"

The prosperity of the later 1950s and early 1960s was also matched by the influx of large numbers of young people who were the first products of the comprehensive secondary schools and the ongoing expansion of universities. The expectation of a meritocracy also gave birth simultaneously to critical studies of the Establishment and to the altered image of the working masses in such media phenomena as *Coronation Street*.

The emergence of the Socialist Humanists (or Ethical Socialists) was also part of the same. While it is true that they had little directly to say about religion (except perhaps E.P. Thompson in his attack upon Methodism in the 'Chiliasm of Despair' section of *The Making of the English Working Class*), their critique of existing society was moralistic. A new generation of socialists, the New Left, as some described them, emerged as figures such as R.H. Tawney disappeared and moderates such as Roy Jenkins moved toward what would later be called the Social Democrats. Political differences existed within this grouping. Most had departed from the Communist party by the late 1950s as a result of the Soviet invasion of Hungary as well as the excesses of Stalin. An exception to this was the University of London historian Eric Hobsbawm.

At the centre of the Socialist Humanists was the Welsh writer and Cambridge academic Raymond Williams. His early views, as expressed in *Culture and Society* (1961), showed a strong commitment to popularizing truth and beauty by broadening the conventional confines of what was largely high culture. This more democratic culture would still preserve civilization in his view, and thus oppose views that legitimized the domination of the ruling strata of society. It was ethically based. In a similar fashion E.P. Thompson, in *The Making of the English Working Class* (1963), described the historical birth of a radical collective culture of people rescuing it from the condescension of traditional history writing, including its victimization in the service of Marxist theory. Both Thompson and Williams shared a belief in progress based upon reason. Later in his career Thompson continued Bertrand Russell's work combating the threat of nuclear warfare. Indeed he held many of Russell's assumptions.

Richard Hoggart might also be included in this number, as he shared the same background in support of adult education, as well as socialism, seen in Williams and Thompson. Hoggart's way of looking at literature was inclusive, and recognized the difficulties of integrating the perspectives of the working classes into higher education. He also supported the publication of *Lady Chatterley's Lover* along with John A.T. Robinson. Through their approach to culture, the Socialist Humanists pointed to a world vision that would no longer be manipulated by the power elite, pursuing truth and beauty, as well as social justice, for all.

In the same period, the advancement of the Christian agenda through literature could include everything from Eliot's poetry, to the allegorical writings of J.R.R. Tolkien and Lewis, to Greene's so-called Catholic novels. It was often difficult to fathom a clear and unified message beyond the reprinting of Lewis's *Mere Christianity*. On the other side of the Atlantic, the Cambridge-trained Marshall McLuhan contributed new insight into the understanding of the effects of visual media and their messages. How this related, if at all, to McLuhan's strong Catholicism is unclear, and indeed he may have been deliberately ambiguous.

New attitudes to sexual behaviour were enabled by the pill as the moves to deregulate the intervention of church and state in the bedrooms, entertainments, and lifestyles of the nation were made possible by the sheer number of youthful protesters and their potential votes. The pill and deregulation of sex each had an impact upon the social control aspect of religion. However, this did not necessarily amount to a godless age. Christianity would not be fully displaced. It was clear that Christian leaders could no longer set the nation's morality. As Keith Robbins has stated: "The churches could make statements and pass resolutions which were not without significant insight into the social consequences of what was taking place ... Late twentieth-century democracy in the United Kingdom functioned, at least to some degree, as a market place of competing but also negotiating moralities. Just as Christian leaders said that Christianity could only be freely accepted, so, whatever morality or moralities, stemmed from it had to be an example not an imposition."[119] Perhaps, as Thomas Luckmann has suggested in *The Invisible Religion* (1967), individuals could now build a private system embracing a purpose for living from whatever was available in the market place of ideas. This would apply even within the most rigidly organized churches as observed for Roman Catholics by the late 1960s.[120]

These choices, which according to Brown were taken collectively in the recrafting of morality,[121] involved a *popular* adoption of new positions, "not something handed down from above," and these positions were "largely free from intellectuals." For Brown it is why there was the cataclysmic "death" of Christian British culture (McLeod calls it a rupture). Jeremy Morris, however, dislikes Brown's use of the word death, preferring "displacement" given that the churches remain the "largest voluntary organizations in the country" and that "no single alternative viewpoint to that of Christianity has yet emerged as a referent of public and private morality."[122] There is also the transformation of the role of religion within communities which is not always "a straight-forward process of decline."[123]

Is Brown correct in so diminishing the influence of intellectuals? In an age of mass media is it not possible that their ideas could have a rapid trickle-down effect? As Charles Taylor has stated, we live in "an extraordinary moral culture" where we are awakened by "world-wide movements of sympathy," aided by the media, and nowhere more than in the Western world.[124] Who directs our attention to these matters?

Into the context of the decline, but not demise, of British Christianity, the heritage of the unbelievers and the dynamics of the long sixties now enter the four figures under consideration. Each had something to offer Britain and the Western world, both in their heyday and, in legacy, for decades thereafter.

2

One World, One Faith:
The Quest for Unity in Julian Huxley's Religion
of Evolutionary Humanism

Before Julian Huxley, there had been others, such as Auguste Comte, who had advocated replacing older religious traditions, especially Christianity, with new, non-theistic, rationalist systems of belief. What was unusual in the system proposed by the celebrated British scientist and philosopher, Sir Julian Huxley (1887–1975), was its extraordinarily strong penchant for unity. With an urgent message that humankind was master of its own fate, and at a time that was pivotal in the history of the planet, Huxley offered a new vision, or secular religion, that was necessary for the future. An analysis of the quest for unity in his belief system and the purposes which it was designed to serve, as well as the effectiveness of his message, form the substance of this chapter.

Early in his professional career, Huxley had sketched what he meant by religion. He described "scientific," and later, "evolutionary," humanism in his longest dissertation on the subject, *Religion without Revelation*, published in 1927. A substantially revised edition appeared some thirty years later. Huxley believed that a new faith was needed in a modern world marked by the rapid decline of existing religions. His inspiration came via a casual reading of a volume of Lord Morley's essays while he was awaiting surgery in Colorado. Morley's observation that "the next great task of science will be to create a religion for humanity,"[1] as well as his use of the word "science," were both crucial for Huxley. Morley made it clear to him that "any real progress in religion nowadays would be the slow product of generations of thinkers and workers reacting on the common thought and practice of the times."[2] Huxley did not envisage himself, initially at least, as a Luther or a Wesley, let alone a Jesus, and he presumed that evolutionary humanism would continue to develop during his lifetime and after. While at first he referred to his religion more as an "attitude of mind"[3] than anything else, he would develop an enduring set of principles in the years that followed.

Huxley's initial venture into this arena came in 1916 when, at the city auditorium in Houston, he delivered a lecture touching upon religion as part of a series on the theme of "Biology and Man." A recent graduate of Oxford, Huxley was employed as an assistant professor in the newly founded biology department at Rice Institute. The lecture was covered by the local press and, for the first of many times, he had to face a hostile reception from orthodox believers. In a letter to the editor of the Houston Chronicle, Huxley took pains to defend what he argued was an attempt to overcome reactionary views toward science and evolution that "stand in the way of any religious advance." Though he argued that his criticisms were only of "low types of religion," it was not altogether clear that his stance was friendly to traditional faiths.[4] It was a valuable, though perhaps painful, lesson in the need for effective persuasion, albeit one not well-learned.

While his *Memories* (1970) do not record this early incident, they do describe Huxley's feelings at Aldershot about one year later, when he was in training for the British Intelligence Corps. There Huxley found time away from his career as a scientist and the chance to read a large volume of religious publications, in order "to understand how the religious mind works, and what induces changes in doctrine."[5] His diary for the period corroborates these interests.[6] Among the persons with whom he consulted about matters of faith was William Temple, the future archbishop of Canterbury. Huxley had first encountered Temple at Oxford as an undergraduate while attempting "to spill over the edge" of his "scientific specialism (Honours School of Zoology) and dabble in philosophy."[7] Exactly what advice Temple provided at college or during the training period in 1917 remains unclear – though on the latter occasion Huxley acknowledged that Temple's theology got "things into black-and-white," which was apparently a "great crystallizer of dissolved thought."[8] A subsequent observation that Temple's beliefs were "radically different" from his own emerging concepts was an understatement.[9]

By the early 1920s Huxley was ready to formulate some of his own concepts and to add more content to his religion. In 1923 he published the *Essays of a Biologist*, one of which contained his earliest definition of religion: "Religion itself is the reaction between man as a personality on the one side, and, on the other, all of the universe with which he comes in contact."[10] At first glance, this definition pictures an enormous gap between two very different realms. Indeed until this point in his life, he was struck by the dysfunctions of psychological division within himself and in the world about him. But from the start Huxley felt that through science a truth had to be conveyed for building a better world: "not only does the unity of nature demand a unity of religion, but such unity of religion would be of the highest importance as a bond of civilization."[11] Ironically, while he would derive much from science, especially from Darwinism, Huxley saw the means of harmonizing the individual with the universe by organizing "our knowledge of outer reality after the pattern of a personality" and "our experiences of the universe in relation with the driving forces of our soul or mental being."[12]

Huxley's adherence to Darwinism followed in line with that of his father, Leonard, and his grandfather, T.H. Huxley, "Darwin's bulldog." Julian Huxley once called his grandfather a "religious" man, although the latter was well-known for his unpleasant confrontation at Oxford with Bishop Samuel Wilberforce in defence of *On the Origin of Species*, and for his attributed coinage of the word "agnosticism." Nonetheless, he described T.H. Huxley as "a man deeply and essentially religious by nature," referring to his "reverence for truth and for moral virtue"[13] rather than to a conventional belief in God. He subsequently observed that T.H. Huxley was "bred by nineteenth-century humanitarianism out of traditional Christian ethics."[14]

Julian Huxley also displayed a well-ingrained tendency toward Idealism, as did many in his generation.[15] Indeed, a commitment to some sort of higher realm of truth and beauty and a strong sense of the need for moral development in himself and others was evident throughout his life. Here he was influenced by members of the other side of his family – the Arnolds – in particular the "moral – religious – literary combination" to be found in the works of both Matthew Arnold and Mary Augusta Ward.[16]

Reading a full range of such texts in the family library undoubtedly inspired the literary bent in young Julian, which won him the Newdigate Prize for English verse and balanced his first class degree in Natural Science at Oxford. The same propensity to excel in both science and literature can be seen in the early life of his younger brother, Aldous, who intended originally to be a physician but disease destroyed his eyesight and turned him exclusively toward writing. These were also the realms that Julian hoped to bridge both for himself and others. As science progressed, he hoped that literature would also develop and at some point the two would meet and mix. But this conjuncture was of even greater urgency than an improved dialogue between the cultures of science and literature. It was inextricably bound to that attitude of mind which underlay his scientific humanism.

This gap concerned him as late as the mid-1950s when Huxley suggested a solution in a letter to Umberto Campagnolo:

> I would say that the real problem today is not that of my linking up a separate field of study called classical culture with modern culture, including scientific thought, but that of introducing the historical approach into all studies. In this way the role of the classics in the development of human thought and feeling becomes clear, but in addition science is seen not merely as a static collection of facts and principles, but a developing adventure of thought. In other words, both the Humanities and the Sciences could come to be regarded as part of a comprehensive humanism. The history of man is the progressive realisation of new possibilities, and this applies both to literature and the arts and to science.[17]

He had already led an international effort to produce the History of the Scientific and Cultural Development of Mankind under the auspices of UNESCO. To Huxley, evolutionary humanism would end the schism between the cultures of science and the arts that C.P. Snow and others described. He also emphasized the importance of understanding scientific facts and ideas in relation to history: "The biologist knows that they will not be directly applicable in detail to cultural evolution, but he can be sure that they have their human analogies, and that equally important ideas will emerge from the study of human history as an over-all unitary process, ideas that will escape detection so long as history is treated merely as a record of separate sequences of events."[18]

To achieve the ultimate goal of fusion, there was much that needed to be done in the ranks of science itself. As Huxley moved toward founding his religion he was also assuming a leadership role among scientists. Pure scientific research had led to his appointment to the chair of zoology at King's College, London, in 1925. His agenda, however, was much more comprehensive than simply earning a good reputation among his fellow biologists. Huxley worked very hard in this period to rekindle support for Darwinism among scientists, or more particularly, to counter the doubts that had arisen over natural selection from roughly the mid-1890s to the 1920s. To that end, he wove together work in a number of specialties, including genetics. Huxley saw progress in the development of many species through their successful control of the environment. Though internal elements did not predetermine such developments, he did find many examples of unidirectional evolutionary trends as revealed in particular by paleontology. This updated version of evolutionary theory ultimately led to the publication of *Evolution: The Modern Synthesis* in 1942. While troublesome to some at the time, and to many more biologists and other scientists thereafter, it contributed much to the unification of biology, and also aimed at the unification of science in general.[19]

In the early twentieth century, as Roger Smith explains, "there was at no time a united and separate science community in spite of the way common language tended to imply the existence of a distinct social entity."[20] He credits Huxley as being one of the most important figures of the interwar period in moving scientists to think beyond their narrow specialties. While science was his principle guide, Huxley also sought a ground in modern philosophy, especially in French philosopher Henri Bergson's *Creative Evolution* (1907). This did not please some Darwinians, who objected to criticisms by Bergson, a non-biologist, of mechanistic explanations of evolution through natural selection. Yet, according to Marc Swetlitz, Bergson's ideas about individuality and its progress through evolution to man as the most independent of creations made an early and lasting impression upon Huxley.[21] As Michael Ruse has pointed out, Huxley's biological progressionism was grounded in his humanism and "the link between the two was a phenomenon of culture rather than straight science."[22] Vassiliki Smocovitis has suggested that Huxley's modern synthesis of evolution contained an "articulation of a liberal, humanistic and secular world view."[23] John Greene has also demonstrated in more concrete terms how Huxley's worldview shaped much of his work in biology. For Huxley, "biological progress was important only insofar as it validated faith in the progress of mankind."[24]

To that end, Huxley also worked to improve his skills in communication, and learned much from his association with H.G. Wells and his son, Gip, (G.P. Wells) in the production of *The Science of*

Life (1929–1930), a work of rationalist thought that attracted a wide lay readership. Indeed, developing these communication skills was sufficiently important to Huxley that he resigned his chair at London in 1927 to devote himself full-time to writing. As Bowler has pointed out, Huxley was "one of the few professional scientists who actually abandoned an academic career for writing and other forms of social engagement."[25] In time, he had his own literary agent who helped build better links and financial remuneration from publishers. But for this he also had to face the charge of dilettantism from some scientists.[26] As a populariser of science through books, lectures, and broadcasts Huxley attempted to reach the general public and provide them not only with specific knowledge but with an attitude toward life. The latter was decidedly secular, a necessity if a science-based faith was to succeed. In due course he became the foremost scientific generalist of his time. As a prominent authority on science and many other matters by the 1940s he was, as D.L. LeMahieu has put it, an "intellectual as celebrity."[27]

Huxley maintained a high profile nationally and internationally to the end of his life. His writing talents and his close association with Aldous brought Huxley into the company of the literati. It was Julian who led the memorial service for Aldous in December, 1963. Huxley also enjoyed the company of the rich and famous, such as the actress Greta Garbo. He was interested in the new media of broadcasting and gave talks about science and religion on the radio in the 1930s. Often reinforcing the more select fame in such publications as *Evolution: The Modern Synthesis* (1942) he broadened his appeal by being a regular contributor to *The Brains Trust* on radio at the same time. In 1943 the BBC received 3,000 letters per week concerning the program topics and had an estimated audience of at least ten million. Huxley became the authority figure on science as well as on a number of other subjects. In the years that followed, his work expanded into television and often involved programs on nature. He had also produced the Oscar-winning documentary film *The Private Life of the Gannet*. Much of his television work certainly served as a model for similar endeavours by colleagues and disciples, such as Jacob Bronowski's *The Ascent of Man* and, in the United States, Carl Sagan's *Cosmos*. As secretary of the London Zoological Society (1935–42), Huxley revivified popular interest in zoos and was often photographed by the press escorting prominent figures – such as Winston Churchill and the family of American Ambassador Joseph Kennedy – around London Zoo. This circle of associates also led him to speaking engagements. In his rejection of crude materialism, he was a companion of Charles Raven, theologian and supporter of science. As Bowler has described, liberal Anglicans and religious modernists welcomed his company, as did the later Fellowship of Religious Humanists.[28] Ironically, as Bowler has also pointed out, Huxley's belief that emotions must be part of one's worldview divided him somewhat from the more aggressively rationalistic modernists who were also losing ground in church circles.[29]

His attempt to bridge the gap between science and the humanities likewise opened other avenues for addresses to a host of organizations. He began touring the United States on behalf of the Allied cause before Pearl Harbor in 1941, and continued to appear regularly there at the podium or on television until the 1960s, speaking on many subjects. Huxley was prominent at the World Conference of Intellectuals held in Poland in 1948 and at the World Conference of Scientists in London in 1955. He joined the Pugwash Movement in the 1950s in the company of Bertrand Russell and Cyrus Eaton. In relation to his Evolutionary Humanism he was a leader of the Humanist Press Association and was President of the International Congress on Humanism and Ethical Cultural which met in Amsterdam in 1952. The latter activity was a consolidator for much that might seem disparate on first inspection of so much public activity. It also reinforced allied engagements with the Eugenics Society (1926–64) and various British and American branches of Planned Parenthood. Even the attacks of conservative Christians, and later Creationists, gave Huxley a form of immortal fame well after his death in 1975.

The specific approach which Huxley took in his theoretical constructions was to find meaning in the processes of nature and then apply these meanings to everything else. Encouraged by what he saw as the important factor of progressive individuality within animal behaviour, he now expanded this to include the entire living world. Diversity was important as a mechanism of progress within nature, including man, and ultimately as the basis of religion. Thus the construction of Huxley's new religion in this period was directly related to his view of science, infused with philosophical insights from Bergson. John Greene has also noted the importance of psychology in providing a link, for Huxley, between biology and human values and desires.[30]

Many of the specifics of the new faith were offered in *Religion without Revelation*. As Huxley had learned in Houston and elsewhere, the method of presentation was key to the success of the message itself. In keeping with a spirit of unity, he presented the study as an attempt to reconcile and find a middle ground between the extremes of bad, limited religion and a negative, hyper-critical science. He maintained that he wanted religion once again to come to the "forefront of civilization,"[31] and insisted that it must be made appropriate to the advanced, science-based minds of the twentieth century. But he also observed that "complete skepticism does not work"[32] and that it was "an important duty to know when to be agnostic."[33] The agnostic Huxley recognized nothing beyond the world of natural experience; he did not believe in Heaven, Hell, or a Last Judgment, he had no knowledge of another life, and he dismissed any information derived from spiritualism as trivial.[34]

For Huxley, theism was tied to the observable decline of traditional faiths and would not be part of the new religion. Yet he acknowledged that old ways died hard; as biological evolution demonstrated, older forms could co-exist with new species for extended periods.[35] But Huxley, unlike Comte, refused to adopt organizational schemes, techniques, or sentiments from existing churches. Syncretism was not an acceptable option, even in the short run.

Nevertheless, Huxley did find one theistic doctrine attractive: the Trinity. It combined some interesting features of diversity-in-unity: the Father representing the external universe; the Son personifying human nature; and the Holy Spirit standing for the "ideas of value,"[36] partly internal and partly external and transcendent. The first two features were, in a sense, what he posited as the purpose of religion in his 1923 definition, which linked the individual with the universe. But it was clear to Huxley that such dated, theistic concepts must disappear. Religion must evolve like all other things;[37] stasis was not an option, and a failing religion would do well to assist in the inevitable transition.[38] The Trinity had been an "elastic and vital doctrine"[39] in its time but greater things could be achieved by accepting the unity of all nature.[40] Everything was built upon the same matter. Mind and body were thus linked in the unity of one fundamental substance.[41]

Since the loss of religion was the greatest defect of the modern world, a new religion was a moral necessity for Huxley.[42] The intellectual basis of religious thought needed to be constituted by the power of nature, with suitable goals and ideals for humankind.[43] Even the term "god" might be employed to denote unity in the universe if the notion of a supernatural entity was removed.[44] In 1927, and subsequently, Huxley would suggest a number of ways for reforming theology. Initially, he recommended a threefold approach that involved accepting agnosticism, promoting natural science, and expanding the field of psychology.[45] In the last two areas science was depicted as the means for shaping the religion of the future,[46] with psychology as a special tool for exploring individuality or personality within the natural world.

The science of the mind was also important to Huxley for personal reasons. Since mind and matter must unite, mental breakdowns were seen as the product of "the mental house being divided against itself."[47] Huxley experienced seven such episodes during his life. The first was certainly linked to sexual frustrations nurtured in the smothering guilt of the late Victorian ethos. Acknowledging that Freudianism was a useful approach in this and other situations, the root explanation for this case seemed to lie in the basic "biological disharmony" of sexual maturity being reached prior to overall maturity.[48] Huxley dismissed the Freudian notion of the father-complex as the origin of theism. However in a celebrated 1959 address on "The Evolutionary Vision" delivered at the University of Chicago's Darwin Centennial Conference, Huxley did state that "evolutionary man can no longer take refuge from his loneliness in the arms of a divinized father-figure whom he has himself created."[49] For Huxley, who never believed in a personal god,[50] religion would preserve a sense of awe in communion with the universe. Awe would include appreciation of truth, beauty and mystery.[51] Here, again, his Idealism seems to have resurfaced.[52]

Huxley would work out the component elements of "evolutionary humanism" from the late 1920s onward. The 1957 edition of *Religion without Revelation*, for example, contained two new chapters as well as a few revisions and deletions. In this and in other publications pertaining to his faith, he continued to pursue a unitary vision and increasingly employed the language of modern psychology. As a writer and radio commentator, Huxley was at times willing to forgo standard prose in favor of more arcane appellations: on one occasion he referred to the common substance of the material and the mental as "world-stuff,"[53] with due credit to William James. Under this new rubric, Huxley both reworded and reconceptualized religious terminology. A divine "conscious purpose" was replaced by an "adaptive function" which connoted that "the old theological teleology" was being substituted with a "scientific pseudo-teleology" as the mechanism of purpose in the evolution of life.[54] The soul, of course, was really personality. Mysticism and meditative acts were now seen as based upon the desire to escape the self.[55] Faith required psychological analysis as it was the "sum of our beliefs as they predispose us to thought and action."[56] A Freudian "super-ego" was the developed moral sense that replaced the conscience. Consciousness of sin resulted from the conflict of our instincts with self-restraint and altruism. It could be overcome by blending all "into a unitary mental organism."[57] "Evil," the destructive aggressive impulses within us, could be also be transcended in this way and replaced by "wholeness." These were the "higher reaches of personal development" in the mental construction of personality.[58] The social psychological aspects of religion were to guide individuals and move them toward convergence in "a single organic world of society and culture."[59] This was mankind's destiny, "his position and rôle in the universe."[60] Huxley was adamant that this quest to place man within the natural order needed to be based on the progressive discovery of scientifically established truth, which would combat the influence of a dualism created by the persistent belief in the supernatural or "daimonic."[61] "Scientific," and subsequently "evolutionary" humanism meant that humankind was part of the natural world of plants and animals, subject to the same laws governing their world and not under the control of any supernatural force.

In his crusade for unity, Huxley identified Darwin as one figure who had demonstrated the unity of all life.[62] Huxley also maintained that his grandfather had made a fundamental error in embracing a too limited definition of evolution, and endorsing an essentially static view of ethics.[63] T.H. Huxley's intuitive theory, like all similar ethical systems, had been superseded by modern psychology.[64] Moral systems were based upon societal systems, which must themselves adapt to change. In this way they were part of the evolutionary process.[65]

A closely related issue was the perplexing question of purpose in the evolutionary process. A number of historians have pointed out that, at least at the time of the publication of *Evolution: The Modern Synthesis* in 1942, Huxley had conceded that natural selection did not reveal any purposive mechanism in evolution for nature as a whole.[66] Pure science, therefore, could not provide this element for the new religion. In Huxley's system this could also be supplied by the human side of the partnership with science, a valid move since what was human, including the mind, was part of nature. John Greene has pointed out that Huxley considered this to be most important in laying the foundation for a worldview and inspiring the march of progress.[67] As Bowler has also noted, from Huxley's collaboration with Wells in the production of *The Science of Life*, and through the inspiration of Bergson, "For Huxley, the new Darwinism did not rule out a role for the idea of a moral purpose in the history of life."[68] Man, as Huxley put it, was "the only arbiter of his destiny." The "source of all truth, beauty, morality and purpose is to be found in human nature."[69] But as William B. Provine notes, Huxley's categories for the modes of evolution in this mid-century synthesis also limited any future attempts by Christians to search for a *modus vivendi* with Darwinism.[70]

By positing an evolving moral system rooted in the cosmic process, Julian Huxley was moving toward a stance taken by Herbert Spencer, as Greene reminds us.[71] But Spencer's social philosophy was certainly not part of his worldview. Rather, Huxley presumed that laissez-faire was breaking down.[72] Planning, instead, was the hallmark of his approach to society's needs, as indicated by his membership in the independent research organization Political and Economic Planning (PEP) from the early 1930s on.[73]

Perhaps the best guide to his opinions in these matters is *If I Were Dictator* (1934), published as a volume in a series in which authors were asked to describe how they would create an ideal society. Far more than a utopian novel could, this text reveals Huxley's agenda. On the basis that man was the only arbiter of his destiny, he held that "the time is ripe for spurring my people over the hedge into the new country of scientific humanism."[74] In this new setting governance was to be invested in a Central Science Council which would oversee more specialized councils that dealt with different areas. A welfare state providing health care and many other social services later introduced by Britain's post-war Labour government was discussed in terms of a scientific method "by which large improvements in our control over nature (including human nature and its products such as social systems) can be made rapidly and without appalling waste."[75] Huxley made it quite clear that as dictator he would ensure "an organic, stably progressive, balanced community" and would "not want laissez-faire individualism, for that is not organic."[76] Notwithstanding this rejection of laissez-faire, there remained a tension in Huxley's overall social vision in which *Gesellschaft* (society) seemed to triumph on many occasions over *Gemeinschaft* (community).[77]

Huxley was rather creative when proposing a reorganization of all media into a system that would ensure a balance of biases, as well as introduce American-style methods of polling public opinion, "to find out what his people are thinking."[78] A public discourse based upon "intellectual gentlemanliness"[79] would be encouraged by means of an education that avoided dogmatism. To Huxley, dogmatic assertions were often the result of an old-fashioned religion that provided escape mechanisms: a faith still popular, but nonetheless in decline.[80] He would hasten this decline by disestablishing and disendowing the Church of England.[81] Still, there was to be no "artificial unity of opinion"[82] and traditional beliefs would not be eradicated. The state would be given broad powers to oversee parenthood, which was an "essential upward step in man's progress towards full control of nature and destiny," and to provide means for contraception, which was "not purely a private matter"[83] – although Catholics would have the right of opting out. New rules on divorce would be written[84] and the effects of legalized abortion would be tested.[85] Julian Huxley's optimism in these matters contrasts sharply with his brother's dystopian vision in *Brave New World*.

Huxley was less concerned with reactions against the ambitiousness of his plans than with "the danger of a revolution engineered against me by those who think my progress is too slow."[86] Here he addressed the challenge of the "social religions" of communism and fascism, especially the latter, which he viewed as "only a short-cut, and a very dangerous and disagreeable one" with "its crude nationalism, its racial and class spirit."[87] His project would move beyond them and, unlike them, would proceed in the spirit of a "broader humanitarianism." Even if in trying to connect with the masses he was influenced by Fascism – in particular Mussolini's "getting his finger on the pulse of the populace"[88] – Huxley regarded the new totalitarianisms as an early state of societal development, a primitive reaction that followed in the wake of the abandonment of the idea of God.[89]

In the real world of the 1930s and beyond, Huxley emerged as a powerful advocate for many of the proposals made in *If I Were*

Dictator. First and foremost, he championed the eugenics movement. Underlying this support was, once again, the goal of achieving
unity. Huxley viewed the contemporary social situation as essentially dysgenic: "the present state of mankind is unstable, at war
with itself."[90] "The most immediate thing to be done," he announced
in 1931, was "to ensure that mental defectives shall not have children" by whatever means necessary including, of course, sterilization.[91] He classified such actions as negative eugenics for "preventing
degeneration."[92] Positive, or long-range, eugenics aimed at improv-
ing the human stock and featured new techniques of artificial
insemination based upon the realization that "it is now open to man
and women to consummate the sexual function with those they love,
but to fulfill the reproductive function with those whom, on perhaps
quite other grounds, they admire."[93] But birth control remained as
the most "indispensable tool of eugenics as well as of rational control of population."[94] A lifelong advocate of contraception, Huxley
would lead a campaign for its adoption by international agencies,
especially in underdeveloped countries, would lobby for a Nobel
award for his friend, Margaret Sanger; and would clash with a number of prominent figures, including Lord Reith, when attempting to
promote these views on the BBC.

Huxley was also concerned with the misapplication of eugenics.
He came to believe that modern racial theory was unscientific, dangerous, wrong-headed, and divisive; in addition, it offended his sense
of the unity of the human race.[95] However, this position held by the
mid- 1930s was not where Huxley had begun. Indeed as Elazar
Barkan has pointed out,[96] his early days in Texas had made him a
supporter of segregation. This was reinforced by a general racism,
linked with scientific racisms, until he travelled to Africa and experienced direct contact with blacks. His breakthrough work was *Africa
View*, published in 1931 by Harper and Brothers. From this point
onward Huxley argued that the concept of race as used in popular
discourse was not credible. As he stated: "Let us also remember that
'race' is in any case a term of mere convenience to help in pigeon-
holing our knowledge of human diversity. The term is often used as if
'races' were definite entities, sharply marked off from each other. This
is simply not true."[97] For Huxley to not recognize that race is a "complicated subject" was "self-delusion" leading to the "unfortunate dissemination of much pseudo-science" such as the "great Nordic myth"
propagated by Houston Stewart Chamberlain and others.[98]

In touring Africa he concluded that "what concerns us at the moment is the improvability of the black, and this is an undoubted fact."[99] Huxley feared that a good future for Africa was in doubt unless colonial governments and missions supplied the necessary education for the people to forge ahead. Governments, in the name of Westernization, might supply training in trades but left "the mind and habits of the natives" unaltered. Missionaries, also in the name of Westernization, concentrated on theology and morals but discouraged "science or literature or liberal thought."[100] He thought the solution was "to make the Christianizing process, which he preferred over Islam, "a gradual one," "to temper it with that combination of science and humanism which is the new spirit of the post-war age, and may one day form the basis of some religion as yet unborn."[101] The latter suggested, along with what he regarded as the primitive state of African civilization, that this was a sort of *tabula rasa* situation where perhaps even the religion of evolutionary humanism could leap forward at a more rapid pace than elsewhere.

Huxley amplified this urgent call in an article in the *Fortnightly Review* a year later when he asserted that "Africa is the only continent the main lines of whose destiny are not yet decided."[102] As he argued concerning the very presence of whites in Africa:

We are there because we are a higher race; by right of conquest; by virtue of our superior gifts and powers. That is what is usually asserted. This may be true; but let us at least beware of arrogance. Even granted some degree of inherent superiority, that superiority is certainly not of a great order of magnitude. A century ago, the Dutch at the Cape, or the whites in the Southern States, quite sincerely believed that black men were separated from white by a great gulf which could never be bridged; they were predestined slaves, the whites predestined masters. Such ideas, though they linger on in many quarters, are simply not tenable today. The progress, educational and practical, of the negro in the United States, or of the native African where he has had proper training and opportunity gives it the lie. White and black overlap largely in regard to intelligence, energy, ability and character.[103]

Certainly by the early 1930s Huxley's general position toward blacks had shifted; he noted the importance of regional racial and cultural distractions, and believed that environment explained most of the instances of backwardness. But as Barkan has concluded, while Huxley now maintained a position against general racism regarding blacks, his pseudo-scientific racism remained, for example in his view that the intelligence of blacks is slightly below that of whites.[104] However, in *Africa View* Huxley did qualify even this, questioning if we will ever "devise a really satisfactory method of measuring inborn mental attributes" and concluding: "But – and the but is a big one – I am perfectly certain that if this proves to be … [possible] the differences between the racial averages will be small; and that they will be only an affair of averages, and that the great majority of the two populations will overlap as regards their innate intellectual capacities."[105] For all intents and purposes Huxley now presented a different face to his general audience. Certainly, as Tony Kushner points out,[106] in Huxley's disparaging comments about African culture there was latent racism that left room for concepts of racial types and hierarchies, but nevertheless he did urge changes in colonial policy. The mandate system could be extended along with more economic self-development, as Huxley saw no future for large-scale European settlement in Africa.[107] This was reinforced by his pamphlet, co-authored by Phyllis Deane and entitled *The Future of the Colonies* (1944), which argued that the damage done to colonial areas must end: "And so long as the colonial peoples can be treated as inferiors, whether explicitly by colour-bar legislation or implicitly as not entitled to the same standard of life and living as ourselves, we shall still be to that extent bound by the ideas of the economics of scarcity and the consequent exploitation of some sections of the human race by others"[108]

In the 1940s the anthropologist Ashley Montague suggested the elimination of the term race altogether for scientific purposes. While Huxley mentioned that the debate was now more in the realm of social science than in physical science he was reluctant to do so. In a recent article Michelle Brattain has argued that Huxley resisted such sweeping statements citing the controversial British geneticist C.D. Darlington.[109] This was in the period of his headship of UNESCO. Brattain notes that Huxley at the time sided with the "enablers" who seemingly attempted to issue moderate statement but who also helped to perpetuate racial stereotypes. Huxley at the time, for example, suggested that blacks' "rhythm-loving" might be genetic.[110]

However, Huxley's outward shift toward liberal ground and away from general racism directed at blacks, as Barkan has pointed out, was followed by his departure from earlier, crude eugenic beliefs by 1936.[111] He was equally aware of how the Nazis, in particular, had mixed their theories with eugenics, and applied the admixture with devastating consequences. The publication with A.C. Haddon of *We Europeans: A Survey of "Racial" Problems* in 1935 by Jonathan Cape was intended, in spite of its complex authorship, as a popular weapon against Nazi racism.[112] Notions of racial purity were contrary to the diversity in populations which Huxley approved from both cultural and biological points of view.[113] Thus, as Diane Paul has explained, Huxley was one of those eugenicists who attacked the moral and class distortions of those on the movement's right.[114] A later, equally serious, conflict occurred during the Cold War in disputes with left-wing, especially Soviet, scientists, who emphasized environmental factors to the point that they sacrificed proper science in the service of their ideology. Once again the "religious elements" in Communist Russia, as in Nazi Germany, would have to be adjusted to internationalism in the interests of the unity of humanity.[115]

Huxley did come to realize that many of the older elements of liberalism were increasingly ineffectual. But liberalism also promoted a doctrine of progress that was necessary for humanity. Huxley, however, also claimed on many occasion that progress was not inevitable without hard, scientifically based planning. Just as in earlier phases of evolution, change was not completely random; since change was guided by the environment, "relevant analogies from evolutionary biology"[116] would have to be taken into account. Mankind's evolution needed to be crafted by the wisdom and efforts of humans if progress was to be made.[117]

From the late 1940s, Huxley helped to lead the Ideas Systems Group (ISG) in projects designed to serve this evolutionary cause. For Huxley, the examination of general ideas systems or "the ideological pattern of ideas and knowledge, values and beliefs" was a necessary first step in a "unitary" psychosocial process of exploring both the material and mental resources of humankind, a process which needed to occur before scientific planning could ensue.[118] Jacob Bronowski, the mathematician and humanities scholar, was among the group's most active members. Huxley's evolutionary humanism constantly surfaced within the ISG, although its mandate was to consider the most useful of any and all ideas. Huxley's approach was favored because the group feared "the number of unrelated, competing and even conflicting ideas" in the Western world.[119] Instead, unity and dynamism – the hallmarks of Huxley's thought – were needed. Huxley and company spoke in terms of a "humanist" (the new word for rationalist) agenda and advocated a New Humanist Institute and access to a reasonable share of the religious broadcasting activities of the BBC. The ISG brought together elements of the older PEP and a new lobby among the intelligentsia, and helped Huxley gain support for his continuing campaign for the new religion. By the 1950s, he had become president of the British Humanist Association. He was convinced that evolutionary humanism would become the spearhead of a "Humanist Revolution of thought, and [was] destined ... to become the dominant idea-system" of the next phase of world history.[120]

Huxley was also a pioneer in the emerging field of ecology, with particular interests in the dangers of overpopulation and the depletion of natural resources. Since the clashes within the eugenics movement in the 1930s, he had been concerned with the chronic conflict between environmentalists and hereditarians. Once again, he played the part of an apostle of unity: "Evolutionary biology provides us with another unifying idea of the greatest importance – the ecology idea. Ecology is scientific natural history; it is the science of relations par excellence – relations between organisms and their environment, and of organisms with each other. It helps us to understand how life makes a living."[121]

For Huxley "we are on the threshold of another major revolution, involving a new pattern of thought and a new approach to human destiny and its practical problems."[122] This new approach entailed "two rather distinct fields" of ecology and ideology, generating "linked currents of thought and action, that may be called the Ecological Revolution and the Humanist Revolution."[123] The population explosion was giving "a powerful impetus" to both, and as ecology is "the science of relational adjustment – the balanced relations of living organisms with their environment and with each other,"[124] this was understandable. On the humanist side, as humanity was part of nature, including emotions, as Bowler has stated, "evolutionism would provide a spiritual ecology" in relating our lives to the rest of nature.[125] Indeed in a paper delivered to the Idea Systems Group on 10 February 1951 Huxley seemed in agreement with an unidentified man that "the idea of Ecology was destined to have the same sort of importance for general thought in the next fifty years as the idea of Evolution had had in the half century after the publication of the *Origin of Species*."[126]

Huxley believed strongly in the notion of dynamic equilibrium. This notion of equilibrium depended on respecting the complexity of life in terms of its physical environment. As a scientist his work in bird physiology and embryology had made him acutely aware of regional environment before and after man's occupation. Even earlier in his teenage years, as he noted in an interview on the BBC on 19 December 1973, following the publication of volume two of his memoirs: "My most important interests were in wild life and its preservation. Actually it helped to get my scholarship – the main papers were in biology – by my answer to an essay "What would you do if you had a million pounds?" And I said – and they thought this was rather unusual for a boy of eighteen – I would buy up as much as possible the British coastline to keep it safe."[127]

Huxley's visits to Africa in particular inspired a blend of aestheticism and biology in his respect for nature as well as belief that ecology must be the basic science for emerging African societies. As he wrote in *Africa View*, "humanity does not live by bread alone; in East African wilds a stream of men and women down the generations may find quickening, refreshment, inspiration."[128] However, much of his work was also highly practical. Years later in *Man Stands Alone* (1941) Huxley took much time to explain ways in which the grasslands of the world could be increased, noting that "by proper attention to the ecology and genetics of grasses we could double the output of the world's pastures."[129] Such a development would benefit food production affecting both man and beast. Likewise in a chapter entitled "The Way of the Dodo" he argued that "two types of measure are of vital importance for the saving of the wild life of the world. One is the framing and ratification of international conventions for the protection of the fauna of large areas ... The other main measure is the establishment of national parks."[130]

In Africa he had encountered opposition, especially from spirit hunters, to his plans to protect endangered species. As he once described it: "With such people, brought up since childhood in an atmosphere of sport for sport's sake, it is impossible to argue. They find in the idea of wildlife sanctuaries a mere sentimentality, and those who disagree with them simply killjoys or sinister, 'Socialists.' And finally, worst offenders of all are those who kill only to make money out of killing, and value wildlife solely in terms of their own pockets."[131]

Thus Huxley, as was only to be expected, was one of the founders of the World Wildlife Fund and a prime supporter of Nature Conservancy. But ultimately it was the conservation of the habitat more than the preservation of individual species that concerned him.[132] This he believed was the very essence of the ecological approach. Huxley spearheaded this cause in a very direct way when he stated: "with the support of scientific naturalists like Peter Scott and Charles Elton, I helped to put Ecology on the biological map by founding an Ecological Society, which would lay the scientific basis for conservation in Britain."[133] Charles Sutherland Elton, the eminent British biologist and former pupil of Huxley, was seen as the scientist who established ecology as a distinct area of biology.[134]

A sense of emergency permeated Huxley's thoughts and work in these various organizations. As he stated concerning the world's food resources: "We talk a great deal about safeguarding the food supply of the country in time of war. In fifty years' time we are much more likely to be talking about safeguarding the world's food supply in time of peace. And we shall not be looking to machinery for our safeguard, nor even to light cruisers or other forms of naval strength, but to the laboratories of entomology, mycology, and all the other branches of pure and applied ecology."[135] Human ecology also included views such as birth control as well as attention to food supply.

Huxley in these endeavours believed "in some cases man even improves on nature; in any event he can contemplate the possibility of building up new types of ecological community, adjusted to the presence of civilized man, and yet capable of creative self-renewal, leading to conservation not to the destruction of any resources or values."[136] Though man's ultimate destiny was that of the sole agent for the forward progress of evolution, he required the best knowledge of his own environment in this role. Huxley stated: "In any case ecological adjustment is part of the process of evolution, and man cannot hope to plan his own future until he has mastered the idea of ecology."[137]

In the era of Orwell's *Nineteen Eighty-Four* Huxley expressed concern that his insight that evolving moral systems reflected evolving social systems might be misused by authoritarian regimes. This is how he put it in 1947: "So far I have spoken almost wholly of such external components of an ethics as change with the changing times. But there are others which are more lasting and may indeed be considered permanent ... These permanent standards deriving from the nature of human society as we know it are those which proclaim the primacy of the individual over the State or any other social organization."[138]

Yet in a paper on "Evolutionary Humanism" delivered in 1952, he again emphasized that fully developed individual personalities must harmonize with social systems as "the human individual attains his highest development by transcending the separateness of his ego in some form of unitive experience."[139] By the early 1960s Huxley had become convinced that the guidance of humanity would entail a redirection of traditional social patterns. In *The Humanist Frame* (1961) man's evolution was seen to be "psychosocial" through the mechanisms of cultural adaptation. Huxley deemed the organization of ad hoc ideas and scattered values into a unitary pattern all the more necessary at the current evolutionary stage.

Huxley's advocacy of eugenics continued well into the 1960s, and remained predicated upon the belief that, in one form or another, it was the primary means by which humanity could direct its own destiny, infusing purpose and progress into evolution. Some of his bolder statements about the prospects of artificial insemination by admired donors in service to the greater good were met with derision in the press.[140] Departing from the technical discussions, Huxley held that "genetics and education must join hands." A "comprehensive selection system to catch as many potential geniuses and top people as possible" was needed, as was a means to insure their proper education.[141] He noted that in both communist Russia and capitalist countries "people with higher intelligence have, on the average, a lower reproductive rate," but admitted that the success of mankind had not depended on sets of special types in breeding pools.[142] Nonetheless some deliberate selection for desirable hereditary characteristics was needed. At present, however, "large-scale eugenics is outside the range of practical possibility; but already, on the basis of our present knowledge, the eugenic idea can become an incentive and a hope."[143]

Such speculations could cause concerns beyond conservative-minded circles. In 1963 Bertrand Russell explained to Huxley that "I am entirely with you as to what eugenics could achieve, but I disagree as to what it would achieve."[144] But for Huxley, eugenics was a necessity not an option. As John Beatty has observed, it was the guarantee for man, as trustee, of the continuance of evolutionary progress.[145]

Huxley's religious vision, expressed in various international conferences, became increasingly more global in the years after the Second World War. In his capacity as the first director-general of UNESCO he maintained that "the general philosophy of UNESCO should, it seems, be scientific world humanism, global in extent and evolutionary in background."[146] Indeed he ventured further and suggested that tensions between East and West could "be reconciled along the lines of some such evolutionary humanism."[147] These remarks received stiff criticisms from the historian Sir Ernest Barker as a rather heavy-handed attempt to introduce a personal religious position into a world organization. In retrospect, Huxley agreed.[148]

The passion with which Huxley advocated population control often brought him into conflict with Catholics, Muslims, Jews (he complained about the ecological damage caused by overcrowding in Israel), and the Soviet Union – he objected to idiosyncratic genetics theories based on the gospel according to Stalin. Quite frequently his remarks led to open and bitter acrimony, in particular with the Roman Catholic Church, which he denounced on many occasions for opposing birth control. Here again, Russell cautioned him about dismissing too readily the "silly myths which make up orthodox religion,"[149] and underestimating their hold on much of the world's populations. Huxley endorsed the Russell-Einstein Manifesto and the Pugwash Movement, which rallied the scientific community against the dangers of atomic warfare, the greatest of dysgenics. But Russell never reciprocated by supporting Huxley's specific agenda for furthering the rationalistic cause, let alone embracing his religion.

When dealing with Christian movements that sought a compromise, or some compatibility with aspects of his creed, Huxley was increasingly, but politely, dismissive. The social Christianity of the 1940s, with its emphasis on religiously inspired social reform, seemed to Huxley to be a form of retreat from traditional concerns with salvation and preparation for the hereafter.[150] He dismissed the Rt Reverend John A.T. Robinson's *Honest to God*, which attempted to create a more rationalistic approach to Christianity in the 1960s, as a futile attempt at "trying to ride two horses at once."[151] It is not altogether fair to say that this was what Robinson was trying to do, of course. While such developments within Christianity were generally to be encouraged, they were still on the wrong side of the theism question.

Huxley frequently displayed poor tactical sense when presenting his views to the public, many of whom still cherished traditional religious sentiments. The BBC, for example, spent a great deal of time in late 1943 debating whether to broadcast a Huxley lecture on scientific humanism. Eric Fenn, the assistant director of religious broadcasting, composed a memorandum on the draft script: "I think, personally, it is a terribly bad advertisement for Rationalism – but that is not my business. It goes to show that Rationalism has very little positive content and lives by its attack on other views."[152] His supervisors decided that more balance was warranted, and opted instead for a three-talk series which included Professor Gilbert Murray on classical humanism and the Reverend J.H. Oldham on Christian humanism.

In 1951, staff at the BBC exchanged memoranda about scheduling a revised version of Huxley's *Third Programme* series on "Humanity and Evolution" on the Home Service. Lawrence Holme, head of religious broadcasting, warned that even if reworked the material might produce a "violent controversy." Though he recognized that many Christians had accepted evolution and that their numbers outweighed "the noisy minorities who still maintain a fundamentalist point of view," Holme also noted that, "[o]n the other hand, there is much in the Huxley talks which goes beyond the mere description of scientifically demonstrated facts concerning the process of biological evolution, and of some of these speculations Christian thinkers would have severe criticisms to make."[153]

Huxley's chronic communication difficulties culminated in "The Evolutionary Vision" address which he delivered from the pulpit of the Rockefeller Chapel of the University of Chicago in 1959. On this occasion his diplomatic skills entirely failed him, with serious consequences. His strident call for abandoning theistic religion elicited widespread condemnation from traditional believers as well as others.[154] In a threatening, complex age of impending "superscientific war" and overpopulation, Huxley argued that it was imperative "for us to cease being intellectual and moral ostriches and take our heads out of the sand of willful blindness."[155] This meant that humankind must assume control of its destiny and acknowledge that "there is no longer either need or room for the supernatural."[156] Although the Darwin Centennial may have furthered the cause of unity among biologists, and extended the new evolutionary synthesis by including anthropologists, in the religious realm it had largely the opposite effect. As Smocovitis has observed, "it would be matched only by the Scopes Monkey Trial in highlighting the tensions between science and religion for vast American audiences."[157] Yet Huxley seemed incapable of realizing that in his efforts to organize ideas and values "into a unitive pattern, transcending conflicts and division in its unitary web"[158] he was actually generating more conflict.

By the 1960s, Huxley had, due to negative publicity, become more sensitive to the objections of Christians. On a number of occasions he reemphasized that his was a legitimately "religious" outlook. He employed such terms as "transnatural" – that which "grows out of ordinary nature, but transcends it"[159] – to describe his religious thinking. The transnatural was something approaching supernatural, but without any hint of old-fashioned divinity. In an extraordinary passage in his highly popular *Evolution in Action* (1961), he even granted that "in a broad sense, evolutionary humanism, it seems to me, is capable of becoming the germ of a new religion, not necessarily supplanting existing religions but supplementing them."[160] Despite this gesture towards reconciliation, in the long run Huxley no doubt did presume that supplanting was the actual process. How much more could have been done at this late stage in his career to develop what Andrew Wernick has called "a more agnostic vocabulary, the sense of a discursive field that includes theology and all its post-theological continuations" is open to question.[161]

One contemporary whom Huxley used as a possible bridge to his critics was Teilhard de Chardin. Teilhard's broad acceptance of evolution and his paleontology strongly appealed to Huxley, and he regularly invoked the Catholic theologian in such late works as *The Humanist Frame* (1961) and *Essays of a Humanist* (1964). Huxley's admiration for Teilhard derived from their shared affection for Bergson, and also from the maverick Jesuit's mysticism, which coincided with Huxley's interest in extra-sensory perception and other similar phenomena in the field of parapsychology. These latter interests were not entirely new, since Huxley had been a member of the Society for Psychical Research in the late 1920s.

At least one historian has also suggested that Teilhard de Chardin was important to Huxley in that he reemphasized purpose in evolution.[162] Yet these expanded approaches did not lessen objections from more orthodox Christians, and in some instances such approaches also created new opponents in the ranks of quite secular-minded intellectuals. Huxley's uses of "humanism," almost always in non-standard ways, were now subject to fresh criticisms. Hugh Trevor-Roper added to these by observing in one widely noted review that "Sir Julian has swallowed whole the extraordinary, pretentious, anti-scientific mumbo-jumbo of a French priest, the late Fr. Teilhard de Chardin."[163] The failure of evolutionary humanism to gain adherents, despite Huxley's proselytizing, also received notice in the 1960s and 1970s. These reinforce Brown's recent observation that some cultural theorists see, in the 1960s, a "new skepticism about the science-derived nature of 'progress,'" which made science, and social science, joint victims with Christianity in the "disappearance of an agreed 'reality.'"[164] In reviewing *Essays of a Humanist*, Philip Toynbee remarked that "general statements, all forms of polymath eclecticism, all Religions for Modern Man and Free Men's Worships are as useless in our time as are all attempts to restore or modernize traditional religious beliefs."[165]

Until the end of his life, Huxley continued to believe that his gospel provided the correct path for the social and political salvation of the world. He was convinced that scientific research and knowledge in general were already demonstrating this unifying trend. But diversity-within- unity was often hard for others to see. Regarding a world religion Quincy Wright, a renowned authority on international law, explained to Huxley that attitudes and values would vary from person to person and "that everyone ought to be encouraged to roll his own instead of buying the most popular or even the best recommended brand."[166] Philip Toynbee offered a similar suggestion: "Simply to wait – on God or whatever it may be, and in the meantime to leave the general alone and to concentrate all our natural energies and curiosities on the specific, the idiosyncratic, the personal."[167] But in his determined pursuit of a unified vision for all of humanity, Huxley, to the last would not accept such advice.

3

Bertrand Russell: Reason, Love, and the Conquest of Fear

While Bertrand Russell's detached agnosticism seems to contrast sharply with Julian Huxley's religion of evolutionary humanism, Russell's strong commitment to liberal rationalism, fused with certain other ideas, also exhibits many features of a secular religion. In roughly the same period of the 1920s as Huxley was formulating *Religion without Revelation*, Russell had more or less come to the same conclusion that Christianity was on the way out. Before the end of the Great War, he had also concluded that Christianity was detrimental to any advancement of Western civilization. However, as he also wrote before the Great War, "when the dogmas have been rejected, the question of the place of religion in life is by no means decided."[1] Christianity might be waning, but it could still have much influence in its twilight years.

In his own autobiographical accounts Russell mentions that much of his early intellectual journey was motivated by the desire to find a suitable religion. His daughter, Katherine Tait, and his biographer, Anthony Grayling, have both attested to his religious temperament throughout his life. T.S. Eliot once noted, in a letter concerning his friend's most famous essay attacking Christianity, *Why I Am Not a Christian* (1927), that he detected a person who remained evangelical in mentality, and indeed this is in keeping with Russell's upbringing. This condition Eliot contrasted sharply with his own outlook, which was that of an Anglican who had been brought up as an atheist. It is interesting that Russell himself, many years later in 1941 in a letter to Gilbert Murray, said that he admired the Church of England as it was "the most purely Platonic form of Christianity."[2]

It is therefore possible to view Russell's framework of moral philosophy and social action as at least in part derivative of Christianity – in spite of his frequent philippics against that same Christianity. As we shall see, Russell's upbringing and early education were solidly within Christianity, which allowed for Unitarian influence being slightly to the margins of traditional orthodoxy as well as unusually early exposure to the challenges of science. Later in his life his adversarial, at times emotional, but nonetheless continuous, dialogue with Christians helped to define the direction of his ethical thought.

Terry Eagleton has recently argued that the liberal rationalism, which grew by leaps and bounds within the youthful Russell as he exited the formal ranks of Christians, and remained with him for the rest of his days, "has its own metaphysical articles of faith, and to that extent, has something in common with the religious belief it excoriates."[3] Eagleton goes on to pose the question of whether liberal rationalism, with Russell as its most prominent champion, entertains a dream of a future, thoroughly rational world that is almost "a substitute for heaven," with "Progress" as its version of an "after-life."[4]

Outwardly Russell clearly rejected the attainment of real knowledge by any means other than the use of reason. Certainly Russell believed that whatever could be accepted with complete certitude as true must be established by reason. This is why science, the tool of reason, must be embraced and religion, based upon unreason, must be rejected – any alliance between the two is impossible. In 1921 he wrote that "religions are beliefs with many dogmas which direct human behaviour and are neither based on – nor contradict – real evidence." In the same piece, while admiring Buddhism as "almost reasonable" and among the least harmful of religions historically, it too would have to be rejected along with every other religion. Like the others, it did not really pursue the truth.[5] However, in terms of Russell's definition of religions, could liberal rationalism be a form of "secular religion"?

Russell at other points clearly had further thoughts about the nature of man, thoughts that would allow for the addition of other elements to blend with liberal rationalism, forming a religion of his own. He argued in one article in 1914 that "human beings cannot, of course, wholly transcend human nature; something subjective, if only the interest that determines the direction of our attention, must remain in all our thoughts." He was quick to add, of course, that "scientific philosophy comes nearer to objectivity than any other human pursuit,"[6] which will lead to the humble acceptance of our fate.

Two years earlier, in *The Essence of Religion* (1912), Russell reflected upon the "two natures" in the soul of man, which were at odds with each other. "The finite" was situated in the "here and now" and its views, loves, and hatreds "based upon some service to the self."[7] The infinite part, in contrast, did not see the world from one's separate, individual perspective but rather looked impartially to what is general to all humankind. The effect of the latter is that there can be no essential conflict between the infinite nature of individuals. As such "in proportion as the infinite grows strong in us, we live more completely the life of that one universal nature which embraces what is infinite in each of us."[8]

The breaking forth from the prison of the finite self to the infinite part of our other nature produces a deeper insight and "this experience of sudden wisdom" is the source of "what is essential in religion."[9] Russell acknowledged that this self-surrender to the infinite life might be made easier for some by a belief in a God. But this is not necessary and indeed the concept usually accompanying theism of a world division into good and bad "in hostile camps" is inferior to "what is felt to be real" in "the oneness of the world in love,"[10] which seeks no boundaries. As he concludes "wisdom is only free when it asks nothing."[11]

According to Taylor, "Russell's sense of inspiration" gives expression "to the experience of being lifted to a higher, more universal moral place."[12] In so doing, it can "empower some people to beneficent action" which is "a new development of this period."[13] As Russell says, "its impartiality leads to truth in thought, justice in action, and universal love in feeling."[14] Taylor argues that Russell's "idea of universal benevolence" gives for the first time "an opening to the universal which is not based in some way on a connection to the transcendent," being instead "a purely immanent sense of universal solidarity."[15] In moral action it could produce a melting down of social divisions as well as new movements, such as the culture of youthful rebellion in the 1960s.[16] It could also lead to a peaceful unification of the world under one government – a cause Russell espoused late in life.[17]

Influenced by the American pragmatist philosopher and psychologist William James, Russell believed liberation comes through resignation to the processes of the universe. Such reverence has parallels with Julian Huxley's thought. But Russell also held that belief grounded in reason alone could not work. His agnosticism, for example, could never be based solely upon reason.[18] The hope for the good life takes human beings into the realm of feeling and emotion, beyond the criticisms of science. It was this life of the spirit that rejected the domination of "power philosophies" of the Church in its heyday, or today in the modern state, or even in uncontrolled science. This supported the link with liberalism, which safeguarded and ensured this progress through liberty. In this teleology, the result for the individual, as for society, would be the realization of love or compassion on the widest scale, which he once stated is "all that anybody should need in the way of religion."[19] It must be at the root of civilization in order to have progress, not fear, which was the basis of so much of the pattern maintenance in societies, especially Western civilization, in the past.

Certainly Russell's crusade to conquer fear in modern society, a situation which he heartily ascribed to Christianity, supplied the impetus to much of his public life in pursuit of universal benevolence. Bertrand Russell was undoubtedly the most revered figure within the ranks of those who protested against the proliferation of nuclear weapons, the Cold War, and a host of other social and political policies pursued by entrenched power in the mid-twentieth century. Often it was also framed in the name of youthful love. Given Russell's advanced age, and the fact that his greatest and earliest intellectual achievements lay in the field of analytic philosophy – something few had heard of and even fewer understood – he was a very unlikely representative for this essentially youthful protest movement. His great work with Alfred North Whitehead, entitled the *Principia Mathematica*, was published in three volumes (in 1910, 1912, and 1913) before the First World War. In the decades since the outbreak of the First World War and even before, of course, Russell had also turned to wider considerations of philosophy, as well as social, political, religious, scientific, and religious subjects, and produced a very large number of publications (including seventy-one books) designed for a more general readership. He won the Nobel Prize for literature in 1950. Indeed he was already widely known for both his diverse writings and for the controversies they engendered by the Second World War. However, it was in the 1950s and 1960s when, in his eighties and nineties, Russell gained celebrity status through his vigorous involvement in the issues of the day. Especially interesting was his appeal to the post-war generation. As a BBC admirer wrote to one of his assistants in 1966, "somehow he seems more contemporary and relevant to the spirit and ethic of the young than most people half his age."[20]

Much credit can be given to Russell's successful use of radio and television, as well as print, to enhance his reputation in this period. But it was the message as well as the media. I argue that it was his views on particular questions, as well as a moral philosophy developed over the previous decades, which ripened at precisely the right time to position him at the centre of controversy at the mid-twentieth century. Though rooted in the late Victorian generation, and in many ways still admiring aspects of that age, by the 1950s Russell possessed the intellectual framework to galvanize successful arguments against the policies of government and the mores of the establishment. In that sense, post-war baby boomers caught up to where Russell had already arrived, long before in his message of "the oneness of the world in love." As important as these particular ideas was his overall attitude, which exuded a type of bravado and assurance necessary in those challenging authority. It was the age of fear. The counterforce of authority was prepared to use its best techniques of control, including the promotion of fear over social disintegration, as well as the image of strength in leadership, given the possibility of nuclear annihilation, if the principles of the Cold War were not followed. And there was also the possibility of nuclear annihilation if indeed those Cold War principles were followed.

Russell always remained a Victorian liberal with a strong belief in personal liberty. Born into the distinguished Russell family, he was raised by the widow of Lord John Russell of Great Reform Act fame. His grandmother was a strong believer, unlike his father, Lord Amberley, and his godfather, John Stuart Mill. Initially a Presbyterian, she became a Unitarian at the age of seventy and Bertrand was later instructed in that faith as well as being given exposure to the Presbyterian and Anglican churches he attended. Though he eventually rejected the strict Puritan morality of his grandmother, he admired her courage, which was grounded in her frequent use of the Biblical admonition: "thou shalt not follow a multitude to do evil."[21] He was also exposed to a degree of skepticism through tutors and his grandmother's liberal attitudes toward learning and the Bible.[22]

By his mid-teens Russell began to experience the classic Victorian Crisis of Faith doubting personal immortality and other concepts central to Christianity and this carried into his student days at Cambridge. He noted in his *Autobiography*, regarding his adolescence: "my nature may incline me to disbelieve free will, and there may be very excellent arguments for free will which either I have never thought of, or else have not had full weight with me."[23] This position on the Judeo-Christian concept of free will remained with him when in 1930 he stated "The free-will question remains just where it was. Whatever may be thought about it as a matter of ultimate metaphysics, it is quite clear that nobody believes in it in practice."[24] He moved to the position of seeking "certain knowledge," with mathematics as a guide to his philosophical investigations. This was largely his thinking until he was almost forty years old. His moral convictions were strong and he wrote in areas where applied ethics were in operation. Yet, as A.J. Ayer has pointed out, Russell contributed little to the pure philosophy of morals beyond his essay on "The Elements of Ethics," written mainly in 1910, and his *Human Society in Ethics and Politics*, written in 1945–46.[25]

Some thirty years after Russell's death, Charles Pigden initiated a challenging reappraisal of Russell's work in theoretical ethics. While Russell may not have excelled in this field to the degree that he did as a logician or philosopher of mathematics, Pigden argues that Russell's work in theoretical ethics formed an important component of his thinking – even beyond the two works cited above – and made important contributions to emotivism. Emotivism, the view that moral statements are expressions of attitudes or desires rather than truths, has not been treated with the same respect as other branches of philosophy, of course. The same was also true, at least in his later life, for practical ethics, something that certainly was linked to Russell's activism. And then there is the troubling question of how activism can be generated by a philosophy that does not hold that it is based upon moral truths.

Pigden has skillfully argued that Russell's moral philosophy evolved through many phases as an enquiry that led to a more sophisticated position in which he made many original contributions.[26] Michael K. Potter has further developed this line asserting that Russell ultimately produced an "enlightened emotivism" of considerable value to philosophers.[27] Certainly in *Human Society in*

Ethics and Politics, produced in his later career, there is evidence of emotivism in seeing moral judgments as the result of a desire or emotion.[28] But there is some distance to go in convincing most philosophers of the importance of Russell's emotivism. And there is Russell's own overall assessment, when he was very old: "I do not myself think very well of what I have said in ethics."[29] But there is little doubt of the emotional aspect to Russell's moral activism. The spirit of love and the combating of fear, albeit in the service of reason, attest to this.

Russell's moral philosophy was essentially grounded in the same concepts as those of David Hume, in a determinism that viewed motives as causes, not founded on Divine authority. It was further refined from the basic utilitarian view that all action was rooted in the seeking of pleasure by the Humean concept of the calm passion of benevolence, in that right actions were also influenced by the approval of others (and thus ultimately satisfactory to society). But there were difficulties in this, concerning issues of justice as they applied to individuals or minorities. A.J. Ayer sees in the later Russell, after the 1930s, changes in his descriptive view of trying to mold ethical propositions into scientific propositions. As Ayer states, in the last regard, Russell's theory of ethics "falls short as a descriptive theory" but "as a prescriptive theory, which is predominantly but not entirely utilitarian, I find it altogether acceptable."[30]

In spite of his repeated criticisms of the shortcomings of the Victorian age, such as its superficial religiosity, treatment of women, and such, overall he continued to have positive feelings about the world as it was prior to 1914. As he later wrote: "The Victorian age, for all its humbug, was a period of rapid progress, because men were dominated by hope rather than fear."[31] Freedom of movement from country to country as well as of thought, neither controlled by governments, was remembered and admired. For Russell the coming of the Great War "extinguished the Liberal hopes and the creed of inevitable progress which expressed themselves in the optimism of the nineteenth century."[32] For Russell, however, such hopes were not personally extinguished, and he maintained an optimism rooted in the doctrine of progress, though of a more qualified variety and no longer viewed as inevitable. The First World War, for Russell, as for so many liberals, was a turning point. As he later wrote in his *Autobiography*,[33] he got into "the habit of thinking of … [himself]

as a non-supernatural Faust for whom Mephistopheles was represented by the Great War."

Already distinguished in academe as a founder of analytic philosophy while at Cambridge, Russell also engaged in other activities in the Edwardian and pre-War period, including standing as a candidate for Parliament on behalf of the women's movement. His writing style was also made more readable for the general public using the twin models of Milton and Baedeker's guidebooks.[34] He embraced wider topics in his writing beyond analytic philosophy or indeed philosophy itself. As a philosopher of mathematics he became interested in other areas of science, including Einstein's new theory of relativity. By the 1920s he was learning more about the results of experimental science and was keen to popularize it. By the 1920s he accepted offers from C.K. Ogden, a Kegan Paul editor, to write *The ABC of Atoms* (1923) and *The ABC of Relativity* (1925) – both sold thousands of copies and made considerable money for him.[35]

Into the period of the First World War doubt also overtook Russell's original certitudes concerning logic and mathematics, and what he called his "mathematical mysticism." As he stated concerning the latter, "But in the end I found myself obliged to abandon his doctrine also and I have never since found religious satisfaction in any philosophical doctrine that I could accept."[36] Thus his "religion" came to be one of general outlook rather than specifics. It became easier to communicate to others. Forging ahead as a public figure toward the end of the war he confessed in a letter his urgent need to appeal to a much larger audience than technical philosophy could engage. Indeed he aspired to be a European intellectual power in the fashion of Voltaire.[37] Thus the public intellectual was born, with great communication skills and an even greater motivation to use those skills.

But if the First World War brought a sea change in his attitudes, it was already evident that he was gravely dissatisfied with some aspects of pre-war life. Russell's move away from theism was predicated upon his belief that religion, in this case Christianity, had suffused men's minds with authority-imposed superstition. In his essay "A Free Man's Worship" (1903) he urged, in a poetic fashion of the heroic sort, that men must disdain "the coward terrors of the slave of Fate"[38] posing the question to god-given authority "shall we worship Force, or shall we worship Goodness?" And in the fashion of

James Mill, father of John Stuart Mill, who saw the Biblical God as a perfect concept of wickedness devised by men, Russell raised a related question – "Shall our God exist and be evil, or shall he be recognized as the creation of our own conscience?"[39]

However, Russell also quoted from John Stuart Mill's *Autobiography* concerning the fact that James Mill's rejection of religious belief was primarily on moral grounds more than intellectual. Russell wrote that he had "no doubt that James Mill remained a Protestant," noting that the Reformation was a great victory over "priestly tyranny for liberty of thought."[40] The same could be said of Russell himself; T.S. Eliot, in his formal review of *Why I Am Not a Christian*, said of Russell that he was a "Low Church Atheist," not having joined another faith in simply saying he was not a Christian.[41]

Russell conforms overall to the master liberal narrative, professed by John Stuart Mill and others in relation to religion, which R.J. Helmstadter describes in his introduction to *Freedom and Religion in the Nineteenth Century*.[42] In this master narrative, modern freedom – with its democratic serving of the largest degree of individual liberty – originated in the end of the medieval church's monopolistic power during the Reformation. "The results of the Reformation and Counter-Reformation, in the intellectual sphere, were at first wholly bad, but ultimately beneficial" Russell wrote of the sixteenth-century. In the next century "disgust with theological warfare turned the attention of able men increasingly to secular learning, especially mathematics and science."[43] The events of the sixteenth century also led to the concepts of religious tolerance in England by the end of the seventeenth century. But in the eighteenth century Anglican-dominated constitution, tolerance was not the same as liberty and equality in the eyes of the state. Those conditions had to wait legally for the nineteenth century through the repeal of the Test and Corporations Acts, Catholic Emancipation, Jewish Emancipation, as well as a host of other concessions in the process of crafting the modern state, largely by liberals. The final agenda of advanced liberals was the introduction of complete secularism and free thought; ironically this revealed Protestantism, or the different versions of Protestantism, as merely stages in this higher and more perfect goal.

As Lewis Greenspan and Stefan Andersson have stated of Russell's writings "in this account Protestantism seems to supersede science as the moral and intellectual source of modernity." As a result of Protestantism, truth no longer required a "consulting authority" as it had with the Roman Catholic Church during the Church's hegemony in the Middle Ages.[44] In this sense, Russell, like Christopher Hitchens, was what the latter described as a "Protestant" atheist.[45]

Russell himself noted that there were "remarkable" differences between skeptics of Protestant background, like himself, and those of Catholic background. As he stated, his attitude of not following the crowd in formulating his independent moral stance was the product of his education as a Protestant, which led to the view that goodness was "individual and isolated" as compared with the more "social" attitude of former Catholics or those so influenced.[46] Taylor has described that the end product of the "synthesis" of Britishness, Protestantism, law, freedom, and civilization in the nineteenth century exemplified in its great spokesman, historian George Macaulay Trevelyan, whose abandonment of faith amended it, was "to make Protestantism the penultimate stage before liberal, disciplined unbelief."[47]

Following the war Russell began to build his case against existing traditional religion, essentially Christianity. His focus was how it exercised such control over so many people. In *What I Believe* (1925) he stated: "Religion, since it has its source in terror, has dignified certain kinds of fear and made people think them not disgraceful."[48] Three years later he restated this position with even greater vigor and with no attempt to discover any of the positive allurements which drew people to the fold: "My own view of religion is that of Lucretius. I regard it as a disease born of fear and as a source of untold misery to the human race."[49] And finally in his most famous work on the subject, first published as a pamphlet in 1927, he amplified his feeling: "Religion is based, I think, primarily and mainly upon fear. It is partly, as I have said, the wish to feel that you have a kind of elder brother who will stand by you in all your troubles and disputes. Fear is the basis of the whole thing – fear of the mysterious, fear of defeat, fear of death."[50]

Against the fear allegedly created by Christianity and similar theistic influences, Russell expended great energy for the rest of his long life examining its effects and suggesting remedies largely in the realm of inculcating his worldly version of hope, which he deemed "the creative principle."[51] This also entailed the development of a system of ethics which could combat the claims of traditional religion, as well as other alleged progenitors of fear, and provide guidance in combating the varied effects of those threats in the world of public affairs. His method was largely one of combative engagement and dialogue, in the style of a controversialist. While at times unsettling and damaging even to his livelihood, overall he seemed to enjoy it.

By the late First World War Russell had moved solidly into the realm of specific social and political issues in his writings and suffused these writings with his loosely constructed alternate faith. As he stated in terms of his opposition to war: "I have never been so whole-hearted or so little troubled without hesitation in any work as in the pacifist work that I did during the war. For the first time I found something to do which involved my whole nature."[52] His thinking on the disparate issues of ethics, sociology, and politics now became more synchronized than in the previous decade. The first convergence of moral thought and action in this period resulted in the *Principles of Social Reconstruction* (1916), which he described as the "least unsatisfactory expression of his own personal religion."[53]

The *Principles* originally delivered as lectures in 1916 were to suggest that politics was based upon "impulse" rather than "conscious purpose." He then made the important distinction that the state, war, and property were the chief political products of the "possessive impulses," while education, marriage, and religion embodied the "creative impulses," with the "liberation of creativeness" being "the principle of reform both in politics and economics."[54] Harmony was the objective between the principle of liberty and the life of the community[55] in what ongoing modifications were necessary to political structures. Useful thought must also prevail over utopian visions for the present time. The thrust of Russell's suggestions was taken by one admirer as late as 1964 as the exercise of thought over "fear."[56]

Edging toward state socialism, in a quaint blend with guild socialism, Russell envisaged local government by trades as well as in regions, with the cost of raising children and the pay for emancipated housewives both assumed by the communities as well. Many of these ideas were further developed in *Roads to Freedom* (1918) and *Power* (1938), with the latter advocating for a world government to counter war mongering and unrestrained nationalism. In relation to individual states, if collectivism was the way of the future, Marxism was too far along the lines of control. It also had suppressed Victorian liberalism while encouraging class hatred.[57] At the opposite extreme, however, pragmatism was to be avoided as it could create a vacuum leading to the rule of naked force.[58]

While already obvious to him through experience, Russell received additional reinforcement in his suspicions about the growing Leviathan of the state from Harold Laski. While a visiting professor at Harvard in 1919, Laski suggested in a letter to Russell that the state had now exchanged places with the church in aiming at some evil, unified control as part of its ultimate technique of governance.[59] In addition to this, Russell began to experience worries about the thrust of modern science – in spite of his use of the term "scientific moralist" to categorize himself. Generally considering himself a follower of science, he had seen science as a tool in his quest to combat fear.[60] By the late 1920s, however, Russell had some reservations. As he surveyed the scene in 1928: "As these traditions and beliefs grow weaker, the influence of science over men's thought and feelings will increase. I do not feel by any means certain that the world produced by science will be better than the world in which we live, for after all, science will have to be embodied in scientists, in whom love of system may easily lend to repression of much that is good but not easy to organize. But for good or evil the scientific world is pretty sure to come about, and any resistance that we may offer to it is not likely to make it better when it comes."[61]

For one who spent a considerable amount of time upon the subject of appropriate social behaviour, he once conceded that "theoretical ethics has little effect on social systems, as a rule." He also described moral law as "entirely temporary, accidental, and dependent upon the circumstances in which you are brought up."[62] In other words, a moral agenda could well be set by a state-directed science. But Russell made a clear distinction between science and scientific technique, the former being the use of reason through empiricism in the systematic acquisition of knowledge. Scientific technique, however, in the hands of a misguided state could have unfortunate results, which he envisaged in Part II of his *Scientific Outlook* (1931).

Entitled "The Scientific Society," Russell stated that this section of his book was "an attempt to depict the world which would result if scientific technique were to rule unchecked."[63] The dystopia that then unfolded was a description of the symbiotic relationship between unbridled science and state power, which then led to a world state of one military, one language (Esperanto), and the complete regulation of industry employment, raw materials, and population growth. Unlike for Julian Huxley, for Russell a unity so achieved through science was a nightmare. While encouraging in some respects, this organic society would unfortunately come to diminish liberty as based upon an ethic beneficial to the organic whole but not necessarily the individual.[64] While exhibiting an illusion of democracy,[65] such a scientific society would be in the control of an oligarchy, whether capitalist or socialist.[66] In fact, the closest model might be that of government by experts manipulated by plutocrats, originating in America, who then extend control over Europe.[67]

Scientific reproduction and education would form a base to much of this. The streaming of children based upon intelligence tests, after selective breeding[68] would result in the education of the most intelligent in adventurous, research-oriented instruction for the best jobs.[69] The discouragement of serious thought among manual labourers was the other route, though some exceptional individuals might be later admitted to the higher instruction. Security was the goal in such a society, in terms of both economics and social attitudes. Difficult individuals could end up in the "lethal chamber."[70] This reflected the general dispensation from "traditional sentiments," where "public moralists" would set general rules which removed affection even between biological parents and their offspring[71] and sterilization would remove any possible consequences from adult love affairs[72] after reproductive service. Sadistic impulses would probably increase within society in Russell's scenario.[73] The result was power over love.[74]

Russell believed that veracity demanded skepticism about science as in all else as a safeguard.[75] A new moral outlook would be required to bring out the best in humanity, including the need for culture and beauty.[76] Here, as always, it was important to adhere to his faith in liberal rationalism, to safeguard liberty, and to look toward the achievement of true progress. Russell later raised the question of possible plagiarism of these ideas in the novel *Brave New World* (1932) by Aldous Huxley.[77]

Unlike in *Principles of Social Reconstruction*, in "The Scientific Society" the dangers of an interventionist state bolstered by science, indeed of a science-directed society, were emphasized. But both *Principles of Social Reconstruction* and "The Scientific Society" shared the common belief that balance would be required in the governance of any future society, in order to preserve the spirit of John Stuart Mill's *On Liberty*. This was in keeping with, and informed by, Russell's own belief in the tenets of liberal rationalism.

Further works, especially in the 1920s and 1930s, indicated specific areas of life where the infusion of freedom could be the basis of improvement in the interest of social progress. In the case of education this began in a very practical way with the establishment of Beacon Hill school in 1927. As Russell indicated in the *Principles of Social Reconstruction*, in the future education must help students "to think, rather than to make them accept certain conclusions" and "to rouse and stimulate the love of mental adventure."[78] As he had also noted in *What I Believe* (1925), above all types of courage that would allow someone "to think calmly and rationally in the face of danger and to control the impulse of panic fear or panic rage"[79] must be developed early in life. Education could help to achieve this attitude.

In a letter written to H.G. Wells soliciting a donation for the school, Russell described the purpose of Beacon Hill as a "training initiative," having "long held that stupidity is very largely the result of fear leading to mental inhibitions." In this Russell was well aware in 1928 of the danger of too much liberty in the curriculum as witnessed in the school led by A.S. Neill. Russell's stress on "intelligence," he claimed, was unusual in a reformer's school.[80] In this he undoubtedly had in mind the Victorian Master of Rugby College, Dr Thomas Arnold, who reformed the great public schools. In *On Education* (1926) he depicted Arnold as one who would create "humbleness of mind" through the use of the rod. Essentially the duty of Christian educators had been to compel children to learn through terror.[81] In this Russell obviously sided with those in the late Victorian period who felt the stress on manliness would crush emotional development, spontaneity, and with it the aesthetic.[82]

For Russell, "children are not naturally either 'good' or 'bad'" and, through creating the appropriate environment, "happiness" could be built, which was "absolutely necessary to the production of the best type of human being."[83] Indeed, Russell not only indicated, throughout his book, ways in which fear in its various manifestations might be overcome in the child, he also devoted an entire chapter to fear. According to Russell most problems were rooted in fear, such as untruthfulness.[84] New educational approaches, based upon love, could conquer fear in its various conscious and unconscious forms.[85] Though Beacon Hill school was plagued with problems involving discipline and finance, Russell continued to adhere to his basic educational ideas. In *Power*, written in 1938, he again contended that, if democracy was to work, the task of education must be to make the population "as far as possible free from hatred and destructiveness, and also from fear and subservience."[86] The end product was his version of the *Kingdom of Heaven on Earth*, in which individual creativeness would be maximized in a free community. One can see in the later reprinting of these works how his ideas resonated in the aspirations of youth in the 1950s and 1960s.

There was also a crossover into the subject of human sexuality in his frank desire to discuss sex education, which he believed was necessary. This view was in accordance with his frequent observation that fearlessness is the essence of wisdom. In agreement with many aspects of Freudianism, in *Marriage and Morals* (1929) he believed that "it is not guilt and shame and fear that should dominate the lives of children."[87] Naturally, this advocacy of more open marriages and the questioning of certain underlying principles in sexual relations raised voices of disapproval in many quarters. In this work he attacked the thinking of many "conventional moralists" particularly regarding the inequality of women in relation to family and society.[88] Such stances not only increased his following decades later but also, as he himself realized, contributed to the character attack on his candidacy for an academic appointment at the City College of New York in 1940.[89]

In relation to eugenics, Russell expressed qualified hope that both negative and positive approaches in their application might, with the aid of science, improve the human stock. In a passage in *Marriage and Morals* Russell did sanction sterilization of the "mentally defective."[90] But he opposed anything beyond that, as in the case of criminals or perverts who might be better treated through psychoanalysis.[91] Stephen Heathorn has argued that his foray into this area was in keeping with broader discussions of such questions, not the result of experiences with his second wife, Dora, or a personal phobia about his own possible mental instability.[92] Russell was also careful not to encourage state involvement along any further lines. As he stated: "Mental deficiency is, to my mind, the only thing at present sufficiently definite to be safely made the subject of legal enactment in this region."[93] Overall he expressed caution about the right of eugenicists to intervene in personal human relations. Science persuasively had challenged the hegemony of the church and therefore had the potential to be a better guide. But he foresaw "the time when all who care for the freedom of the human spirit will have to rebel against a scientific tyranny."[94] While he could write works in the field of popular science such as *The ABC of Relativity* (1925), he continued to be skeptical of a world ruled by science, especially in relation to sexual questions, in opposition to the ways favoured by his friend Julian Huxley.

In the growing tensions of the 1930s he continued to work with those who opposed war and to support the ideas of conscientious objectors. In *Which Way to Peace?* (1936), however, he did indicate that a future world government might need to suppress rebels. Later, in his *Autobiography*,[95] while conceding his drift to support for Britain against Nazi Germany in the Second World War, he did argue that, in his earlier actions in the First World War, he had never asserted that *all* wars were unjustified.

A strong objection Russell had toward theists, especially advocates of Christianity, was that "it affords justification to their sadistic impulses."[96] At root Russell suspected that the true believer was aware "however dimly, that his opinions are not rational, [and] he becomes furious when they are disputed. He therefore adopts persecution, censorship and a narrowly cramping education as essentials of statecraft. In so far as he is successful, he produces a population which is timid and unadventurous and incapable of progress."[97] Linked to this was fervent dogmatism, which has its emotional source in fear. As Russell noted elsewhere, "every fanatical creed essentially involves hatred."[98] This was also the same under the new dogmatic systems of the authoritarian regimes of Nazism and Communism.[99] In this way emphasis on these so-called spiritual values destroyed compassion, and Russell on one occasion even stated "I think the Nazis concentrated on spiritual values."[100]

Politically, while Russell had moved toward socialism in the early decades of the twentieth century, he argued in *Power* (1938) that, even in a more socially just society of redistributed wealth, the state must be democratic. The economic determinism of capitalism or collectivism was never the whole story for him. As he later argued, "the only philosophy that affords a theoretical justification of democracy in its temper of mind, is empiricism."[101] He also asserted that empiricist liberalism "is not incompatible with *democratic* socialism."[102] One must note the continued adherence to the word liberalism, the touchstone of his faith.

Returning to scientific publications, an overall positive picture was presented in *Religion and Science* (1935). As he stated, "Whatever knowledge is attainable, must be attained by scientific methods; and what science cannot discover, mankind cannot know." He did conclude, however, "that science cannot decide questions of value."[103] In another publication he also pointed out that "science can help us get over this craven fear in which mankind has lived for so many generations."[104] While our animal, physiological needs are important for happiness and while he always conceded prosperity diminished cruelty, cruelty being "an outcome of fear and the struggle for life,"[105] Russell argued further that our desires are, in fact, more general and less purely selfish than many moralists imagine."[106] At root, Russell believed that "human beings are capable of love, they are capable of suffering because others suffer. And that is a plain fact of human nature; it does not require mystical explanation, we are just made that way."[107]

Most fully developed in *Human Society in Ethics and Politics* (1954) he stated "the best hope for the future of mankind is that ways will be found of increasing the scope and intensity of sympathy."[108] Rejecting once again the claims of Christianity and other religions as custodians and originators of the code of good behaviour, he stated "professional moralists have never considered, and do not now consider, that kindliness, generosity, freedom from envy and malice, are as important as obedience to the rules imposed by a traditional code."[109] It is by constantly examining actions by these criteria in their general and probable societal consequences that "right" actions could be determined. This was not inconsistent with his notion that moral law was entirely temporal. This was the basis of the so-called subjectivist ethics that guided Russell for the remainder of his career.[110] But such a position, as Charles Taylor has observed, was very much within the rewriting of Evangelization into an aspect of unbelief emphasizing self-control and an "ethic of duty and altruism" through figures in the high Victorian period such as Leslie Stephen and John Stuart Mill.[111]

With his steadily developing moral philosophy now reaching a more or less definitive position by the early 1950s, with an outlook very much in alignment with the trend toward causalism already penetrating even the ranks of establishment, Russell was well positioned to articulate a clear alternate vision to Judeo-Christian ethics. He gave a constant reminder of this by the publication of the book *Why I Am Not a Christian* in 1957, essentially a compilation of lectures and writings going back at least thirty years. Some have also speculated that the timing of its publication may have been aimed at discouraging an anticipated Christian revival.

There is no evidence that he saw himself as the key figure in the downfall of Christianity. He always insisted that he was agnostic rather than atheist. By this term, he meant that he was open to the arguments of theists, and that there was still the possibility, though not a probability, of a deity. Unlike Julian Huxley, Russell seemed to propose no developed religion in its place. Yet, with its specific assumptions, feelings, and hopes for the future, his liberal rationalism amounted to a type of secular religion. Russell of course would have disagreed. Indeed he feared that "new systems of dogma, such as those of the Nazis and the Communists, are even worse than the old systems," but added "they could never have acquired a hold over men's minds if orthodox dogmatic habits had not been instilled in youth."[112] The image of Stalin starting his career in a Christian seminary was alluded to more than once. And of course he could not resist the periodic attack against old religion. In 1957 in a radio discussion with Malcolm Muggeridge over the notion of progress, a cardinal article of Russell's faith, he made it clear that Christianity and all religions were "horrible."[113] Muggeridge later recalled, with some exaggeration: "I had spoken in praise of Christianity, and he [Russell] rounded on me with unexpected ferocity, shrilly insisting that everything most cruel and destructive and wicked which had happened in the world since the end of the Roman Empire had been due to the Christian religion and its founder."[114] Russell never lost his sense of passion about these and other issues.

Man's being was subject to many forces. As Russell wrote in 1928, "the decay of morals among the young, which our older generation are continually deploring, is, I am afraid, due as much to the automobile as to the decay of theological belief."[115] The social developments of mid-century in that sense were nothing new. It would be a stretch of the imagination to say that Russell was the architect of what later would be called counter-culture. What he did maintain was the need for the presentation of alternate views in the free market of ideas, believing that his faith would predominate, of course. Thus he supported the concept of shared time for ethical humanists in broadcasting on the BBC in the late 1940s, or in their protection under the constitution under trying times of McCarthyism in the United States. What blossomed forth in the 1960s in the new movements of youth, women, and those discriminated against, was what he had so long advocated in past decades – that "courage must be democratized before it can make men humane."[116]

While the power of the church and the village had weakened, there were still many threats to freedom. In reviewing *Nineteen Eighty-Four*, for example, he made perceptive comments on the intention of the author: "GEORGE ORWELL'S 1984 is a gruesome book which duly made its readers shudder. It did not, however, have the effect which no doubt its author intended ... They rather enjoyed the *frisson* that its horrors gave them and thought, 'Oh well, of course it will never be as bad as that except in Russia! Obviously the author enjoys gloom; and so do we, as long as we don't take it seriously.' Having soothed themselves with these comfortable falsehoods, people proceeded on their way to make Orwell's prognostications come true. Bit by bit, and step by step, the world has been marching towards the realization of Orwell's nightmares." With these comments written in 1956 was also that nostalgia for Victorian times in his added sentence "only those who remember the world before 1914 can adequately realize how much has already been lost."[117] Viewing the twentieth century he still saw the importance of the individual, even in these circumstances. As he stated in the same period: "What has happened in the world since 1914 has proceeded with a kind of inevitability that is like that of a Greek tragedy. It is an inevitability that is derived not from external circumstances, but from the characters of the actors."[118]

The various forms of oppression were becoming more sophisticated including the use of the media through the twentieth century. As he had noted earlier in the *Conquest of Happiness* (1930): "Fear of immediate neighbors is no doubt less than it was, but there is a new kind of fear, namely, the fear of what newspapers may say. This is quite as terrifying as anything connected with medieval witch hunts." As he pointed out "fear of public opinion, like every other form of fear, is oppressive and stunts growth."[119] There is no doubt that he was fully aware of such things given the extensive file of negative, even hate, mail in files among his papers at McMaster University Library, some under the title "Christian Charity."

In spite of his age, Russell was also most willing to engage all forms of media, including television, to further what had always been the didactic aspect of his writings since the interwar period. The battleground was a host of issues, the vast majority being related to the Cold War, where he willingly was part of the physical activism of the age. His apotheosis was at hand.

Though interconnected, there was also a ranking given to his areas of public discourse. Aside from the basic questions involving the meaning of life, about which he was always willing to discuss, he set about to address the most fearful of all issues – the danger of nuclear war. The fear engendered by this issue cannot be overemphasized. Though it engulfed youth, of course, it affected thinking persons of all ages.

In 1954 Russell delivered his famous broadcast "Man's Peril," which heralded in a host of writings, broadcasts, and activism on the subject of the dangers of nuclear war. Mankind had reached the point where continued existence was questionable. The duel between the two powers in the Cold War required mediation under these circumstances. The importance of neutrals in this was central, according to Russell, in order for Western political leaders to avoid being accused of appeasement.[120] For Russell, "the study of history from the building of the pyramids to the present day is not encouraging for any humane person." The application of ethics to politics was extremely difficult but most necessary, including even a consideration of "the well-being of those whom we hate."[121]

But as he also pointed out "it is not immorality which is the really novel feature of modern weapons. The really novel feature is the absolute certainty that, in a war, *both* sides will be defeated."[122] In 1955 the Russell-Einstein Manifesto was issued by eleven eminent figures following in the footsteps of "Man's Peril." Most were nuclear scientists and all condemned the use of nuclear weapons in any future conflict between East and West. Soon the American industrialist, Cyrus Eaton, sponsored the idea of a conference of scientists to be held in India on this subject. The location changed because of the Suez crisis, and this gave birth to the Pugwash Conferences on Science and World Affairs. The location of the first was to be in Eaton's birthplace, the small Nova Scotia town of Pugwash. Among the initial participants were to be Russell (who could not attend because of illness) and Julian Huxley. The core idea of the Pugwash Movement was that of establishing a channel of communication among scientists from all parts of the world to discuss current issues of urgency and providing a means of informing both governments and the public on these matters.

By 1960, to this end, and given the possibility of a Third World War, Russell was often dismissive of pleas for involvement in other subjects of discussion. To a request from the BBC to engage with Julian Huxley on the future of mankind he stated: "I am afraid I have nothing to say about the future of mankind that would take as long as 8 minutes. I think the Great Powers of East and West will see to it that no human beings exist at the end of the present century, but it will not take 8 minutes to say this."[123] In the same period he gave similar responses to pleas from the Divorce Law Reform Union. To the Homosexual Law Reform Society he also wrote "I entirely support the aims of your society, but my energy and time are devoted primarily to the struggle against nuclear annihilation, and I am afraid I cannot take an active role in your work."[124]

In November, 1957 the Campaign for Nuclear Disarmament (CND) was founded by J.B. Priestley and others in part to protest against the abandonment of unilateral nuclear disarmament by a number of figures in the left wing of the Labour Party. This led to a meeting in which Canon John Collins of St Paul's Cathedral, London, a leader in Christian Action, was chosen as chairman and Russell as president of the CND. By 1958 the CND began to rapidly grow into a mass movement beyond what the sponsors like Julian Huxley and prominent members like E.P. Thompson and A.J.P. Taylor had envisaged as a more discreet ginger group. Cohesion was also hard to maintain between secular leaders and religious figures, as well as a growing host of other interest groups. The March to Aldermaston at Easter, 1958 was one of its most famous mass actions.

Some historians, such as Richard Weight, have argued that the CND was not very popular with the majority of the population in Britain in spite of the appearance of support by many middle-class young people.[125] Whether this is true or not, Russell gained the attention of world leaders on the question of nuclear disarmament in the late 1950s. In the early months of 1957 he made many appearances on BBC, and by November had penned the famous open letter to Eisenhower and Khrushchev, addressed to "Most Potent Sirs," which urged co-operation over the path to war through confrontation. Khrushchev replied almost immediately, with Eisenhower's reply coming through the US secretary of state, John Foster Dulles; the latter revealed his "righteously adamantine surface."[126] Russell had succeeded in at least placing the peace initiative on the table before the most powerful world leaders. For a time the Labour Party was also committed to Britain joining the non-nuclear club, and a unilateral nuclear disarmament declaration was made at the party's annual conference in 1960.

In October, 1960 Russell resigned from the CND to form the Committee of 100. He was reacting to the timidity of the CND in engaging in protests, civil disobedience, and other forms of direct action. The formation of the Committee of 100 was also the result of a split between Russell and Collins, partly through miscommunications[127] as well as because of differences in approach. Collins, though of the Left politically, believed firmly in parliamentary democracy. Collins did not support civil disobedience and maintained that the ending of nuclear weapons was very much a moral issue for Christian persuasion under the rule of law.[128] He revealed this position further in a lecture shortly afterward entitled "The Christian and War" (given 4 November 1960, Stafford Cripps Memorial Lecture) and in a broadcast on 23 September 1962.[129] Russell worked upon a different basis from Collins, who had also taken a public stance in upholding the banning of the film *Lolita*. Collins, more fundamentally, believed that "the building of our contemporary society into the pattern of the Kingdom of God is our daily task."[130]

Russell was generous enough to appreciate that politicians could on occasion rise to the challenge, as in the Cuban missile crisis. He wrote to the general Secretary of the British Communist Party: "as you might appreciate, the crisis was such that it was not at all clear that we should survive the week, but I can assure you that the solution to the crisis made the week one of the most worthwhile of my entire life."[131] Though support for the Ban the Bomb movement began to wane, possibly as a result of the success of President Kennedy's diplomacy, including the Test Ban Treaty of 1963, Russell nevertheless continued in his advocacy against the nuclear stockpiles.

The terror inspired by the danger of war was itself a debilitating way of controlling populations in pattern maintenance on both sides of the Iron Curtain. As he wrote "Fear, at present, overshadows the world. The atom bomb and the bacterial bomb, wielded by the wicked communist or the wicked capitalist as the case may be, makes Washington and the Kremlin tremble, and drives men further and further along the road towards the abyss. If matters are to improve, the first and essential step is to find a way of diminishing fear."[132] He wrote on another occasion of the necessity of disarmament: "I would put first among the gains to be expected the removal of that terrible load of fear which weighs at present upon all those who are aware of the dangers with which mankind is threatened. I believe that a great upsurge of joy would occur throughout the world and a great store of energies now turned to hate and destruction and futile rivalry would be diverted into creative channels, bringing happiness and prosperity to parts of the world which, throughout long ages, have been oppressed by poverty and excessive toil."[133] Russell, ten years earlier, had advocated more concern for the economic plight of the Third World, and had even made a visionary statement about the need for conserving natural resources, as he was concerned that shortages of oil could contribute to war and the substitution of nuclear energy would ultimately result in depletion of uranium and thorium supplies. As with the soil upon which agriculture depends, the "wasteful expenditure of natural capital" must stop.[134]

For Russell, the containment of conflicts with nature, between men, and within one's self required "the gradual approach of man towards wisdom."[135] Systems of morality were intended to deal with conflict but had to involve changes with changing circumstances, in this case moving toward co-operation from competition.[136] This was in keeping with his hope and faith in progress.

The removal of Kennedy and Khrushchev from the diplomatic scene again set off the alarm bell within Russell. The Vietnam War, in particular, was attacked as both war mongering and racist on the part of the US in the Third World.[137] Such positions, of course, engendered criticisms of Russell as being a tool of Communists. His formal political involvement with the Left in Britain had in fact ended at this time when he publicly renounced his membership in the Labour Party because of the Harold Wilson Government's tacit support of American foreign policy. Since the end of the Great War Russell had never favoured traditional market economics as the best path to prosperity, instead adhering to his general concept of "socialism." But "disciplinarians, whether Nazi, or Communists, or of brands to which we are accustomed nearer home" were always his enemy. As he indicated in an essay entitled "Have Liberal Ideals a Future," "it should be the problem of political theorists in our time to think out ways by which mental freedom can be combined with economic regulation."[138] Individual freedom remained the cornerstone of creative work in science, literature, and art, which could never flourish in a totalitarian environment. A Communist triumph was never his goal, though "better Red than dead" might have to do in the short run.

In one broadcast he revealed that he still held on to the Victorian liberal idea of progress, however tenuously. He said: "you are not to understand that I foretell that there will be progress. I do not know whether there will be or not. I hope there will be."[139] In 1955 Russell wrote to his American editor, when the latter attempted to entitle an essay "The Philosopher in Retirement," that the title was inappropriate as he had never been so much in the public eye.[140] When asked two years later what the function of a philosopher is, Russell replied: "I am not quite certain whether in the modern world there is much that a philosopher can do unless it is to offer a certain comprehensiveness, a bringing into one consciousness of things which generally are held separately in different people's consciousness."[141]

Russell maintained a high profile to the end of his days assisted by royalties paid by Allen and Unwin, his principal publisher, for some forty-nine of his books prior to his best-selling *Autobiography* at the end of the sixties.[142] However, he never assumed that his reputation as a great mind among his peers gave him complete protection from the powers that be. As he stated to Julian Huxley in 1963: "You seem to think that governments will be composed of wise and enlightened persons who will have standards of value not unlike yours and mine. This is against all the evidence. Pythagoras was an exile because Policrates disliked him; Socrates was put to death; Aristotle had to fly from Athens as soon as Alexander died. In ancient Greece it was not hard to escape from Greece. In the modern world it is much more difficult; and that is one reason why there are fewer great men than there were in Greece."[143]

There is no question that Russell achieved celebrity status in the last decades of his life, and that status in itself offered protection. World political leaders, intellectuals in Britain and abroad, regularly corresponded with him and appeared in broadcasts with him. At mass rallies celebrity figures such as the actress Vanessa Redgrave were frequently at his side. Paul McCartney has recently claimed that he politicized the Beatles, moving them to their stance against the Vietnam War after his meeting with Russell in the mid-1960s.[144] Given the volume of mail Russell received, as he grew increasingly infirm his assistants had to likewise increase their involvement in his correspondence and had to set up his appointments for him. His endorsements were eagerly sought for many causes. It is true that he was denounced by as many for a host of other reasons. He was never ignored. In all of this there was no sign of any disdain for publicity, especially as it served what Russell saw as worthwhile causes.

In conclusion, a theme clearly running through so much of Russell's writings and actions was the exhortation to conquer fear in the pursuit of love, including compassion for all of humanity. For him nothing truly creative could come from an atmosphere of fear. The tool in conquering fear was the use of reason in a free atmosphere. As he states in the first sentence of the "Prologue" to the first volume of his *Autobiography*: "Three Passions, simple but overwhelmingly strong, have governed my life: the longing for love, the search for knowledge, and unbearable pity for the suffering of mankind."[145] Such a life was not, to his mind, sedentary or without vitality. As he wrote in *The Conquest of Happiness* "No man need fear that by making himself rational he will make his life dull. On the contrary, since rationality consists in the main of internal harmony, the man who achieves it is freer in his contemplation of the world and in the use of his energies to achieve external purposes."[146] Yet Russell also realized that such an approach had historically been rejected by most people. In a discussion broadcast in 1957 he was asked "do not most of us fear freedom." Russell's answer was "I agree entirely with that. I think there are a great many people in the world who like bondage with ease, but I think it is base to be like that."[147] In the end perhaps Russell's greatest flaw was not to appreciate that most people saw happiness in the protective womb of church or state, rather than in a lifetime of demonstrated courage. Outwardly his quest energized his engagement with the issues of the world and made him extremely popular with those who did the same. His disdain for those who could not follow this path was always present, and he once stated: "There is something feeble, and a little contemptible, about a man who cannot face the perils of life without the help of comfortable myths."[148]

Did the private person beneath the public façade ever indulge himself in fear in any significant way? Once, while at sea in a period of personal despair on Christmas Day, 1931, he appears to have experienced fear. Undoubtedly, in part, the result of seeing the toll of his ways in personal relationships, he wrote: "When I speak of fear, I do not mean merely or mainly personal fear: the fear of death or decrepitude or penury or any such merely mundane misfortune. I am thinking of a more metaphysical fear. I am thinking of the fear that enters the soul through the experience of the major evils to which life is subject: the treachery of friends, the death of those whom we love, the discovery of the cruelty that lurks in average human nature. During the thirty-five years since my last Christmas on the Atlantic, experience of these major evils has changed the character of my unconscious attitude to life. To stand alone may still be possible as a moral effort, but it is no longer pleasant as an adventure."[149] He did not remain in this state of mind for long, and soon resumed his normal duty as a warrior against the "coward terrors of the slave of fate" for more than thirty-five years to come. He revealed to the Indian writer Ved Mehta in late life: "there were many boys cleverer than I, but I surpassed them, because while they were dégagé, I had passion and fed on controversy. I still thrive on opposition."[150] This undoubtedly helped to make Bertrand Russell an outstanding voice for change in the twentieth century. His obvious empathy for people's worries propelled his passionate engagement with the immediate state of affairs in the here and now. In that engagement he became a major architect in devising a bolder vision for the public, which was in effect proselytizing his own faith. As an individual Russell displayed little concern for his own safety given the threatening tone of his opponents. He was also financially fairly fearless, giving away money earned in journalism to his school and other causes despite his lack of steady employment since the loss of the Cambridge Fellowship.[151]

Russell was capable, on occasion, of giving credit to the past achievements of some Christians for finally resisting some suppressions of liberty, for assisting in the abolition of slavery, and for alleviating certain forms of economic injustice.[152] But to his mind the Christian churches, like governments, historically had mostly been in the business of maintaining power through the manipulation of the impulses of conceit, hatred, and above all fear.[153] As such Russell had little comprehension of the positive impulses that generated Christian leaders' actions, nor of the optimism that they could also engender in the masses for a better day. It was his luck in the fearful decades of the mid-twentieth century, when those rival Christian voices were divided, introspective, and sometimes filled with doubt, that liberal rationalism coupled with Russell's message of the oneness of the world in love would appear to give hope with great authenticity.

4

Heaven in Heaven:
The Cultural Apostasy
of Malcolm Muggeridge

Throughout his life Malcolm Muggeridge identified with *Gemeinschaft*, in contrast with *Gesellschaft* and all the values entailed therein. The primitive socialists of South Croydon; the Anglo-Catholics of Cambridge University; the iconoclastic anti-establishment pundits of the 1950s; the defenders of unfashionable virtues in the turbulent 1960s; the small company of staunch Christians (with Muggeridge as their "St Mugg" in the seeming collapse of Christendom); and the minority Roman Catholic Church in Britain were all his communities. Dominant ideologies and institutions of church and state were never friendly territory for him. The outsider, the skeptic, the man of the Left (or, as he defined it, defender of the underdog) were his fortes.

Muggeridge would probably not be pleased by this description if he were alive today. Ever engaged in self-fashioning, which was a constant exercise throughout his life, he made the repeated observation – in various forms – that he felt that he was never truly a part of this world, and was instead "a stranger in a strange land."[1] In his later writings, and affirmed by the observations of others, Muggeridge saw much of himself in the life of St Augustine. Certainly the sinner who sinned in excess in youth, the hedonist, then the conspicuous rejection of such, the latent Manichaean, and the final progress to the City of God would be more to his liking. But this latter script implies a greater degree of discontinuity than actually was present in Muggeridge's life story. It also fails to take into account the dissimilarities to Augustine, namely the North African bishop's conflict with the purist Donatists, his *modus vivendi* with the Roman Empire as a church administrator, the overall necessity of the City of the World, and his admiration of the dominant classical culture of his time.

The spiritual actually came much earlier to Muggeridge in his life, and with it, the role of an Elijah. One suspects that Augustine's City of God as an end product, if not a steady path of righteousness, was in his heart from the beginning, as an alien in this world. This would be translated later in his life to the belief that true happiness lay only in God's Kingdom, and that Kingdom was not of this world.

A more apt parallel in life progression was that of the great Victorian religious figure John Henry Newman. The conversion to Roman Catholicism is but one similarity. Frank Turner's brilliant study of Newman's life has stressed that the great cleric's cultural apostasy was at the centre of his thought. In Newman's early rejection of Protestantism (and Erastianism), first as leader of the Oxford Movement within Anglicanism, and later as a Roman Catholic, Turner argues that the future cardinal anticipated a vision of a pluralistic intellectual and religious environment that was at odds with a central element in the contemporary ethos of Victorian England.[2] In that way, Newman's significance was more than that of a champion of a rejuvenated Catholicism; he was among the first modern cultural apostates who paved the way for wider cultural transformations that would follow into the twentieth century for believers and non-believers alike. Newman perhaps would not have anticipated or sought that distinction in his conscious self-fashioning. Like Muggeridge, he sought the smaller community in this life whether among Anglo-Catholics or Roman Catholics, minorities in his homeland.

Muggeridge's constant berating of liberalism also shares much in common with Newman a century earlier. An important element in British intellectual life in the twentieth century, as in the nineteenth, liberalism was the worm that ate away at the best of traditional beliefs, and contributed to the declining influence of Christianity in the eyes of both men. This in turn would lead to the ultimate collapse of all in the near future according to Muggeridge. As he stated late in his career: "I am personally convinced that our Western civilization is approaching its end. This is an absolute basic part of my thinking which governs all my feelings about the world that I live in."[3] The elderly Muggeridge believed that only the community of true Christians could survive the demise of Christendom, as he termed Western civilization. Accommodationist Christians, such as social Christians in the image of Archbishop William Temple (or social Catholics like Barbara Ward for that matter) only served the collapsing Earthly City.

Charles Taylor has pointed to the tendency in many converts, such as Evelyn Waugh, to see the errors of modernity, the close companion of liberalism, as eroding Western civilization through its subjectivism and denial of its moral roots derived from Christianity.[4] This was certainly in Muggeridge's mind well before becoming a Christian. He acknowledged in a letter to Archbishop Geoffrey Fisher of Canterbury on 29 February 1956 that he was "not ... a believing Christian," and he went on to say of Christianity that "our civilization was born of it, is irretrievably bound up with it, and would most certainly perish without it."[5] In one of his many retrospectives, this one to his friend, the American political conservative and conservative Catholic William F. Buckley, he conceded that he knew he should be a follower of Christ much earlier in life, and had suffered "the self-reproach for putting off his subservience to the Cross."[6]

Throughout his life the medium by which Muggeridge delivered his messages was important. Of all the major figures presented in his book, none had a more intimate knowledge of the mass media of the twentieth century than Malcolm Muggeridge. A lifelong print journalist, he was also a consummate broadcaster, particularly in television. Pioneering the various roles assumed by professionals today from host or anchorperson, to guest commentator, to interviewer, to producer, and writer, Muggeridge served as a model for later broadcast personalities throughout the globe. As Julia Stapleton has stated, "in exposing large radio and television audiences to issues and debates of serious import his role as a public intellectual should not be underestimated."[7]

Reaching beyond, but also including those who would normally tune in to the BBC *Third Programme*, Muggeridge was probably able to engage a higher proportion of the citizenry who watched television or listened to the radio in Britain than any before or since. Given the great expansion of broadcast receivers during the middle decades of the twentieth century, and then the fracturing of those audiences through the proliferation of channels, cable, and satellite by century's end, it is doubtful that these circumstances could ever be replicated. Muggeridge won much praise at the time and, as Noel Annan has said, "for over ten years he became a celebrity on British television, known to so many millions that he received the ultimate accolade. A waxwork was made of him at Madame Tussaud's."[8]

Remarkably, in the first decade of the twenty-first century, Muggeridge is not very well-remembered by many Britons. Whether this outcome is the product of the very nature of the short-term memory of a media-saturated public, or of the increasingly less charming, somewhat pessimistic image of the man presented to that public in his late career cannot be determined. In defining Muggeridge as a celebrity, one of his biographers, Ian Hunter, made the distinction that being a celebrity was not the same as being popular. Celebrity "virtually guaranteed an increase in ratings" on a television program.[9] Not being rooted in a specialized field, besides journalism, as public intellectuals would normally be today, or as Russell, Huxley, and Ward all were at the time, and certainly having no university attachment, in retrospect Muggeridge could also be seen as lacking a certain gravitas. His last days as a conservative Christian also lessened his standing among the national intelligentsia, even among some Christians in those ranks, thus contributing to the diminution of his general reputation. Abroad, especially in conservative Christian circles in the United States, he continues to be revered – but more as a cult figure who appeals especially to conservative Catholics and the Christian Evangelical Right.

Laying aside the question of legacy for the moment, Muggeridge must be viewed as one of the most successful communicators of his time. Though his activities might be seen as disparate in today's world of more specialized journalism, especially given the sharp contemporary divide between print and television, Muggeridge nonetheless supplied a unity to his activities. Often his broadcasting became the basis of later publications (or vice versa), which helped what would have been an impossible schedule for a reasonably prolific writer. It was more like Victorian writers who serialized their books in the press before final production. Writing for broadcast came early in his overall career. He noted with satisfaction in his diary, regarding the sale of his first story to the BBC in 1937: "I am seldom afraid now as I used to be. This is because I know that no evil can happen to me except by standing away from life."[10]

Given such comments and his choice of career, one can say that Muggeridge, more than anyone considered in this book, sought the limelight both for its own sake and as an integral part of a successful journalistic career. Narcissism is endemic in such a situation, but Muggeridge in his cultivation of a charming persona, at least until his last years, had the ability to laugh at himself. Later, resting upon his laurels, he could afford to set such things as money aside and speak of the relative unimportance of fame. Charm, of course, gave

Muggeridge both popularity with a wide audience and access to interesting and important friends who could be written about and interviewed.

However there was much not contrived in his career. Impulsive actions and passions also ruled at least the first third of his life. Later one can see a more directed life, assisted by the production of repeated self-narratives, of his life both partial and full, in print and on radio and television, beginning at least in the late 1930s and continuing almost to the end of his days. Indeed no modern figure comes to mind who shared his life's journey so repeatedly and with such a wide audience as Malcolm Muggeridge.

By the late 1960s this self-narrative had taken on a religious conversion theme, though the final chapter, Roman Catholicism, was not set down until close to the end of Muggeridge's life. The role of narrator and of self-observer developed quite early in life, and along with it a feeling of alienation or detachment from the world about him. As he stated many times and in many ways: "I can tell you in all honesty, almost the first thing I can remember as a conscious child was this feeling that somehow or another I didn't belong here; that here is not my home."[11] Though this feeling would later be linked to the notion of the other Kingdom, not of this world, alluded to by Jesus, its initial origins were probably rooted in personality. Again, quite early, the notion of a slightly mystical or otherworldly journey, though not necessarily involving Christian conversion, came into the picture. This journey began earlier than most commentators on Muggeridge in his heyday would have imagined.

Born in 1903 into a social level somewhere between the proletarian working class and the lower-middle class in South Croydon, a London suburb, his initial exposure to Christianity was quite tangential. This was by design as his father, Thomas, saw the teachings of Jesus as merely a forerunner of socialism, the true liberator and moral guide of humanity. As Muggeridge later put it in 1975, the New Testament was not deeply studied but used as an example – like using Shakespeare's *King Lear* as a commercial for good geriatrics.[12] While Muggeridge developed some deviant tendencies from his upbringing in agnosticism, like reading full sections of the bible in secret, he was on the whole very comfortable with this plebeian culture of the Left as supervised by his kindly father. As confirmed in a later television documentary, *A Socialist Childhood* (1966), the sense of community or *Gemeinschaft* was very strong in this early part of his life.

In his late teens Muggeridge won an entrance scholarship to Cambridge, being one of only about three percent of borough secondary school graduates to do so. Before that, he had displayed his brilliance to some of his teachers, including Helen Corke, a former companion of D.H. Lawrence. Lawrence, of similar social background to Muggeridge, but from the North of England, had also come to Croydon as a teacher. Muggeridge was to become an enthusiastic fan of Lawrence's writing, though he experienced a rather prudish reversal toward his hero later in life.

Malcolm's period at Cambridge was amongst the worst of his life. Attempting to become part of the establishment, he now addressed his parents in letters as "pater" and "mater" while reinventing himself into the erudite personality so familiar to radio listeners and television viewers decades later. Letters preserved, however, especially to Alec Vidler, show that this transition was accompanied by some guilt over such things as the trivial nature of discussions at Selwyn College (for example about the wine list) when friends and relatives back in Croydon were on the dole. In a letter concerning college life he stated: "We have nearly everything for our material comfort that we can want and outside people are dying of starvation."[13] At times he placed his hope in the Labour party which "has Great and Christian ideals but <u>at present</u> it fails in its methods."[14] On other occasions he described himself as "Bolshie" believing this might shake things up, but adding "yet I know that kind of thing would never solve the problem."[15] Perhaps for this reason he first turned to Christianity in this period to supply a new sense of community, as well as action, at Selwyn after duly being baptized in the Church of England. This Anglican phase was also the result of his admiration for the work of High Church, Ritualistic Anglo-Catholics (who also predominated at Selwyn) as slum priests, as they were called, in the East End of London. He developed a lifelong friendship with Alec Vidler, one of them, and even spent time at one of their community houses in Cambridge while preparing for his last examinations for his pass degree in science.

He then went to India to teach at a Christian school associated with the Syrian Church, but had ended his dalliance with High Anglicanism a little earlier. Thereafter he became hostile to Anglicanism as a whole in its capacity as the Established Church of England, with moderation as its "watchword," for the remainder of his life.[16] In India he was not impressed by Christians in general as much as by Mohandas Gandhi, whom he came to know personally after the Mahatma made a short visit to the school. He never broke his links with India and later returned there for another period as a newspaper reporter at an Indian newspaper. In fact Muggeridge broadened his Third World perspective with a stint as lecturer in English at Cairo University after his first departure from India.

Abandoning any idea of further association with Christianity, when he returned to England he began to pursue a full-time career as a journalist, joining the staff of the *Manchester Guardian* as a leader writer. He was also reunited with the Labour Party through marriage to Kitty Dobbs, the beautiful niece of Beatrice Webb. But this was entrance into the intellectual aristocracy of the Party, not the humble rank-and-file he had known through his father. It was also supplemented by much drinking and womanizing. The latter must have been noticeable earlier as Gandhi wrote him a letter on the benefits of curbing excessive sexual appetites.[17]

The renewed commitment to socialism also prompted the Muggeridges' departure for the USSR in 1932, with the possible aim of becoming Soviet citizens as well as Malcolm being the resident *Guardian* correspondent there. Disillusionment came swiftly with the new board and through the revelation that Stalin's empire was hell, not heaven, upon earth. Muggeridge's subsequent attack upon the regime not only led to his firing but even a libel suit by the *Manchester Guardian* for a book he hoped to publish back in Britain that would display the attitudes and actions of his employers. Needless to say, he became a pariah in the eyes of the intelligentsia of the British Left.

In the 1930s Muggeridge utilized his ease of prose to turn out books. The *Earnest Atheist, Autumnal Face, Three Flats, The Thirties, Winter in Moscow,* and *In A Valley of This Restless Mind* were all produced in this period. In the *Earnest Atheist* (1936), he explored the life of Samuel Butler, a man who like himself left detailed notes of his life and who also went to Cambridge. In the case of Butler, he lost his Christian faith there. Though debunking the traditional image of Butler, the iconoclastic author of *The Way of All Flesh*, there were ways in which Butler's life could have served as partial model for Muggeridge. However Butler, for Muggeridge at least, was not an authentic outsider, but rather the ultimate conformer to Victorian conventions including the discreet role of unbeliever. *Winter in Moscow* (1934), a piece of fiction, with its bleak fear about the dangers inherent in any man-made utopia, was later seen by some as a rebirth, for Muggeridge, of interest in things spiritual. He compared the belief in Jesus of Christians with the public veneration of Lenin: "Their living Christ was ethereal; but the living Lenin was dead Lenin embalmed and brushed and manicured."[18] The message from his Moscow days was that any attempt to create the Kingdom of Heaven on earth would always end in disaster.

Orwell, in a letter many years later, having himself just finished "a story about the future," offered comment upon both *The Earnest Atheist* and Muggeridge's Soviet experience to this friend. He stated: "I know that you feel that people like Butler, who are disintegrators, prepare the way for dictatorship etc., and I can see the connection between Butler's revolt against his parents and your experiences in Moscow. But I do earnestly think you are wrong. The real division is not between conservatives and revolutionaries but between authoritarians and libertarians."[19]

Muggeridge's wider attack upon the Soviet Communism included especially Western sympathizers such as Bernard Shaw, Julian Huxley, and the Webbs. Russell had seen problems with the Soviet Union earlier. As he addressed them, "your attitude towards the Soviet régime is, at any rate for the moment, more significant and illuminating than the regime itself."[20] For Muggeridge, they collaborated in the denial of rights to Russian workers and upheld show trials of dissidents that exploited the very emotions they deplored in the West and in "a more savage and unrestrained form."[21] He concluded that the "friends of the Soviet Union," but a small community in the West, were "frustrated revolutionaries" who "would like to be a dictatorship of the proletariat" which is "all-powerful and mouths your aspirations."[22] Further "it shows you an attainable bridge between the abstract and the concrete"[23] with divorce and abortions free for all and "the degradation of every kind of value, moral and spiritual and aesthetic."[24] At base, Muggeridge believed "Karl Marx and you have provided the General Idea"[25] and "a General Idea is the most terrible of all tyrants. Individual tyrants have their moods, and must at last die; it is inflexible and immortal" attacking "the soul of a society."[26] This concept of a civil society could spell the death of European civilization[27] if it spread beyond the borders of Russia.

In the same period Muggeridge also opposed political moves that would assist the extreme Right, such as appeasement. Ironically in his opposition to both the totalitarian Left and Right, he and his friend, Hugh Kingsmill, had written of a fictitious, cynical alliance between Hitler and Stalin in *Next Year's News* (1937) before the actual appearance of the Non-Aggression Pact of 1939. While an intelligence officer for MI6 during the war, and during a period of continual disillusionment, Muggeridge had even attempted suicide. By this time his political inclinations appear to have moved to the right, though he displayed little consistent social philosophy, except that of cynicism.

In the postwar world, Muggeridge began the path to celebrity status, engaging with all the existing media. He quickly joined the staff of the *Daily Telegraph* in May 1945. While he discovered his ability to woo an audience on both radio and early television, Muggeridge continued to write chiefly for the conservative-leaning press. A famous stint as editor of *Punch* from 1953 to 1957 gave his skepticism, mixed with wit and charm, a large following. The Left, then the Right, even the Royal family, could not escape his barbs. By the 1960s he had evolved into a more international figure, becoming a frequent guest on popular American television shows (especially with Jack Parr), selling books on a global basis, and acquiring, as always, droves of friends. Much later in his visits to North America he aimed more at a select audience, such as *Firing Line* with William F. Buckley. He also increasingly revealed his antipathy toward the age in which he lived, especially the direction taken by British society. He described the years from 1951 to 1964 as "political, economic and moral free-wheeling" with records established in road accidents, hire purchase, juvenile delinquency, and television watching.[28]

In the early 1960s Muggeridge's topic choices for print and broadcast journalism seemed to move increasingly into the realm of religion. The thrust of his arguments was ambivalent with criticism of religion only on a selective basis. The Church of England was the prime target, depicted in the process of final decay and prodded by secular rationalists who were contaminating its programs. As early as 1951 he also wrote to Archbishop Fisher that the clergy were linked to Stalinist Communism (perhaps with the Red Dean of Canterbury in mind).[29] He felt that the Roman Catholic clergy would, in time, surely face the same fate – with their own reformation (possibly with the calling of Vatican II) coming at the "wrong time and in the wrong way."[30] Along the same line was a talk he gave to religious broadcasters in Birmingham in 1962 when he pointed out that it was the most mystical versions of Christ which now flourished, not the rationalist versions that would please the likes of Julian Huxley and UNESCO.[31] He became a vehement critic of social Christianity with its notion of a collective Kingdom of God upon earth, ahead of individual salvation. For him it was but another pathetic, and compromised, attempt at a man-made utopia.

In fiction, in the same period, he produced the screenplay for the Boulting Brothers motion picture, *Heavens Above*. In his diary account of a meeting with John Boulting in 1961, Muggeridge noted that the producers misunderstood his theme and dropped the conversion story from it. For him they were captivated by the "almost universal fallacy" that the good Christian is engaged only in trying to behave in what he supposes to be a Christian way.[32] In this, as Noel Annan has concluded, Muggeridge essentially took the Augustinian position that one is justified by faith not works,[33] or, as Muggeridge himself put it, that "the changed man" puts away the old Adam to be reborn. But at this stage Muggeridge still spoke as a bystander, albeit one who made references to all the great Christian authors from St Augustine onward and made no secret of what sort of Christianity he preferred.

Certainly St Augustine's *Confessions*, which Muggeridge termed "the first great autobiography" in the modern sense,[34] was a model both in writing and a guide for an ultimately righteous life. The public persona, with a gift for words, the remaking of a man with lustful pursuits into a powerful advocate of Christianity, were all striking parallels to Muggeridge's later life, as was the tendency to see a good deal of humankind condemned. However, while the *City of God* may have been a shared goal, there was no similarity in the admiration of a contemporary earthly city. Twentieth-century Britain was not Rome.

Intellectual inspiration for Muggeridge's line of thought was a complicated business. In general he felt that all forms of recent literature were part of the decomposition of the Western civilization. He did not identify with an intelligentsia, and was particularly disdainful of established academics. Of course, he was not immune to ideas, but they had to reflect true wisdom learned from the slow process of experience. He explained: "I have never, I should add, learnt anything from any exhortation or homily; any political, ethical, theological or philosophical exposition; any presentation in any form of plans, programmes or blue-prints for happy living. Nor from any supernatural visitation or sudden Damascus Road prostration. Only from the experience of living itself, or – what is the same thing – the distillation of that experience in the visions of mystics and the productions of great writers and artists. Learning from experience means, in practice, learning from suffering; the only school master. Everyone knows this is so, even though they try to persuade themselves and their fellows otherwise."[35]

Blaise Pascal championed virtually all Muggeridge's major views. First emphasized in his diaries back in the early 1960s,[36] Muggeridge repeatedly made reference to the *Pensées* thereafter. Initially attracted to a brilliant mind who made a shrewd assessment of the possibility of a God and what should follow from it, he became a disciple of Pascal's doubts about what science could accomplish, and with it, the pretensions of rationalism in general. This was all the more credible given Pascal's actual scientific accomplishments, and was somewhat similar to Augustine's ridicule of his own achievements in the field of rhetoric as "the chair of lies."[37] Deeply impressed by Pascal's quest for heaven, Muggeridge saw a path that entailed a relationship with the poor and humble, and not one of self-aggrandizement and egomania (or erotomania). It was also obviously one that did not involve compromises with existing institutions, *Gesellschaft*. The latter he identified with the Jesuits in the seventeenth century who "favoured tempering the severities of Christian doctrine and practice in order to make them more palatable."[38]

Tolstoy similarly rejected the link between church and state. Dostoevsky reinforced the point, going further in opposing any attempts to establish an earthly paradise. Muggeridge admired both Russians greatly. Closer to being a contemporary, he also venerated pastor Bonhoeffer, who illustrated the dangers in acquiescing to such experiments and the ultimate price paid. Simone Weil was another of his admired martyrs. William Blake, certainly not the easiest of inspirers to fathom, introduced the key element of imagination in Muggeridge's spiritual journey beyond earthly passions. He also seemed to be the basis of Muggeridge's repeated concept of striving to see through the eyes to the essence of things by way of the imagination – the gateway to truth. Kierkegaard supplied, for Muggeridge, an early analysis of the dangers of the communication media (in that case the press), when turned against the individual seeking the truth. Muggeridge said of Kierkegaard, "his profound sense that if men lost the solitude or separateness that an awareness of the presence of

God alone can give, they would soon find themselves irretrievably part of a collectivity with only mass communication to shape their hopes, formulate their values and arrange their thinking."[39] Like Pascal, and most of the others, he reaffirmed that no earthly kingdom can ever bring about a just society, even if placed under the banner of Christ's Kingdom upon earth.[40] For those Christians who interpreted the Incarnation as the inspiration for social justice, Muggeridge remained a source of frustration more than inspiration. In essence, there was a complete non-meeting of minds between Muggeridge and a succession of Christian figures of the Left from William Temple, through Michael Ramsey (see chapter 5) and Lord Soper,[41] to Barbara Ward.

But the framework of John Henry Newman's writings, which Muggeridge rarely mentioned, comes far closer to the nature of Muggeridge's ongoing self-narrative. Here the choice between complete skepticism and the embrace of Catholicism in Newman's *Apologia* seems to be similar to Muggeridge's thought. But so is what Frank Turner has described as Newman's pioneering cultural apostasy (against the conventions of Victorian society in Newman's case). Parallels can also be noted in their mutual loathing of liberalism. Unlike Augustine's lament for the decline of Roman civilization, Muggeridge saw little lost in the final destruction of what he termed contemporary Christendom. For Gauri Viswanathan, as for Turner, Newman's philosophical writings "probed the possibilities of conversion as a critical practice" and "what appears to emanate from a religious discourse is as concerned with negotiating secular parameters as it is with establishing the claims of religious subjectivity."[42] The same applies to Muggeridge in the twentieth century.

In some statements moving well into late career, Muggeridge indicated that there was no sudden, sharp break from skepticism. In his case, as compared with Newman's, there was more of a "phasing in" of belief. Muggeridge stated: "I've always been a skeptic. I instinctively disbelieve almost everything but because I disbelieve much I find it possible to believe … As for myself, I can't say, it would be impossible for me to say, that at that point I believed or that at that point I disbelieved."[43]

Such religious instability has often characterized the situation of those who have gone the opposite way into disbelief. Timothy Larsen's recent book, *Crisis of Doubt* (2006), involving case studies of the reconversion of secularists back to Christianity, illustrates the thin barrier between faith and doubt and examines those who moved back and forth across it. It is also interesting that Muggeridge linked this situation with his feeling of being a stranger in this world.[44] It therefore would seem a rather harsh comment made by Paul Johnson in the *New Statesman* that "Malcolm Muggeridge's return to Christian belief is one of the more exotic show-biz events of our age."[45] Perhaps this was a function of his public narrative. Were there any incidents which came close to Paul's road to Damascus experience? Such was not acknowledged in Muggeridge's narratives but there is one possibility.

In 1965 Muggeridge devised a documentary program for the BBC on Lourdes. His proposal was for himself and a film crew to accompany a group of Britons, who were presumably seeking cures for their ailments, to Lourdes. The proposal was accepted as he had a knack for drawing good audience numbers and approval indexes. The events that unfolded in connection with the making of the documentary may have been a major turning point on the path to conversion. Fortunately, thanks to his own papers, and the BBC written archives containing the original scripts, production notes and project correspondence, much light can be shed on this process.

In his book *Conversion* (1988) Muggeridge speaks of the beauty of a dying girl that touched him on this Lourdes journey.[46] This was not a prominent feature of the documentary over twenty years earlier. This book was a somewhat unreliable account produced late in life when he was quite feeble. In fact one could argue from the records that it was more the comradeship of a shared experience with modern pilgrims – *Gemeinschaft* – that was the basis of his transformation. His first interview in the documentary was with a rough customer who, when asked by Muggeridge what he would do with his crutches if cured, replied that he would wrap them around someone's throat.[47] Another early encounter was with a terribly disfigured boy who wanted Muggeridge's autograph. The boy lay on a stretcher unable to speak or see. Muggeridge wondered why he wanted his autograph and was quickly informed by friends that the boy could hear. Humanity thus emerged, in others and himself, in its fullness and with all its imperfections. As he stated on board the pilgrim train to Lourdes: "On this train the sick are the centre of attention – not shunned, as they tend to be in our humanitarian societies, where they remind us of the fallibility of all human endeavours."[48]

On arrival at Lourdes Muggeridge was not particularly impressed with the words of priests and what he regarded as the theatrical display of crutches – in other words, anything involving mental manipulation by church authorities. Certainly he interviewed enough authorities to determine cures were few and far between.[49] But again, the source that moved him was the people themselves, especially in their determination to return to Lourdes because of the changes they had experienced. Clearly those changes were metaphysical. The pilgrimage was about faith more than actual cures. But it did entail the miraculous in its ability to transform.

What was also particularly important for Muggeridge was that these were voices of the people. Increasingly his script refers to the working class or proletariat, rather than to pilgrims. They are also invested with a type of superior authority, learnt from their sufferings. As he states in one late script concerning the poor condition of most of the pilgrims: "Can these poor souls, one asks oneself, sometimes in outward appearance, barely human, really wish to go on living? The scientific answer of course is emphatically no. In a broiler house, there's no place for such poor specimens ... If the Christian view is correct, and mankind are a family, with a father in heaven, who can't see even a sparrow fall to the ground without concern, when these twisted, tangled bodies have as rightful a place in the human family as any others ... I as it happens believe them more readily than I do the pronouncements of experts on population and eugenics. It can be argued, it seems to me, that no lives are worth living or that all lives are worth living but not that some lives are worth living and others not."[50] These sentiments were later repeated in *Something Beautiful for God (1971)*. This text also points to the importance of seeking meaning and purpose in life beyond any explanation that could be framed within the limits of rationalism.

An authority was thus bequeathed on these working-class pilgrims with their strong sense of community, a sense of community also linked to the Divine. Their wisdom, born of experience, had to be respected and ultimately, in his case, adhered to. In the same year, 1965, in which the Lourdes documentary was produced, Muggeridge started another called "A Socialist Childhood," which was an equally revealing piece that follows some of these same themes.

Unlike his Lourdes documentary, "A Socialist Childhood," was ostensibly autobiographical, running up to his early married days. It clearly reinforced the strong need, seen throughout his life, for a sense of community. As a "socialist toff" he embraced a set of warm relationships that seem to exist among socialists in South Croydon. As Raymond Williams has described D.H. Lawrence's childhood among the working classes of the North of England, Muggeridge's childhood was one that gave a "sense of close quick relationship which made for 'a whole attachment'" to the workings of life.[51]

Muggeridge likened this primitive socialist world to that of early Christians waiting not for the end of the world but for the collapse of the capitalist order, and to be reborn in a more virtuous collectivity. He identified strongly with his father seeing him as a Socialist David battling the Capitalist Goliath. The realization that his father was also a solitary figure in the wider society, whether in the borough council or later in Parliament, may have contributed to Muggeridge's own sense of "being a stranger in a strange world" which he mentioned repeatedly in his writings.

In this narrative, leaving his proletarian childhood world in South Croydon for Cambridge University exposed him to university life that "had the rank stench of a decaying class in a society which was itself in the last stages of decomposition."[52] He also noted how "proletarian boys tend to succumb to Cambridge's allure. Instead of manning the barricades, they hang around in the corridors of power."[53]

Muggeridge's later association with the Webbs, though they were of the Left, was more with a hierarchy, "more Ducal"[54] as he put it, which included condescension exhibited toward his beloved father (also noted in the biography of his friend A.J.P. Taylor[55]) by the Webbs. All socialism, of course, would fail. But the failed colony at Whiteway in South London exhibited the best in socialism as compared with the evil structure of the USSR. As Muggeridge observed in his documentary, a perfect society on earth is too difficult to construct as it would necessarily be the work of imperfect beings. It is "mad."[56] In *Winter in Moscow* the same theme had emerged but with more frightening consequences.

It is then conceivable that what the Lourdes experience represented was a new bridge back to Muggeridge's proletarian roots, through religion rather than politics. As Raymond Williams said of D.H. Lawrence, his tragedy was that he "did not live to come home to his working class roots."[57] John Worthen describes D.H. Lawrence as the "outsider" unable to be close to middle-class friends, while lacking the emotional identification and support of his original community.[58] In that sense Lawrence was to remain a narrator only, unlike Muggeridge. For Muggeridge, the Lourdes pilgrims were a "living, organic, believing community,"[59] a description which both Lawrence and Williams would agree with. So perhaps Muggeridge had returned home, in contrast with Lawrence who never did. *A Socialist Childhood* therefore completed the cycle of redemption, reclaiming his roots in a fused, ultimate *Gemeinschaft*.

The reaction of British television viewers was generally quite positive. At the time of the first transmission, on 13 October 1966, the size of the audience within the general population of the UK was estimated at 8.6 per cent, compared with an average of 19 per cent for competitors Tom Jones and David Frost. The Reaction Index, compiled from questionnaires completed by a sample audience by the BBC audience research department, was a respectable 72 – the same figure as for *Twilight of Empire*, in week 46, 1964.[60] The summary of written comments revealed a cross-section of opinion from enjoyment to hostility. It seems that it evoked much interest in the socialism of that period but a consistent view of Muggeridge's identification with his earlier self in that period was not revealed to all.

It is significant that the Reaction Index to the "Pilgrims to Lourdes" documentary was 75, "a highly satisfactory figure" (share of the national audience market was 9.8 per cent). As the report of comments indicated, "the whole programme, many said, was for them a most impressive and moving experience, inspiring not only compassion, but admiration and respect for the stricken; the scenes in Lourdes were of the utmost interest and they also much appreciated what Malcolm Muggeridge had to tell them about the Pilgrimage."[61] Clearly Muggeridge had displayed something to his audience that seemed very authentic. A month later, on 21 October 1965, another documentary by Muggeridge, also produced and directed by Michael Tuckner, entitled *The American Way of Sex*, received a poor Reaction Index of 51 (though the market share of audience was 15.3 per cent). There were "divided opinions" on Muggeridge, who was described in one comment from the processed questionnaires as a "pompous prude."[62] Similarly, a later series of *Three Films of a Life of Christ* (10–12 April 1968) on BBC 2 received a Reaction Index of only 67, with many negative comments about Muggeridge. It appeared not to be the subject matter (the market audience share reached 22.5 per cent for the second film on BBC 1) as it was noted that John Betjeman's similar *Journey to Bethlehem* program in December 1966 had received an index of 72.[63] Again, among those filling out questionnaires, viewers could not connect with the sort of consistency of character in Muggeridge that was displayed in the Lourdes documentary.

At Lourdes, reconnecting with his working-class roots, and linking it with religion, found a unifying principle for Muggeridge. From this, his path to Mother Teresa two years after Lourdes can be more readily understood. Learning of the work of this Albanian nun with the most abandoned of people – the dying of Calcutta – he ventured to do an interview, later a television special and finally a book, *Something Beautiful for God* (1971).

In his progression toward full conversion, Muggeridge continued to engage the public. This was in the very nature of his role as he wrote in 1972 "We communicators – vendors of words, to use St Augustine's expression – tend to accumulate a lot of waste matter as we go along … The rags and tatters of a professionally exhibitionist ego."[64] But this exercise was more than just ego – it was in the service of his ultimate aim to be a conduit for a type of catharsis.

In his view of the general direction of society he was not alone, sharing much in common with figures such as Mary Whitehouse and Lord Longford, the latter of whom was a personal friend. Such associations would manifest in such activities as the Festival of Light in 1971, which was directed against sexual exploitation in the media and arts, homosexuality, and drugs. Such movements directly challenged the course advocated by figures such as Bertrand Russell (who he had at least one highly unpleasant public encounter with) and by liberalism as he defined it. Muggeridge's concept of liberalism was really a sort of cipher for the vilest concept of the modern world – the dethroning of God by placing man at the centre of civilization. Liberals believed progress was about the evolution of mankind's control of its destiny, thereby eroding the true basis of civilization, which amounted to a death wish. For Muggeridge, connecting with God was true reality. Liberalism, on the other hand, was fantasy and in its pursuit of self-indulgence would lead only to self-destruction. In twentieth-century politics and social thought, he saw no corresponding advocates of the life wish – certainly not in ultra-conservative figures such as Enoch Powell. Western liberals ever praised the wrong people who hastened their death wish.[65] So-called progressive Churchmen aided in emptying Christianity of its spiritual and transcendent content, replacing it with material welfare. Thus eminent Churchmen could praise someone like the agnostic Russell at the time of his death, or permit the moral pollution of D.H. Lawrence. He wrote to Archbishop of Canterbury, Michael Ramsey, enquiring why he did not support the Festival of Light.[66] Muggeridge thought he knew the answer. For Muggeridge social Christian clergy spent too much time promising good things in this.[67] He believed their motivation to be unworthy: "I think the Church, like most institutions of our society, is scared, and is anxious to ingratiate itself with people, rather than to tell the truth."[68]

Situational ethics was coming to rule the day. Sex indeed came to be the closest to a mystical experience in this quest for worldly happiness. Extreme consumer capitalism was as damnable as the false premises of Communism. In the sense of protecting the vulnerable, the sort of people who were on board that pilgrim train to Lourdes, Muggeridge maintained that he was of the Left – so defined as not including liberals like Mrs Roosevelt.[69] Birth control literally assisted the death of Western civilization. Education, the great liberator, was ultimately a deception. The three horsemen of this apocalypse were death, the gospel of progress, and the pursuit of happiness.[70]

Muggeridge's taking up of the largely figurehead rectorship of Edinburgh University in the late 1960s also served as an opportunity to publicly express many of his views on the state of society and culture. Following his invitation in 1966 by students to contest the rectorship, which was successful (he had tried before in his iconoclastic period in 1957), to many of his youthful supporters his investiture speech on February 16 1967 must have been a disappointment. He attacked the modern notion of education as "a sort of 'mumbo jumbo' or cure-all for the ills of a godless and decomposing society." He went on to state that "the so-called 'permissive' morality of our times will, I am sure, reach its apogee" with free birth control pills and abortion, "those two contemporary panaceas for all matrimonial ills," available on the public health, followed by suicide rates "up to Scandinavian proportions." He saw the curtain falling "on all the utopian hopes which have prevailed so strongly for a century or more." In the end he believed that "we shall once again understand that fulfillment must be sought through the spirit, not the body or the mind."[71] Clearly, a secularized version of Victorian morality, "the unbelieving philosophy of self-control," as Charles Taylor has called it,[72] was not working.

Long gone was the public skepticism and agnosticism of the earlier Muggeridge. In the year that followed, issues arose including an article in the student magazine encouraging the use of LSD as well as an incident involving obscenities on stage by student actors. The suspension of the editor of the magazine (who was later reinstated) resulted in Muggeridge being criticized for not defending the editor's right of expression. By the end of 1967 another motion by the Students' Representative Council that the university health service provide birth control pills on request provided a further instance in which the student leaders demanded that Muggeridge as rector must adhere to their views. After fierce public exchanges against student self-indulgence, Muggeridge resigned, following his rectorial address in St Giles Cathedral in January 1968. He stated in that address: "For the Christian religion began, let us never forget, not among brilliant, academic minds, not among the wealthy, or the powerful, or the brilliant, or the exciting, or the beautiful, or the fascinating, not among television personalities or leader-writers on *The Guardian*; it began among these very simple, illiterate people, and one was tremendously conscious of them gathered there."[73] Clearly Muggeridge indentified far more with the Lourdes pilgrims than with the academe, including college chaplains.

In a letter written in the same month to the head of the department of machine intelligence and perception at Edinburgh University, Muggeridge also attacked the legalization of hashish, noting: "Like many other vicious practices, this one in its present form came largely from America, where addiction has been carried much further than here. If you like the result, well and good; I don't. I have little doubt that your view will prevail in the end, being – as I see it – part of the liberal-humanist death-wish which now hangs over our so-called western civilization. Perhaps, by an irony of history, the communist countries (where, whatever other faults they may have, this particular type of degeneracy does not prevail) will preserve some of the essential values in a way of life we are supposed to be defending and they attacking."[74]

There was also another parallel from his own personal life, as just a few years earlier, at age 60, he had given up alcohol and extramarital affairs. Like St Augustine his period of sinning well was over, unlike his student critics. Like St Augustine, or more a supralapsarian at the Synod of Dort in 1618, as Noel Annan has again pointed out, this would be against what he perceived as the current wind direction in society, the direction of the majority who were doomed.[75] But as Frank Turner has also said of Newman, a strict moral life was "the classic compensatory pattern for the Victorian doubter or unbeliever" in that case found in the parallel behaviour of a High Churchman at odds with the predominant Victorian Protestant evangelicalism.[76] Again all of this was in defiance of *Gesellschaft*.

Muggeridge's crafted self-narrative also conformed to a pattern Northrop Frye has described in *The Great Code* as roughly U-shaped – from descent to disaster, followed by repentance, then deliverance, and finally a return to the level from where the descent had begun.[77] In his case he would see it as above that original plateau by joining the community of Christians. Perhaps Muggeridge had read the Book of Judges in his secret Bible reading during his primitive Socialist stage as a boy, from whence he started his descent.

As John Cornwell's recent book on Newman, *Newman's Unquiet Grave* (2010) has argued, the great Victorian cardinal was the ultimate self-absorbed autobiographer, and yet was regarded by many as the greatest writer of his age. This was not the case with Muggeridge. On the whole, Muggeridge's journey did not please his audience. Reviews of some of his books dealing with religion in the 1960s and 1970s could be quite hostile. Television productions, often the basis of these books, could also be badly received, at least in terms of critical response, though his share of the national audience could fluctuate, even at times being fairly good. In any case his persona as a neutral, witty bystander seemed to many people to be merely a posture. As Paul Johnson said of him in this period, Muggeridge was not a Christian "in any meaningful sense."[78] Indeed nothing seemed to come to the standard of honest sincerity of *Pilgrims to Lourdes*, excluding *Something Beautiful for God* which was essentially not about him.

Muggeridge's hostility to the media grew enormously in this period, perhaps fueled by the hostility of his critics and the public. He became convinced that what we still call Western civilization was fast disintegrating and that "the media are playing a major role in the process by carrying out, albeit for the most part unconsciously, a mighty brainwashing operation, whereby all traditional standards and values are being denigrated to the point of disappearing, leaving a moral vacuum in which the very concepts of Good and Evil have ceased to have any validity."[79] The assumption that any other sort of moral system was in fact a moral vacuum was also highly offensive to advocates of other belief systems, including the non-theistic variety. Muggeridge often alluded to the destruction of Christendom as opposed to Christianity. Letter exchanges in the 1970s with Charles Curran, the BBC director-general, contained these themes where he again contrasted liberalism based on "the fallacious notion of progress," and "life as a process" with his own view of faith and the notion of "life as a drama."[80] As he noted in *Jesus Rediscovered* "Moral propositions without action are as sick as sex without pro-creation. That's precisely what's wrong with liberalism – the basic ideology of our society."[81] As with the wider civil society, the *Gesellschaft*, "consensus-making and promoting, I should say, is to be seen historically as an instinctive preparation for some sort of conformist-collectivist society which lies ahead whatever may happen … In this country, the same force has discredited and rendered nugatory the whole structure of Christian ethics."[82]

A number of parallels can be made with C.S. Lewis at this point. Muggeridge, in spite of the fact that Lewis engaged in the "the second-rate activity" of being a university academic, claimed that "no one has presented the Christian faith to the twentieth century mind as clearly as he has."[83] Lewis's most famous work connected directly with his religious views was *Mere Christianity*, a book produced in 1952. It was largely formed from his BBC talks during the Second World War. As a work of Christian moral philosophy, in opposition to atheism and pantheism, it espoused traditional Christian teachings. After his conversion Lewis upheld a moral law reflecting the Creator's will and Christ's teachings. He, like Muggeridge, believed that Christianity rests on supernatural foundations and rejected any attempts to compromise with the secular modernity that would remake Jesus as an ardent humanist. It was God the lawgiver who would judge us, rather than the reverse. In spite of his seeming comfort with those around him in wider intellectual circles, Lewis believed that the values he identified with were disappearing. And in spite of the success of his wartime radio talks he increasingly rejected invitations to broadcast. He rarely listened to the radio, perhaps viewing it, as did the senior devil in *The Screwtape Letters* (1942), as creating a noise that would destroy the solitude that allows us to hear God's voice. Unlike Muggeridge, he had no under-standing of why he had been a radio success, and overall saw the media as hostile, and television, which became so prominent late in his life, as the promoter of materialist culture.[84] For Muggeridge television was the propagator of images and ideas that were not true. This fantasy world was very much in league with the great death wish of liberalism. Occasionally it could be defeated, as "with God all things are possible, and Mother Teresa's appearance on television was supremely useful and successful because, for once, the total dedication of her life broke through the fantasy-proneness of the medium."[85]

Like Lewis, Muggeridge believed strongly in hope. And like Blake, he held that one must see through the eye to the heart, employing imagination. Imagination, of course, was very different from fantasy.[86] Here Muggeridge's thought bears a strong resemblance to that of the ethicist Margaret Somerville, in what she describes as "the ethical imagination."[87] Both would agree that rationalism has been given too much sway over the determination of social mores. Muggeridge would go further, believing that ethical imagination was the product of "the seeing eye which comes to those born again in Christ."[88]

Television was Muggeridge's special target; he saw it as an Orwellian facilitator for a post-Christian society in this ongoing cultural critique. Indeed, as early as his 1967 documentary on Lord Reith, the first BBC director-general, he joined Reith in believing television to be potentially a social menace of the first magnitude, and a contributor to "a lowering of moral standards in our society in recent years."[89] His admiration of Reith seemed uncharacteristically on the side of the Establishment. But he did ask the strongly believing Reith: "isn't working with Christ the opposite of working with the eminent?"[90] Reith later perceived Muggeridge's more despairing view of a decadent, collapsing culture when he stated to him that he must have had the Roman Empire in mind. Muggeridge replied "On that hard pagan world, disgust and secret loathing fell. Deep weariness and sated lust made human life a hell. It's my conviction that that could happen to us in these islands."[91]

Yet Muggeridge also used this very same medium, television, to great effect selling Mother Teresa to the public. He claimed this success had little to do with his abilities; instead, he noted, "The moral would seem to be that what is required to make a successful Christian television programme is merely to find a true Christian, and put him or her on the screen. This, rather than any television skills or devices, would seem to be the key. Though my own part in making the programme was quite small – just doing the commentary, which meant letting Mother Teresa speak, and then producing a book about her, which meant holding a pen for her to write."[92] Reactions in the press to the broadcast on Mother Teresa were very positive, as were later responses to the book. Here the miraculous was joined to the documentary in a much more successful way than ever before as seen in the famous incident of the camera functioning perfectly in the darkened room for the dying without lighting. He conceded later that there was some debate about this luminosity from a technical point of view.[93] Beyond that was the impetus to join the Roman Catholic Church after Mother Teresa critically noted to him his Nicodemus approach to Catholic Christianity (Nicodemus preferred not to be seen with Jesus). As he publicly stated, the Roman Catholic leadership's uncompromising stance on issues such as abortion and contraception was crucial to his ultimate decision.[94] But Mother Teresa remained the focus of his activities as evinced by his ceaseless efforts to win her the Nobel Peace Prize.[95]

Muggeridge, of course, had already become a figure of derision for some, such as Kingsley Martin, long before then. But he fared much better than C.E.M. Joad, the public intellectual turned Christian convert, had in the previous decades.[96] He retained the friendship of figures such as A.J.P. Taylor, though losing a few others, like Anthony Powell.

Muggeridge's actual journey had indeed been a very long one, as fellow journalists began to realize in trying to solve "the great Mugg Riddle," as some at the *New Statesman* called it. The view of Christopher Booker in 1978 in that journal was that the Moscow experience of the 1930s had set Muggeridge on his course to Christianity.[97] George Orwell had also suggested that his Moscow experience was the pivot of his life. Though the term "St Mugg" was coined somewhat derisively by the 1970s, in part because of his association with Lord Longford and Mary Whitehouse in such activities as the antipornography campaign, it was obvious that his seeming transformation from cynic to the company of believers was complex.

Muggeridge's public narrative of conversion was also perhaps being laid, even subconsciously, as early as his biography of Samuel Butler. The conversion process, including to unbelief in Butler's case, had been of interest to him for a very long time. As Paul Johnson pointed out in the late 1960s, Muggeridge was a literary convert as in the nineteenth century there had been liturgical converts: "If the lost Testament of Beelzebub, written in the cadences of Milton, were suddenly to emerge from a heap of Dead Sea scrolls, I am not entirely sure where Malcolm would stand."[98] David Mills also described his later *Chronicles* as those of a literary apologist.[99] Again, this reinforces the idea that Muggeridge was first and foremost a cultural apostate. This was again not unlike Newman, who saw himself as primarily a literary man.

Professor Frank Turner in his study of Newman has cautioned against historians readily accepting any figure's own analysis of their conversion. Both the unreliable *Conversion* (1988) and *Paul, Envoy Extraordinary* (1972) must be handled with care (the latter being written when Muggeridge was in better form in drawing possible parallels to his own road to Damascus). But the point that he makes in both, in opposition to the evangelical habit of exact calculation – that conversion was a slow process – is more in keeping with academic writing generally on the subject.

It also entailed the final phase of his work in promoting Mother Teresa. In this effort he was a great success. It may well have been that he understood that the story of his conversion was not selling well. In spite of his suspicion of modern media, including a misunderstanding of the work of his friend Marshall McLuhan (Rebecca West made the same mistake in believing McLuhan wanted the death of the book),[100] it is hard to imagine that he did not appreciate when he failed to carry an audience. As the *Listener* noted of *Something Beautiful for God*, "the book's impetus is psychological rather than religious."[101]

The motives, social attitudes, and enterprises of both Mother Teresa and the Missionaries of Charity have been the subject of criticism by writers such as Christopher Hitchens and Vijay Prashad.[102] The idea that individual charity must be encouraged, more than social engineering, was certainly also in Muggeridge's thinking. As he stated back in the mid-1950s concerning the very foundation of Britain's welfare state: "Herein lies, perhaps the basic fallacy one senses in the whole Beveridge concept of welfare. It leaves out of account the charity without which, according to St. Paul, benevolence itself is of no account and the service of others no more than yet another manifestation of the demanding ego."[103]

The picture presented by Muggeridge of Mother Teresa was of one who achieved much through individual contact. As she herself stated "I do not agree with the big way of doing things."[104] Muggeridge also made the point about the activities of Mother Teresa in Calcutta "It is perfectly true, of course, that statistically speaking, what she achieves is little, or even negligible. But then Christianity is not a statistical view of life." He also added that there was no real conflict of approaches with, for example, the state: "Mother Teresa is fond of saying that welfare is for a purpose – an admirable and a necessary one – whereas Christian love is for a person."[105] Christian love requires "close contact" with the individual according to Mother Teresa.[106] Thus, it was important that the Sisters live in the slums.

Here Muggeridge also reinforced the lesson, which he took up from his Lourdes experience of 1965 if not before, that the people must be accepted as they are, as God's creations, against the vision of false prophets such as Julian Huxley. Muggeridge stated, "if the eugenist's dream were ever to be realized – the sick and the old and the mad, all who were infirm and less than physically complete and smooth-working, painlessly eliminated, leaving only the beauty queens and the athletes, the Mensa IQs and the prize-winners to be our human family ... God really would be dead."[107] The *Gemeinschaft* is immediate, intimate, and filled with every variety of humanity.

Muggeridge continued to devise and present television programs through the 1970s on public affairs, though often linked to the BBC religious affairs section. A good case in point was the series *The Question Why*, which ran from 1968 through 1972. The format was to invite a panel of public figures to discuss issues with Muggeridge introducing each program, intervening as moderator, and often offering concluding comments. A wide variety of figures participated including politicians (Dennis Healey, Richard Crossman, Enoch Powell, Rhodes Boyson), academics (Max Beloff, Anthony Smith), UN officials (Connor Cruise O'Brien), journalist-broadcasters (including the American Fred Friendly) and the occasional clergyman (Fr Bruce Kent).

The program on poverty included the comment from Muggeridge that "surely, it will be regarded as one of the greatest ironies of history that technological developments which make possible virtually unlimited production of all human requirements should have equally resulted in the multiplication of the hungry and the homeless." Certainly there was no theme of the gospel of wealth noting that affluence "produces it own special miseries; the relentless exploitation of greed in our society can create a longing for abstemiousness."[108] A religious perspective was observed with no particular earthly cure offered.

On the issue of majority rule with places like South Africa in mind, he commented that the phrase has come to be "a magical incantation in our time" but "looking round the world, it doesn't seem to be much in evidence." As he elaborated, "Except in certain Western countries, and then with somewhat dubious credentials. One looks for it in vain in contemporary Africa, Black or White; authoritarian Communism can scarcely sustain it other than on obviously fraudulent terms."[109] For some Christians, in situations like Rhodesia, it could "justify subversion and violence," or in Northern Ireland, "the Protestants are prepared to endure the ravages of IRA terrorists rather than forego what they consider to be their majority rights in Ulster."[110] He noted that it did not exist at the time of Jesus in Palestine nor St Paul and the first churches in Roman cities.[111]

In an earlier program on racialism where he did address "the vile doctrine of apartheid" and other forms of racism, he suggested the following concerning the manipulations of politicians like Enoch Powell at home as well as abroad: "I myself feel that none of the various 'solutions' offered, through legislation, education, etc. are likely to prove effective, or, in the long run, to prevent the polarization of the conflict into Black and White Power. In my opinion the only true racial, or any other, equality that exists lies in all of us belonging to one human family as all children of God. Otherwise, however hard we try, and however zealously pretend, inequality in one guise or another will keep breaking through. Such is my view."[112]

On the question of freedom of speech, Muggeridge added his own experience in broadcasting asking "is freedom of speech as hitherto understood – I mean the classic liberal doctrine – compatible with the camera? If not, how is this strange, powerful, incalculable instrument to be controlled; by whom, and on what principles?"[113] Thus the very value of discussions on these vital questions was open to question given the manipulations of modern media.

Finally, on one broadcast involving the question of the possible breakdown of society in its present form he provided his perspective: "My own opinion has long been that the impending dissolution of our society is due to inward and spiritual, rather than outward and material, causes. Having no longer a sense of a moral order, any order whatsoever – political, economic, social – becomes increasingly unattainable. Or, put more simply, we have been trying to live without God, which means either that we imagine ourselves to be gods, and succumb to megalomania, or revert to being animals, and succumb to erotomania."[114] Britain's pride in being a nation of respect for law and self-restraint was gone. Unlike St Augustine's contemporary Roman Empire, it did not require the invading barbarians to actually bring it down.

Muggeridge's political philosophy seemed conservative, but "other worldly" would be a better description, as he still referred to himself in that special way as a man of the Left in relation to the dispossessed. Clearly the danger of moving to the ultra-Right in the pattern of some European Catholics who uphold the line of defending civilization[115] was not taken by Muggeridge in his homeland. Though he worked closely with Barbara Ward in promoting the cause of Mother Teresa for the Nobel Peace Prize,[116] his differences with her over social Christianity as well as her left of centre politics were considerable.

His upholding of so-called family values, and his opposition to abortion in particular, probably contributed to Muggeridge's popularity with the Christian Right in America (including letter exchanges with Ronald Reagan) and William F. Buckley. This was augmented by mutual disdain for sexual excess. But what was probably overlooked was his dislike of the capitalist quest for materialist progress (which he also felt was shared by the welfare state). Ian Hunter has said of Muggeridge's political outlook that he only distinguished between "bearable and unbearable governments" of whatever sort.[117]

In visiting a small Catholic university in rural Nova Scotia, only three years before his formal reception into the Roman Catholic Church, Muggeridge exhibited the main themes of his thinking in late life during his convocation address. Clearly, he felt at home in this community. He congratulated those assembled for not being affluent and avoiding "those great concrete temples to the gods of the computer, and the mysteries of genetics, electronics and other contemporary fantasies." He then went on, rightly or wrongly, to assume that "no notion of such a ridiculous thing as progress has ever been put into your heads. If it has, dismiss it at once. There are various things that human beings can do; but there is one thing they can't do, and that is progress."

The final part of his address was wrapped in his frequently used image of the cathedral gargoyle. He stated: "That laughter and mysticism, that clowns and saints, that gargoyles and steeples are manifestations of the same essential thing which is a sense of the enormous disparity between human aspiration and human performance. This is what humour does and this is what mysticism is." In his view, this was the essence of our existence, and he urged embracing the virtue of humility "to be able to know it." Humour could act as an antidote to the worldly disarray of fantasy. He concluded: "the fantasy of the world is always there, but the reality of Christ is also always there to challenge it."[118]

In terms of Muggeridge's public image in his last years, especially back in Britain, gone were the days of the popular satirist who could have praised *Monty Python's Life of Brian*, not condemn it. There was a widespread perception of his deep pessimism, at least for the ways of this world. His upbringing had been quite different in this respect as a socialist in Croydon, but he came to believe that life was good only in leading to heaven defined as the next life. There could never be anything approaching a utopia in this life. The secular-minded would never have their heaven on earth. Yet he maintained that he loved life "*because* I disbelieve in the world," looking upon it as a "staging-post" of great significance not as "a destination."[119] This was not very appealing to many people, though it was a recognizable religious position. But unpopularity was also the ultimate price to be paid for a cultural apostasy manifest long before his public conversion – an apostasy increasingly irritating to so many, both old and young, and only later reinforced by his unyielding form of Christianity. His personal survival in this world was in whatever *Gemeinschaft* he identified with – ultimately the small community of true Christians. Perhaps this also explains why so well-known a figure is so little remembered today. The final product of his narrative efforts was not the successful publicizing of his own spiritual progress, of course, but rather the presentation of Mother Teresa to the world – the greatest triumph of Christian iconography of the twentieth century. Like Brother Barnabas in Anatole France's *Our Lady's Juggler*, he had offered his skill, in this case as a vendor of words, to what he believed was a higher purpose.

5

Barbara Ward and the Social Conscience of Christianity

Barbara Ward (Lady Jackson) was certainly well-known to British and global audiences of the middle decades of the twentieth century as a prolific writer and celebrated speaker. She was especially revered in Christian circles; was a guest at many church conferences, both Roman Catholic and Anglican; and was a major figure at the time of Vatican II, the Ecumenical council of the 1960s. Adrian Hastings states in *A History of English Christianity* (1986): "Her life, personality and achievement might seem to provide as good evidence as any of the continuing effectiveness of Christianity. If there was in truth anything of a deeper Christian consensus in this period it certainly owed most to Barbara Ward."[1]

Other historians, particularly those who do not share the perspectives of the Christian Left, of compatriots of Barbara Ward such as Archbishop Michael Ramsey of Canterbury, and equivalent figures in the United States, where she was also well-known, would take a different view. E.R. Norman, for example, sees Ward as one of those who in the 1960s helped "the conflation of Christian morality and Humanist ethics."[2] With Malcolm Muggeridge, eventually a fellow Catholic as well as Christian, she shared almost nothing in common in social outlook. The Christian Right today would view her as an unfortunate period piece. Her global interests, especially in ecology, would place her in the company of Julian Huxley. Among developing world economists and environmentalists her words are still echoed today. Given her overall political and social proclivities, she shared much in common with Bertrand Russell, and to some extent, worked at having a similar influence upon world leaders.

Like Julian Huxley's religion, it may be said that her system of moral principles informed most of her activities from the outset of her career. The daughter of a Quaker solicitor in Felixstowe, near Ipswich, she was raised as a Catholic in the tradition of her devout mother. The prosperity of her family afforded a good education at a convent school in Felixstowe and later at the Lycée Molière and the Sorbonne in France. There, and briefly in Germany, she acquired an excellent background in modern languages. In 1932 she entered the politics, philosophy, and economics program at Oxford (PPE, or "Modern Greats," which had been initiated as an honour school only in 1921) as a member of Somerville College.[3]

In a piece written about women students at Oxford, Ward noted that while equal status had been granted in 1921, "official recognition, however, did not involve any of an unofficial kind. The woman student was still regarded as a curious subhuman species." By the 1930s, however, change had taken place, with the "undergraduette" welcome at most social gatherings with the exception of two clubs – "Of these one is the home of inveterate conservatism – the Union – Oxford's debating club, where women have entrance to the gallery and are permitted to sit under an imposing notice of 'Silence'; the other is the Dramatic Society (or OUDS) closed to women possibly in order that the somewhat broad humour of the 'Smokers' (a yearly entertainment) may not be brought under their refining influence; more probably that the OUDS may continue to preserve its prerogative of engaging the most attractive actresses on the London stage to take part in their productions – a delightful if expensive privilege of which it would be cruel to deprive them."

Ward did note that the October Club, "now unfortunately banned," welcomed both male and female Communists, the latter often its most ardent supporters. She continued, "Communism and Socialism flourish in Oxford. Most students have just enough money to consider the wrongs of others with enthusiasm and just enough initiative to make really striking speeches. Their energy does not however match their eloquence." She did concede overall that "this new recognition of the undergraduette socially, intellectually and artistically adds greatly to the value of a career in Oxford."[4]

Though facing a number of challenges as a woman student, she obtained first-class honours. Somerville had recently been led by Margery Fry, a Quaker, renowned penal reformer, and supporter of the advancement of women in higher education. Fry had left Oxford the year before Ward arrived but undoubtedly the atmosphere of Somerville was still heavily influenced by her. After graduation Ward pursued graduate studies on the politics and economics of Austria under the auspices of the Royal Institute of International Affairs. She also lectured for the Cambridge University extension program for the next three years.

Because of her scholarly pursuits, Ward spent considerable time in Central Europe in the summers. Among her papers can be found an unpublished play entitled "Full Circle" about Social Democrats in the Austrian Tyrol at the end of the First World War.[5] Ward was able to gain some writing experience as a freelance journalist given her linguistic skills and knowledge of current affairs on the Continent. She also began to strengthen her ties with Catholic circles, after a brief waning of her faith while at Oxford.

In the late 1930s there was predictably a growing thirst in the public for knowledge of international affairs. Though she was one of few women journalists, her solid academic credentials improved her chances of landing publishing outlets. The state of a number of European countries potentially threatened by the resurgent power of Germany was of special concern. She felt a firm stand was needed to help "frightened states like Poland and Romania."[6] She defended Yugoslavia, stating: "It is sometimes said that Yugoslavia is an artificial creation, a cardboard state brought into being by the arbitrary fiat of the victors of Versailles. This is quite untrue."[7] Though most of her publications were detailed studies of the current tensions in Europe, she also wrote on other subjects such as the Empire. She contributed to the International Research Section of the Fabian Society, as well as Catholic journals. She was not reluctant to reveal both her political leanings and her religion.

The outbreak of war in September 1939 greatly affected her career. Just as armies, weapons, and economies are essential in total war, so are the objectives of those who must wage war. In the dark days following the Nazi string of conquests from Warsaw to Paris, it became clear that extraordinary efforts would have to be made if Britain were to survive. In examining affairs up to that point, the consequences of being politically divided became clear to some in the dramatic defeat of France. Perhaps it was most clear to those in Britain's minority Catholic community, which had itself experienced severe divisions in the 1930s. In the latter case disputes had arisen over the issues of Italian Fascism, the Spanish Civil War, and how to relate to Germany's new leader, Adolf Hitler. The spiritual leader of Britain's Catholics, Arthur Hinsley,[8] brought out of retirement in the mid-1930s to lead his flock as Cardinal-Archbishop of Westminster by the direct action of the Pope, may have helped heal some domestic issues, but nothing as yet on the foreign policy front. There he even managed to offend his own patron by calling Pius XI "a helpless old man" during the Abyssinian Crisis.[9]

After the outbreak of the Second World War, a number of English Catholic thinkers began to be concerned that Britain must have clearer notions of why it was at war or suffer the same fate as France. Survival was clear and understandable, but not enough for them. Christopher Dawson, a cultural historian, recently appointed editor of the Catholic *Dublin Review,* believed that the basis of Western Civilization and all that was good in it was Catholic Christianity. He had come to the conclusion in the late 1930s that German Nazism, like all forms of totalitarianism, was antithetical to Catholic Christianity.[10] This view was shared by some others, including the young Barbara Ward. More broadly in the country, there were others who argued that Britain stood for "Christian Civilization" by 1940 against the Nazis.[11]

Her personal diaries reveal a series of incidents in this period involving encounters with Nazis when in Central Europe that steadily moved her from an initially favourable view of Hitler to one of hatred. She disliked how the Nazis treated Communists. Though never an outright socialist, she wrote to her parents in August 1937 that all that was good in Communism was derived from Christianity. However, in a dispute with a female Communist she made the following points, recorded in the letter to her parents: "One thing I think my argument with the communists showed me – that's that Christianity must be on the offensive … Communism was a climate of opinion in which I was drawing breath to my own disadvantage. Because one mustn't let the few or perhaps the great elements of truth in Communism (which are entirely purchased from Christianity) blind one to the fact that her general interpretation is radically false."[12]

The major victims of Nazi brutality were, of course, Jews. One particular incident in Freudenstadt in Baden-Wurttemberg involving the survival of Ada, an elderly Catholic lady of Jewish ancestry, aided by a friend in defiance of the racial laws of the Third Reich, seemed to reinforce her belief that in the defence of universal truth there can be no compromise.[13] In a contemporaneous article on Mgr Ignaz Seipel, the deceased Austrian chancellor, while attempting to analyze Seipel's complicated political attitudes, including his relationship with Nazis, Ward did reveal her admiration of his subordination of patriotism to the more ultimate unity of "the community of mankind."[14] In the struggle against racism Ward worked for the cause of Jewish refugees in the late 1930s. At the time, in a detailed draft essay on the Church in Germany, she condemned Nazism and in particular the acquiescence of the Austrian bishops to the Anschluss of 1938.[15] Emotionally and intellectually, Ward was already at war with Nazism by the end of the 1930s.

When the actual war came in 1939, one can understand how impressed Ward, Dawson, and others were with the fierce attack by Cardinal Hinsley upon Nazism in his broadcast address of 10 December 1939. Given the earlier reluctance to speak out on the part of other church leaders, such as the current archbishop of Canterbury, Cosmo Lang, it seemed a breath of fresh air.[16] It was also bold given the continuing pro-Fascist inclinations of some English Catholics. The response was overwhelming. In the same period, even Winston Churchill publicly declared that Cardinal Hinsley was the only person, besides himself, who could be trusted to truly speak to the nation on war aims.[17] Later in 1942 as Prime Minister Churchill supported the replacement of Lang by William Temple as archbishop of Canterbury. Though differing with Temple on social and political issues, in the interests of the nation, Churchill is said to have seen Temple as the only "half a crown article in the sixpenny bazaar."[18]

After the Fall of France, and the establishment of the Vichy regime in June of 1940, Hinsley and his disciples realized the continued danger of Catholics aligning themselves with the extreme French Right as well as Franco and Mussolini, facilitated by the Nazi victory. Thus, by the summer of 1940 Dawson, Ward, and other Catholic lay opponents of Nazism began to organize a Sword of the Spirit movement based upon the warrior metaphor of St Paul used by Hinsley in his speech – the sword of the spirit being the word of God. While Hinsley was courageous and determined, as their leader, he was deemed too blunt for the careful tasks of crafting a specific agenda for the new organization and negotiating with those necessary for its success.

On the eve of the founding of the Spirit, Christopher Dawson, in a personal letter to Hinsley, urged the cardinal to emphasize to the public that this movement would be religious and not political. In recognizing the dangerous pre-war political divisions within British Catholicism, and to some extent in the nation as a whole, Dawson believed that Britain needed unity of purpose based upon the Christian virtues of faith, hope, and charity. He also warned that politics was potentially dangerous, fostering division and confusion. Being a minority within Britain, and in the past frequently misrepresented as an "anti-national force" in English life, Dawson also saw a great window of opportunity in a Catholic movement through collaboration with all the churches. However, in the same letter, Dawson was equally emphatic that there was no need for an elaborate statement of war aims or intentions about the postwar world.[19]

Dawson's ecumenism was shared by some members, including Barbara Ward,[20] but, given her knowledge of so many more issues facing the world (as displayed by such publications as *The International Share-out* [1938]), she also wanted even more from the movement.[21] Ward repeatedly stated then and for many months to come that Britain's reasons for fighting this war must be more specific than surviving the evils of Nazism – it must be a war in which the fight is *for* something.[22]

Following the August of 1940 inauguration of the movement, Sword societies rapidly proliferated and successfully included prominent members of other churches. It also spread into the British armed forces, and to those of the Commonwealth countries, Free French, Free Poles, and others living in Britain. The Sword of the Spirit, as Ian McLaine has pointed out, also "received a great deal of assistance from the Ministry of Information, a fact which the Religious Division was anxious to conceal."[23]

Ecumenical dialogue developed rapidly but it became obvious that it must go beyond general statements of superiority over the Nazis if it was to succeed. In this, Barbara Ward, as secretary of the Sword, operated at the centre – compared with Dawson who lacked any sort of administrative abilities. Friendly voices in other churches, particularly those who supported the principles of social Christianity, soon appeared to offer their contributions. Here Hinsley was able to play a particularly important role in dialogue given his well-established credentials in the field of social justice and in the implementation of social encyclicals. Thus social Catholicism as well as social Christians of various denominations all found a common cause and a cement that would bind them together and the nation with them. It was agreed that Britain was fighting for these principles and not just for its own national survival.

Soon the agenda was hatched. To Pius XII's 1939 announcement of five points for peace among nations was added an additional five standards for testing fairness in economic and social conditions among the peoples of all nations. The latter were derived largely from the Oxford Conference of 1937 which had included important social Christians in the Church of England and Protestant Nonconformist churches. Publicly this ten point document was announced in a letter to *The Times* on 21 December 1940 bearing the signature of Hinsley; Walter Armstrong, Moderator of the Free Church Council; Archbishop Lang of Canterbury; and Archbishop William Temple of York. While successful in the realm of ecumenism and social justice, its absence of reference to Nazism displeased the Ministry of Information which regularly assisted Sword activities.

The Sword advanced rapidly for a time in membership announcing, as it did, that the movement stood for an international moral order not just a preservation of the status quo against something far worse. It was also the most ambitious of ecumenical movements thus far among Christians as seen in the well-publicized Stoll Meetings of 10–11 May 1941. However, this ecumenical aspect was also opposed by some, especially within the Catholic fold. Among Catholics, the issue was the perception that such close collaboration could compromise the doctrinal beliefs of Catholics. Soon it was obvious that Hinsley had very little support from the bishops and theologians of his own church. It led to a forced retreat in which the Sword would become an exclusively Catholic organization, with associated groups in other churches. A second joint statement on co-operation, followed by a meeting attended by Hinsley and the archbishop of Canterbury in May 1942 could not prevent these developments. Much of the force of ecumenism now went toward those molding a world council of churches (also a product of the Oxford Conference of 1937) and the rising national figure of Britain's new Anglican primate, William Temple, in his efforts for social justice. In discouragement Barbara Ward wrote to her parents, following a lecture tour on behalf of the Sword, "I do dislike Catholics and I do think the Church vile, humanly speaking and does very little for England … however, here I am."[24] In spite of all she remained a staunch Catholic. Hinsley died in 1943 and Dawson was removed as editor of the *Dublin Review* in the next year.

But Ward flourished in this period. Employed as a staff member of *The Economist*, after losing a full-time position at the Ministry of Information, she was also introduced to the BBC by fellow Sword founder, Professor A.C.F. Beales of London University, who was already there.[25] In many ways, the BBC thereafter became the chief conduit, along with pamphlets, of Sword's ideas – both being in large measure the work of Ward, who continued as the secretary of the organization, assisted by Beales. Here she developed themes from her writings of the late 1930s. In *The Defence of the West* (1942), which the Sword published as a pamphlet, but first broadcast as three talks on the BBC in December 1940, Ward provided the reasons why Britain was fighting. She argued: "It is a struggle to preserve the traditional order of Europe, that is to say, the whole complex of values and standards which, to an extent we do not always realise, form the basis of our judgments and of our moral actions."[26] She further believed that "democratic practice, liberal values, the very concept of the dignity and worth of individuals" were "devised from Christian doctrine and faith." Nazism, on the other hand, exploited the irrational despair of the Depression, supplying a new set of ideas which produced the Robot – "the man who has lost his moorings – which are the supernatural origins and destiny of man."[27] Ward also argued that "behind all secular evidence, this faith is grounded in the word of God. We cannot argue with those who preach unreason. We can prove them wrong in practice – which is one of the things we are fighting this war to do."[28] Law, reason, freedom, and international order were therefore embodied in the word of God, and the Sword of the Spirit combated the divisiveness and evils of Nazism.

Until his death in late 1943 Cardinal Hinsley, who more than anyone else was Ward's mentor (as revealed in her correspondence), seemed to best embody the concept of the Christian warrior, which Ward also shared. Speaking from the pulpit of Westminster Cathedral his sermons were also frequently broadcast over the BBC. On one occasion in 1942 he alluded to the onset of the Holocaust, which was turning Poland into a vast cemetery for European Jews. He made an appeal to human feelings and Christian justice to swiftly end this campaign of extermination.[29] For Hinsley, as for Ward, the struggle with Nazi Germany was a struggle for the survival of civilization itself.

At the BBC some other Sword members advanced to positions of importance, but none in so spectacular a fashion as Ward. Here the approach, as generally followed by the BBC as a whole, was to inform, persuade, and keep broadcasting no matter the degree of devastation about them. Broadcasts were directed to occupied Europe, the Empire-Commonwealth, and the United States, as well as to the British people. Truth was seen as an ally. Ward produced a remarkably large body of broadcasts beginning in late 1940 and running through to 1945. These ranged from overtly religious topics, to law, political philosophy, world economics, the conditions in various parts of Europe and Asia, and changes in Britain's own society. There was also a series of scripts entitled "Democracy Marches – Inside Nazi Europe" in 1941, including one on the plight of women.[30] While it was acknowledged that Ward had "a remarkable grasp of affairs," it was suggested in a memorandum in 1942 that she might temporarily be confined to "talks for women."[31] It did not really happen although she also produced other scripts that pertained to allied women at war in 1943. Toward the end of the war, she became a participant in the famous program *The Brains Trust*, eventually being rated as one of Britain's most popular broadcasters on a wide-open agenda of subjects.

The road was not always smooth. A draft script by Ward on British colonial policy was rejected for broadcast by the BBC *Talks* section on the advice of the Ministry of Information, seeing it as beyond the possibility of revision. The rejection was on the grounds of its being too critical of colonial administration, including the exercise of the colour bar, for an audience during the war.[32] There were also times when it was difficult to keep American Catholics sympathetic to the cause both before Pearl Harbor and later with the Soviet alliance. Ward made her first speaking tour to the US in 1942, sponsored by the Ministry of Information. Her oratory won her many friends on the other side of the Atlantic.

As the war drew to a close, Ward looked to the dawn of a new age in which many of the aims of the Sword of the Spirit might be realized. In foreign affairs she was among the first journalists to travel to and survey the scene in post-war Germany. She was present for the war crimes trials and was also appalled at the willingness of some ordinary Germans, in conversation, not to reject Nazism.[33] She upheld the United Nations, but also was concerned about the new threat to peace posed by the Soviet Union. She was a strong supporter of the Marshall Plan as a key element in the recovery of the

West. In a lead article in *The Economist*, entitled "Unsordid Act," she called it "an act without peer in history."[34]

Domestically Ward campaigned vigorously for the Labour Party in the General Election of 1945. Though she never aspired to political office it is said that one of her speeches brought tears to the eyes of Ernest Bevin, the soon-to-be Foreign Secretary in the Attlee cabinet. Ward expanded both her print journalistic work, mainly for *The Economist*, and broadcasting for the BBC, eventually becoming a governor of the latter.

She had achieved some special attention at the BBC with her sharp exchanges with Professor C.E. Joad on *The Brains Trust*. As one listener wrote, "I speak for all women in thanking you for your ready and just replies to funny old Dr. Joad. One must say funny in order to keep a right perspective, but it is unpleasing to be a part of a sex which a supposed scientist and sage relegates to the use of a stock-breeding establishment."[35] Not only did she uphold the standing of women in society, but also tried to advance the Christian viewpoint at the BBC to a more modern position. As a governor in the late 1940s, a period of re-evaluation of the role of the BBC in religious affairs, she urged that a lay person should be appointed as director of religious broadcasting. In her note to the board she stated that: "I do not believe that a Director whose experience of life has been on the whole gathered in ecclesiastical circles is likely to be sufficiently sensitive to contemporary lay opinion to meet it adequately in controversy or to know where to call on suitable protagonists of the Christian point of view."[36]

In this period Ward's books became more numerous and substantial, and revealed much more about her moral philosophy as well as her social, political, and economic ideas. Her formal attachments to educational institutions were minimal and transitory, chiefly in later years as a visiting fellow. Her transatlantic contacts grew, enabling her to receive foundation grants, and act as consultant to various agencies and governments, and later to the Catholic Church. She began to lecture on a global scale, so much so that her fairly long period of residency with her husband in Ghana in the 1950s hardly affected her career – if anything it added to her firsthand knowledge of the Third World.

While the late 1940s and the 1950s and 1960s allowed Ward to develop her reputation in the fields of politics and economics, it was also a time when she expanded her moral vision, which informed her views of politics and economics, through writings. Certainly the Cold War was an enormous consideration in this period. Many of her sentiments against the Nazis expressed in *The Defence of the West* (1942) could now be transposed to the Communists. However, she had since the 1930s always seen Communism as a much more serious challenge, appealing as it did to sentiments on an international basis that were far more formidable. In *The West at Bay* (1948) she envisaged a European free trade union to help stabilize and defend Western Europe. But more than that she believed "the need to change, to reform, to expand, to improve Western society is absolute and inescapable. Even if it were not desirable in itself, the hostile witnesses on the frontiers and disgruntled minorities within leave the Western world no choice."[37] For Ward, Western Europe was now "living through a difficult interregnum – the gap between the death of an old, comfortable and familiar world and the birth of a new one of whose nature much can be hoped but little predicted."[38] Nevertheless, society must move forward.

While Marxists could be accused of creating a system inimical to Western democracy, destroying "the belief in the morally responsible and autonomous human being," it was nevertheless in the very soil of Western European democracy that "Marxism first took root."[39] In her historical review of the situation "the chief apostasy lay more with the practitioners of society than with its critics, for as we have seen, the nineteenth and early twentieth century were times during which man built up an inhuman economic system, sanctified it in the name of Christian values, and protected it by the dogma of private property. One may blame the debunkers for defining religion as the means of ensuring a docile working class, but all too many of their contemporaries were prepared to use religion in precisely that way."[40]

For Ward, the United States was unhelpful at times in the post-war years, in spite of the proposed Marshall plan. For example in not encouraging the links between moderate socialists and "the more radical Christians" as in Western Germany, an important opportunity was missed, though British policy and, at times, the "nebulous" ideas of these groups were also to blame.[41] What was the pity in this was that "the fundamental affirmations of Western society are all matters of faith and it is an historical fact that the faith in which they were grounded and from which they derived their deepest strength has been the Christian faith."[42] In short "the only lesson that history gives is that Christianity and democracy grew up so closely intertwined that the languishing of one may well mean the failure and the decadence of the other."[43] The new society would therefore have to enable ordinary people to realize a prosperous and free life in the best traditions of men of good will, including humanists, but especially Christians.[44]

In relation to the United States Ward was also particularly alarmed by the uses of anti-Communism for political purposes. From Accra, she wrote to her family back in Britain with dismay about Senator Joe McCarthy's attack upon the Protestant clergy as a Communist front. Ward referred to McCarthy as a "bastard." But she was also annoyed by the lack of leadership by President Eisenhower on the international scene.[45] In spite of providing John F. Kennedy with a lengthy letter on conditions in Africa while he was a Senator,[46] and generally approving of his policies while President, she was less than impressed with some of his attitudes toward women. As she stated in an oral history interview "my impression of President Kennedy is that, on the whole, he had little empathy for the trained, intelligent woman – he may have but my impression is he hadn't. I think the coolness was mutual."[47] Her favourite American politician was Adlai Stevenson, the Democratic candidate for president in the 1950s, and US ambassador to the UN under Kennedy.

What therefore was the Wardian version of Christianity? There is ample evidence that by the 1950s Ward had successfully assimilated the leading concepts of the Anglican and Protestant social gospel and social Catholicism, which rounded out into what more truly could be called social Christianity. The pedigree was clear from the pronouncements of the Sword of the Spirit, which had pioneered in this ecumenical blend. But neither the rump of what had been the Sword movement nor the leadership of the Church of England and the English Roman Catholic Church were particularly sustaining sources of inspired guidance in this direction into the 1950s, the conservative era of Geoffrey Fisher as archbishop of Canterbury and Pope Pius XII. Indeed the inspired guidance came from within Ward herself, and was reinforced in the real world of action. Ward was also inspired and guided by liberalism.

There can be little doubt that her liberalism was firmly grounded in Christianity, not in the secular, skeptical rationalism of the West that Malcolm Muggeridge so identified with modern liberalism, and condemned. As she stated in *Faith and Freedom*: "Faith is not a matter of convenience nor even – save indirectly – a matter of sociology … Faith will not be restored in the West because people believe it to be useful. It will return only when they find that it is true. But can modern man accept such a possibility? The whole trend of four hundred years of rationalism and science has taken him in the opposite direction."[48]

As I outline in my book *A Kingdom on Earth* (1996), like many social Christians Ward continuously stressed the fatherhood of God and the brotherhood of mankind in her religious thinking. She begins her pamphlet *My Brother's Keeper* for the *Sword of the Spirit* series by stating that "the idea of mankind as a single family under the Fatherhood of God is so much a foundation of Christian thinking that, like many other fundamental ideas, it is simply taken for granted."[49] This metaphysical concept was reinforced again and again in her writings, as was the related concept that "all men are brothers."[50] Early on, as in the Second World War with the Sword of the Spirit, it was related to the move toward religious unity. As she stated in 1962 "Christians have to hasten their own reunion so that they can embark more effectively on the part they could play in discovering a core of unity for the human race."[51] Previously, in the Mott lectures for 1953, she took a Toynbee-esque view (she had worked in global historian Arnold Toynbee's "monitoring unit" of the Ministry of Information based at Balliol College, Oxford before joining *The Economist* in 1939) that "Higher forms of civilization coincide almost exactly with the coming into being of world religions."[52] Unlike some other religions which saw the perfection of the self in union with some higher principle beyond the materialist realm, Christianity "was a religion of the spirit but it was not one that rejected the world as an illusion."[53] While acknowledging the value of studying other world religions, in the spirit of the sixteenth century Jesuit Father Matteo Ricci, who found "in Confucianism a foundation of natural law and morality,"[54] Ward nonetheless believed "in no other religion is the unity of mankind so profoundly, organically preached as in the Christian faith."[55]

The real enemies in any case were "the vast universal pressure of unbelief" – from Nietzsche, who in declaring "God is Dead" "only said what would become a commonplace," to the "dogmatic atheism" of world Communism, which "almost recreates God by the strenuous effort to get rid of Him," to the "waning of faith of a less premeditated kind."[56] The less premeditated would include distractions such as "pervasive television,"[57] and the "advance of aimlessness, rootlessness, a certain shallowness, and a boredom" within abundant societies of the West that may lack "personal restraint and outward-looking unselfishness."[58] In other words, the solution to the problems of the world, as well as some of the seeds of human misery, lay in Western civilization. As she stated in her 1953 Mott lectures, "the impact of the West in the last hundred years has been the main force in the spread of irreligion, and it is well I think to bear that in mind in making judgements about the contribution of the West and the role of the West in modern society."[59]

In the midst of the global struggle to save humanity was "The 'good news' of the Gospel," which was "quite simply that man was not alone in his heartbreaking struggle against social and personal evil."[60] The incarnation was also the good news, "the central fact" of "God Himself deeming human nature worthy to be His dwelling place."[61] This separated Christians from, for example, Muslims,[62] and "with the concept of God incarnate in history and the institution of a sacramental system, we are at the core of Christianity."[63] In the coming of the Second Adam, with Christ as "the prototype of the new man," all the greatest insights of pre-existent world religions were incorporated.[64] This linkage with the sacraments reminds one of the "sacramental socialism" of some Anglican Christian socialists of the nineteenth century. But beyond this special Christian concept, as well as the rejection of any syncretism with other world religions, Ward was also insistent upon the historical, pre-Christian cultural roots of Christianity.

Judaism was the prime precursor of Christianity in terms of their concept of a universal, mystical God who was also concerned with the ethical behaviour of human beings. Their notion of progress in history, breaking with other views of a static experience for humanity, or of cycles of repetitive meaninglessness, was also unique.[65] This gave a "peculiar vitality" to their concept of God,[66] as it was "the progressive revelation of God's will for man which will be realized in the measure of man's free response."[67] Judaism also had dynamism in the vision of "man's social existence here and now." What is hoped for is "the *coming* of the Kingdom," one marked by the replacement of injustice and inequalities with "the recovery of primal brotherliness and good will."[68] Ward believed these qualities were absent from other ancient religions and cultures.[69] It was also accompanied by a sense of moral criticism when not fulfilled. In reading Isaiah, Ezekiel, and Jeremiah is "the extraordinary combination of compassion for the poor with a profound sense of outrage at the rich who will not accept the obligations of compassion."[70] Her appreciation of Jewish heritage may have been the result of her experience in helping Jewish refugees in the late 1930s and in witnessing the Nazi genocide of European Jewry. One of Ward's great heroes was the German Jew, Edith Stein, who converted to Christianity and died at the hands of the Nazis while comforting the women of Ravenstock.

Beyond the concepts of Judaism, there was also the contribution of Greek thought to Christianity. This was not simply the result of her belief in the centrality of classics to Western civilization, nor her continued belief in the value of humanities in modern education, which of necessity required increasing amounts of science and practical training in a changing environment. Nor even was it part of her repeated argument that people must continue to be exposed to the rich heritage of ideas, as ideas were not merely projections of material facts in the way in which Marxists or other economic determinists viewed such things.[71] This classical influence lay in the very particular elements of Greek thought which influenced Christianity, and thereby the Western World, and ultimately the entire world.

The Greeks, like the Jews, did not accept a "static idea of social order," but rather "that the sum of things could by human will be transformed and remade in the image of the divine."[72] For the Greeks this concept of transformation was more a rational vision than a moral one based on the use of reason, and, of course, less mystical and not based upon Revelation. Insisting upon freedom in the use of reason, and driven by curiosity about the earth and its history led the Greek citizen to live "under laws he helps to frame."[73] In this "we can see the early stirrings of the scientific spirit in the Greek intoxication with reason and with the harmonies of mathematics and musical law."[74] The modern concept of liberty grew out of the Christian synthesis of both heritages. Liberalism was therefore well within the Christian tradition whereas rationalism taken to an extreme was not, as in the case of Communism, which was "a bastard of Western rationalism."[75]

The blending of Judeo-Christian and Greek traditions saw full expression in intellectual work such as that of St Thomas Aquinas. Through the Incarnation "God, the remote impersonal Reason, the unconditional Good of the philosophers, had taken human form [Jesus]."[76] Faith was also a function of the mix as "Faith is not an irrational virtue. It is super-rational, adding something that reason needs but lacks."[77] This could be similar to Margaret Somerville's idea of "ethical imagination." Both the immoral and the irrational were enemies to be defeated. Liberty was more than a personal condition for the Christian. Ward stated: "My faith is that the shaping forces of social justice, humane concern, and Christian compassion, which Marx dismissed as worthless bourgeois windowdressing, represent on the contrary the essential expression of the free spirit."[78]

The fusion of the best in Christianity with what she saw as the best in liberalism was already foreseen in Ward's writing during the Second World War. In the post-Second World War decades Ward had laid out not only a much more elaborate philosophical, theological, and historical justification for her positions but also blueprints for the realization of her social Christian vision. In that realization Ward was able to employ her academic training and journalistic experience more directly. Kenneth Gladish in his 1985 thesis believes Ward to have been conservative in her propensities toward the preservation of the state system and turning to the legacy of classical and Christian moral precepts.[79] Perhaps in her alarmism directed against the Soviet menace in the Cold War era, such conclusions could be drawn. But there may be some confusion here in equating Ward's practical, almost pragmatic, approach to certain issues in the short run with her overall philosophy. She was one who was well versed in the experiences of the long, hard road to the attainment of goals whether these goals were winning of the war, attaining rights for women, widening the goals of social Christians, or even revamping the work of the BBC as a governor in the postwar years. Ward was not only an effective communicator but also an effective facilitator, and built friendly contacts with figures as diverse as President Lyndon Johnson of the United States, to President Kwame Nkrumah of Ghana, to Pope Paul VI, in order to attain her goals. As an internationalist, she had no particular love of the nation state system. Her moral foundations compelled her to seek radical change as much as tolerate the status quo.

On the other side, Ward has at times been accused of being almost too idealistic or optimistic in the unattainable tasks she set out for herself in the real world. This is almost contradictory to the first image of one being somewhat conservative in inclinations, and operating almost as a celebrity conscience or, like the liberal Protestant theologian Reinhold Niebuhr, a sort of chaplain to those in power. As in the first judgment by Gladish that she was conservative, such a view does not capture the essence of Ward's strivings. By setting high goals one can be energized. The setting of lower goals can be a formula for acquiescence to the status quo.

In the Cold War, Ward was determined to see the West strengthened by economic and political means against the Communist Bloc. But from the outset Ward was even more concerned that "the moral challenge of Communism is being less urgently considered than its military pressure."[80] While excluding morality in the strict sense in excluding free will by Communists, Ward nonetheless saw in Communism an ethical condemnation of the exploitation of workers by Western capitalism.[81] Likewise this extended to the question of the oppression of Third World peoples by capitalistic imperialism. Communism's dynamism derived from the shared Western "cultural revolution" that was sweeping the entire world. Its "moral outrage" was reminiscent of the moral outrage of the Hebrews. She argued that "socialism came into being as a protest against manifest social evil."[82] Here, of course, she found a contradiction. In so doing, Marxists disproved their main contention that men are moved by the hard effects of economic processes. She stated: "In a word, Marxism, the creed of the determinists is proving to us every day that faith, poetry, and vision are levers of power."[83] Perhaps Ward in this case might have refined her statement that their determinism was really about the primacy of economic processes, not a complete determinism that would deny all else, including free will.

For Ward, the realization of the Kingdom on Earth entailed "a vision compatible with humane and liberal institutions, [it] indeed demands them, since compulsion and dictatorship deny the free spirit of man and cramp his capacity for love. It is in fear-ridden societies that neighborliness ceases to be."[84] In this respect, she would be in agreement with Bertrand Russell that the creation of fear in a population undermines what is most valuable. In spreading "the revolution of liberty," it was important to Ward that "we have to re-examine its moral content and ask ourselves whether we are not leaving liberty as a wasted talent and allowing other forces, not friendly to liberty, to monopolize the great vision of men working in brotherhood to create a world in which all can live."[85] This could again guard us against Communism, but "if freedom for us is no more than the right to pursue our own self-interest – personal or national – then we can make no claim to the greatest vision of our society: 'the glorious liberty of the Sons of God.'"[86]

Ward certainly regarded "the decision to use government as an instrument of greater justice and solidarity" as "fundamental to the change in the West from a narrow class-oriented market to the mass consumption economy of today" as good and no compromise of liberty.[87] "Humane and Christian conscience could no longer tolerate the flagrant evils of an unregulated economy,"[88] operated under laissez-faire in the nineteenth century. As she noted, "some of the basic difficulties in open societies stem from the over concentration on personal interest, and self-advancement which, carried beyond a certain point, makes it all but impossible to achieve a proper and general balance of justice and sharing."[89] Economic liberalism therefore had to be restrained. The achievements of Western European nations since the struggles of the 1840s created standards that would seem utopian to Victorians.[90]

The "interweaving" of different lifestyles and income levels in communities was never "an impossibly Utopian dream."[91] This "old mix" had been the pattern of traditional market towns or merchant cities, and could be for newer communities. In planned economies, as she noted, "segregation by housing and health and education in the ghetto sense is not among the criticisms."[92]

The achievement of wholeness in communities, thereby shrinking class divisions, antagonisms, and distance was well within the grasp of the modern state with a mixed economy. Here *Gemeinschaft* and *Gesellschaft* could meet. In Britain much of this had initially been achieved by Victorian Christian reformers such as Lord Shaftesbury and others who shook the comfortable middle classes into securing government action against social problems,[93] which eventually led to the foundation of the Welfare State. It also took place without the destruction of constitutional liberty. She also believed that the development of the welfare state made good, practical economic sense: "To me, one of the most vivid proofs that there is a moral governance in the universe is the fact that when men or governments work intelligently and far-sightedly for the good of others, they achieve their own prosperity too. Take our Western experience with the welfare state. We did not plan to do it as a good stroke of business. It was a moral decision going back to John Lilburne: it gave 'the poorest he a life to live with the richest he.' Yet one of the consequences has been to reduce business risks. Mass consumption, secured by social security, enables the economy to avoid the booms and collapses of the old economy."[94]

But for Ward the revolution of equality described in her great work *The Rich Nations and the Poor Nations* must engulf the world. Though Western nations had seen much of the glaring inequalities disappear in recent years, such was not the case in other parts of the world. As she observed in *India and the West* (1961), "like the dispossessed urban workers of Victorian times, the peoples of the underdeveloped world have been drawn into the modern economy; but so far, they participate in its labours rather than in its rewards."[95] As she noted, "the world's poor increasingly know that their condition is not an act of God but the choice of man."[96] One option was for the dispossessed to accept the Communist analysis. She states: "It is almost as though the Marxist prediction of the increasing wealth of the few and the growing impoverishment of the many, which has been negated inside democratic society, has reappeared at the world level to create even wider disturbance and unrest."[97] The North-South hemispheric wealth polarization was quite evident.

Apart from the Communist challenge, there were deeper obligations in the revolution of equality. She stated in *The Rich Nations and the Poor Nations*: "The equality of men which is such a driving force all around the world sprang originally from the Western sense that men, as souls of infinite metaphysical value, stand equal before the throne of God. And if we feel this equality of man as a profound, moral fact, can we really be content to see men hungry, to see men die, to see men continue in starvation and ill-health when we have the means to help them? Is this our concept of equality? If it is, do we not betray our faith?"[98] In Ward's view the Kingdom of God upon earth included the entire earth. As she wrote seven years later in *The Lopsided World* "God's fatherhood" is "of all mankind." She argued her moral case: "If Christians allow their conscience to become thus determined by nation and race and culture, they can make no response to the profound and mysterious image of the Son of Man. They will not recognize 'the least of these little ones' if the face is brown or black or yellow."[99]

The path to her position again went back even before the Second World War. In *The International Share-out* (1938) she sought grounds for reconciliation between the "satisfied powers" such as Britain and France and those countries that lost their colonies in defeat as a result of the Treaty of Versailles in 1919. One solution was to extend the mandate system to all colonial areas. However, her concerns over the welfare of colonial peoples who might be returned to even a mandate under Hitler's Germany were obvious: "Distrust of Germany, dislike of Nazi methods, uneasiness over the ambitious scope of the new German 'mission,' all give force to the satisfied Powers' refusal to admit Hitler's case. Memories of the Blue Book mix with tales of the Gestapo to rouse a feeling of indignation at the thought of handing over defenceless natives to masters whose views on race alone seem to disqualify them from controlling alien peoples."[100] She also believed that "it is a great pity that our moral earnestness turns to smug complacence when we turn our eyes on ourselves."[101] She went on to state: "the root of the difficulty lies in the fact that we are applying a dual standard. Most of our own colonies we still work along the traditional lines of economic imperialism."[102]

Later during the war in April 1942, it will be recalled that the BBC had rejected a script she had prepared on British colonial policy because of its critical points, including the racism of British rule. We have no direct evidence of Hinsley's influence in this regard. However, we do know as apostolic visitor to Africa, in the seven years before his appointment as cardinal archbishop, he was more interested in the views of the African people concerning church administrators than any previous authority. This intensity earned him the nickname of "Africanus" at the Vatican. And point six of the ten points of the Sword, the work mainly of the Oxford Conference of 1937 on Church, Community, and State, which Hinsley also supported, called for the abolition of "extreme inequalities of wealth and possessions."[103]

By 1950, with her marriage to Sir Robert Jackson, she became even more intensely interested in the developing world, on a firsthand basis. As an assistant to the secretary-general of the UN, Jackson became head of the development commission in the Gold Coast. In his recent book *The United Nations Development Programme: A Better Way?* (2006) Craig N. Murphy describes the Jacksons' contributions to West African development and their close collaboration with Kwame Nkhrumah.[104] While overseeing the construction of the Volta Dam the couple also spent considerable time in India and other parts of Asia, while residing nearly a decade in West Africa. From the publication of *Faith and Freedom* in 1954 onward, Ward argued strenuously for the sharing of wealth and the strengthening of economic ties between the West and the developing nations, especially those released from colonial bondage.

In service of her moral vision, which was a worldview in the name of social Christianity, she offered many specifics in the area of developing economies. In *The Rich Nations and the Poor Nations* (1961) Ward spoke out about the need for a global strategy, rejecting any fatalistic acceptance of the trends toward increasing wealth disparities between parts of the world. The application of a Marshall Plan-like approach to the world involved capital investments in education, the modernization of agriculture, certain industries related to local conditions, and the production of raw materials, as well as a system of reinvestments. The welfare state was clearly part of this vision, which was related to Keynesian economics, to be shared in an interdependent world.

In *It Can Be Done* (1965) she began to stress the 1960s as the "decade of development" saying it was no time to simply hope for the best in the future, like Dickens's Mr Micawber, but was in fact time to act. In the face of growing world population, it was necessary to raise the underdeveloped countries to self-sustaining growth through surveys of resources, the coordination of donor economies and the encouragement of local manufacturing. A target of 4–5 per cent per annum for donor countries in the expansion of world trade should be backed by a worldwide insurance scheme to avoid fluctuation in prices paid for primary materials. Finally, in *Poverty and Politics* (1968), she warned that such systematic approaches were necessary, with charity being totally inadequate for the expanding 80 per cent of the world's population. She was not blind to the need for population control as seen in *Two Views on Aid to Developing Countries*, 1968.[105] However, undoubtedly because of a possible public compromise of her Roman Catholicism, she refrained from specifics on the matter. She noted that the lessons learned in the experience of the Great Depression from Keynes, the need for public works, the effects of the Second World War, and the failures of international trade and credit all required "demand management." For Ward, the developing world itself had achieved much growth since 1945, most of the investment springing up locally. But they needed much more.

Within all countries, taxation, which entailed some redistribution of wealth into investments in education and health; the creation of more purchasing power in wage-earners (with Henry Ford was a model); as well as government oversight of sustained demand, were necessary. These principles of domestic economic management would affect world planning, backed by a "world tax" upon wealthier countries of 1 per cent of GNP, which would be used to modernize developing countries. This was in line with the suggestion of a World Fund for Development in Pope Paul VI's encyclical *Populorum Progressio* (1967), so loved by planners. In relation to developing countries, the Henry Ford action to help depressed labour would be applied by the developed world to the underdeveloped.[106] It would secure higher prices for primary products, preferential markets for even industrial exports from developing countries, and loans from the World Bank to cover short-term deficits as well as liquidity provided by the IMF.

Ward urged that Christians, in particular, become acquainted with all the facts of the situations, including working with those who might have to be moved more by the realism of enlightened self-interest. Christians must use votes, or any other means, much like abolitionists such as William Wilberforce. A dedicated 10 per cent of the population, even within a nominal but indifferent Christian minority, could achieve much. There was also the example of the Sword of the Sprit of earlier years (now the CIIR). She stated that: "On every possible occasion He told us to see man as he is. We are not agnostics: ours is a very 'unspiritual' religion ... God would never have taken to Himself a human body if He had not cared for it. I am certain He did not build the human body to be starved."[107]

The doctrine of the Incarnation demanded full engagement in the plight of developing countries as human beings – not out of fear but the joy of being creative. Ethical practicality would always be part of the approach. In order to achieve the right outcome she recognized domestically and in international affairs informal alliances would often operate. *In Spaceship Earth* (1966) she noted: "In these changes in the politics of the market economies the pressure of Socialist criticism and attack has been a potent factor. So was Christian reformism whether it appeared in the encyclicals of a Leo XIII or a Pius XI or in the moderate socialism of a line of Anglican bishops."[108] During the food crisis of the early 1970s, which struck Islamic areas particularly hard, she also appealed to newly prosperous Muslims to help those who were less fortunate to avoid weakening "the ultimate moral cement of their own societies." Concerning both Christian and Muslim religions she said: "*The Peoples of the Book* who have monopoly control of what the world most needs – bread and energy – are directly challenged to go beyond the 'idols of the market' and to create instead a moral community for all mankind."[109]

Until her death in 1981 Ward worked within the framework of existing international and national agencies to achieve her goals. She was well-known within the Labour Party (and her memory lived on in Social-Democratic circles) in Britain, receiving a life peerage through Prime Minister Harold Wilson in 1976. Shirley Williams, the Labour MP, wrote to Ward a year earlier stating that the Labour moderates "have been desperately short of any kind of spokesman, or perhaps more important, any kind of prophet or philosopher" since R.H. Tawney. She went on to state "I'm teased by the thought that perhaps you might be that philosopher we are looking for."[110] A year later, Ward, now Lady Jackson, wrote a letter to Williams concentrating on the theme of social democracy in the Labour party. She rejected Marxist totalitarianism, stating: "This is not for us. This is not our tradition and if you ask me to define our roots, they are ethical, not dialectic, free, not deterministic. We believe in the equality and the value of every individual. We seek a society in which men can freely fulfill their capacity for good and fight their inner temptations to evil."[111]

Her final position was as President of the International Institute for Environment and Development in London. Internationally she was an advisor on international economics to UN Secretary-General U Thant. Ward has always been known to prominent Americans, and was frequently a resident there, for the United States could supply much of the necessary aid to the Third World. She continued this connection while being an academic visitor to Harvard and again Columbia, the latter as Albert Schweitzer Professor of International Economic Development (1968–1973). As mentioned earlier, she was close to Democratic party leaders such as Adlai Stevenson, and to President Lyndon Johnson, not withstanding her open opposition to the Vietnam War. She was also special advisor to Robert McNamara at the World Bank.

Ward persistently preached against the dangers of nuclear warfare which often brought her into opposition with some of her American political friends. She would have agreed with Bertrand Russell on this question. Indeed she insisted that: "The point seems to have been reached at which the world must discover enough mutual respect and common purpose to operate as a genuine community or it must face destruction. Scientifically, the instruments of death exist. Only an extraordinary rediscovery of the means and sense of common life can apparently save the human race."[112]

Ward should not be seen as a conduit for the Westernization of the Third World in her activities. While upholding her Western-based values, she was a friend of strong Third World nationalists such as Kwame Nkrumah. As early as 1962, she pointed to the three fundamental preconditions of political order: (1) peaceful settlement of disputes by law, (2) public works and famine relief as first steps to a welfare state, and (3) communal trust – all having been best achieved over the longest period of peace in world history by imperial China.[113]

In relation to the churches, she gave repeated talks to such assemblies as the Lambeth Conference. She was instrumental in including development issues at the Second Vatican Council and worked for the pontifical commission for justice and peace. One of the latter's publications by Barbara Ward was entitled *A New Creation? Reflections on the Environmental Issue* (1971).

Ward's interest in the environment went back at least to the ten points of the Sword of the Spirit issued in December 1940, which included a provision for the protection of the environment. Point ten had stated that "the resources of the Earth should be used as God's gifts to the human race, used with due consideration for the needs of the present and the future generations." This undoubtedly derived from the Oxford Conference of 1937 and the concerns for mother earth expressed first by V.A. Demant and later William Temple.[114] The general record of social Christianity and social Catholicism was even less impressive at that time in this area than their concern for the underdeveloped areas of the world. Lynn White Jr, in a famous article entitled "The Historical Roots of our Ecology Crisis" in *Science* (1967), saw Western Christianity, both Protestant and Catholic, as possessing an anthropocentrism that was to the detriment of the environment. Indeed, he believed this to be a prime source of the environmental degradation in the world since the Middle Ages. Challenges to this view have been mounted by others since the article appeared. Some have pointed to Judeo-Christian influences from Genesis to St Francis of Assisi as being environmentally friendly. In any case, it was obvious that much had to be done in this area by mid-twentieth century by Christians and non-Christians alike. Ward was one of the pioneers in the modern movement of concern over the environment, linking it with her other causes on behalf of developing countries, which were likewise, as always, linked with her moral convictions.

As we have seen, Julian Huxley was also a pioneer in environmental concerns seeing man as very much part of the ecological system. Ward's perspective was rather different and rooted in her theology – about which she stated, in a section of *Faith and Freedom* back in 1954: "This God of the Jews was not a nature god. He was something more. He was the God of nature … Nature's Cause and Creator … On the one hand, God was Lord of nature, separate from it and in no way immersed in its fatalities. The Jews had no part in the polytheism of the fertility religions. But since Creation was the work of God's hands, it could not be dismissed as an illusion, as a mere transitory flux of appearances, as the *maya* of Indian philosophers or the recurring and unchanging cycle of Greek thought."[115] Respect for nature was part of the Judeo-Christian heritage.

In 1972 Barbara Ward and René Dubos, the bacteriologist, co-authored *Only One Earth: the Care and Maintenance of a Small Planet*. The book was an "unofficial" report commissioned for the first UN secretary-general's Conference on Human Environment, held at Stockholm in June of that year. Involving the collaboration of 152 consultants from fifty-two countries, it was an all-encompassing survey of the dangers to the world's environment. It also explored various solutions to specific problems in the spirit of unity among the nations of the earth. The book argued that international agreements were possible, and had even been achieved already, for example with "the first global environmental agreement" – the Test Ban Treaty of 1963.[116] What the authors tried to stress was that the deteriorating environment was also bad for human beings as well as for the earth: "An acceptable strategy for planet Earth must, then, explicitly take account of the fact that the natural resource most threatened with pollution, most exposed to degradation, most liable to irreversible damage is not this or that species, not this or that plant or biome or habitat, not even the free airs or the great oceans. It is man himself."[117] As *The Times* review by Michael Leapman (22 May 1972) pointed out, Ward was with the optimists, for the optimists argued that people will alter their ways if they want to survive.

A more personal, moral note in all of this was struck in Ward's *A New Creation?*, published in roughly the same period. It also pointed to some of the same environmental dangers, arguing for an end to "isolation" and the "recognition of interdependence" in ecology,[118] as well as for planetary co-operation. Ward was clear again in pointing to the Judeo-Christian roots of her stance: "'Taming' nature need not be dominion. It can be the kind of patience and understanding that turns the frightened restive horse into a safe mount or a skilled hunter. Much of man's creativity and freedom lies in the fact that he receives creation in a raw and unfinished state and, in Christian teaching, is called by God to be a co-creator in building a more reliable, useful and indeed beautiful world. The story of Genesis is not one of dominion. It is man 'naming' the animals and learning to cultivate a garden."[119]

In this Vatican-sponsored publication she noted that the past 400 years in the Western world were also ones of increasing secularization, leading to today's "post-Christian" governments, which did little for the environment. In this she emphasized that the Church had tried to provide models of happiness in an ungreedy life, and argued: "if the strong, the rich, the rapacious and the careless 'inherit the earth,' then there is no meaning in the Christian Gospel."[120] The church had certainly issued a clarion call for more international law and world order, noting that "in the struggle between man's new perception of the limits of sovereignty and the old traditional claims of nationalism, it is difficult to exaggerate the emphasis with which, in the last 25 years, the Church has underlined the need to move beyond the nation state." This included "preserving the planet's natural patrimony," through "environmental protection and for the rational deployment of resources."[121]

Ward argued strongly that Christians belonging "to the comfortable majority in developed states or the small wealthy elite in developing lands" must face "the discipline of demanding less and giving more."[122] Like the effort to help the developing world, Christians must join Church leaders in these international efforts and combat indifference. She stated: "This indifference is partly rooted in the tendency of Christian citizens to continue to take for granted the overriding claims of the national state. The leaders of the Christian communions have certainly underlined their support for the world's emerging planetary institutions. But the Christian people have not much followed the lead. They tend to miss the fact that sin can be institutionalized and governments and corporations and unions can do a man's sinning for him.

There are few devoted Christian lobbies working for more effective international action."[123]

In service of that suggestion, in a letter to Archbishop Benelli of the Secretariat of State at the Vatican, Ward wrote of the dangers of wealthy consumerism driving the advances of *nuclear* energy to dangerous levels. She suggested that Christians must take a lead in such matters.[124] In a similar fashion she wrote to Benin-born Cardinal Bernardin Gantin of the Pontifical Commission on Justice and Peace that the US Congress was threatening to cut contributions to the World Bank, thereby hurting poor countries "in direct opposition to the teaching of the Church."[125] As Ward's address at the Midhurst Catholic Church on Women's World Day of Prayers, 7 March 1975 indicated, the "great ethical traditions were not invented out of visions and dreams." They were "rooted in the shattering experiences of mankind"[126] and were down to earth. Thus, as in her entire professional life, ideals must be forwarded in practical ways through action and reaction.

In *The Home of Man* (1976), commissioned by the UN Habitat Conference on Human Settlements, Ward argued for the importance of restoring "use and beauty to the land within and around conurbations" in the interests "both of justice and of environmental decency."[127] Thus there was as much urgency in protecting the ecology of developed as that of underdeveloped countries. She had also produced a series of talks in 1976 on BBC *Radio* 4 covering many of the same subjects. An entire chapter (chapter 17) in *The Home of Man* was devoted to "The Conserving Society," which was also the title of a proposed BBC television series on the subject.[128] She concluded the book by saying that "if man has learned to be loyal to his nation as well as his family and his town, do we have to argue that no further extension of loyalty is possible – to the planet itself which carriers our earthly life and all the means of sustaining it?"[129] Substandard housing, food shortages, and a deteriorating environment were not inevitable. *The New York Times* called it a "trenchant ecology treatise."[130]

Barbara Ward's last book, *Progress for a Small Planet* (1979) was published less than two years before her death. It was a lengthy synthesis of all the needs of the environment, and it advocated recycling, the preservation of clean water, and the development of energy alternatives. In combating global warming and other dangers, she suggested possible ways of conceptualizing new policy initiatives.

She concluded by stating: "In short, no problem is insoluble in the creation of a balanced and conserving planet save humanity itself. Can it reach in time the vision of joint survival? Can its inescapable physical interdependence – the chief new insight of our century – induce that vision? We do not know. We have the duty to hope."[131] Her concept of sustainability through such things as replanting trees or managing fish stocks so that resources can be used again was highly important to the growing worldview of environmentalism in the decades to come. On the threshold of the 1980s, the era of Reaganism and Thatcherism, it was a bold attempt on Ward's part to project her social conscience into the remainder of the twentieth century. As John Kenneth Galbraith stated in a sympathetic review of the book: "She has often in the past been criticized for this kind of optimism, but she has not learned. It strikes an especially odd note at a time when so many are proclaiming so ardently the virtues of self-centred individualism for an increasingly interdependent world and when the really sophisticated politicians are joining the revolt of the rich against the poor."[132]

Certainly Ward can be accused of being too optimistic in her assessment of the feasibility of various solutions to the problems of the world. This stemmed from her view of human nature. *The Economist*, in its final tribute to Ward (6 June 1981) quoted Shridath Ramphal as follows: "Barbara said to me: 'We must all persist. We must never discount the capacity of people to be moved by the argument of goodness.'" This argument of goodness, which must prevail if the earth itself was to have a future, contrasted sharply with what Noel Annan has called Muggeridge's supralapsarian view (a faction at the synod of Dort who believed most men were damned). It was in keeping with the implications of the Incarnation, of the Fatherhood of God and the brotherhood of men, (and sisterhood of women). It was the core of social Christianity and social Catholicism, fused into the soul of Ward since the founding of the Sword of the Spirit.

But Ward also possessed a realistic appreciation of the challenges she had to face. Unlike Malcolm Muggeridge and other Christian writers who saw the demise of Christendom as a recent event, she believed it had actually happened many centuries earlier with the collapse of the "medieval synthesis." This City of God "wanted to create a human order which would reflect in all its aspects the divine will."[133] It failed through poor leadership and was ultimately engulfed in the growing demands of materialism ending "the order of restraint or moral discipline."[134] Nationalism and capitalism completed the destruction.[135]

But the study of history was not debilitating, as other examples, she believed, such as the birth of the abolitionist movement in Britain at its very pinnacle of wealth from the slave trade, could prove the power of the argument of goodness.[136] Indeed Ward saw in the example of Wilberforce and his followers how dedicated minorities could achieve much. As a tactician Ward moved about the world using her enormous communication and "people" skills to woo the high and mighty as well as very ordinary people. She broke through barriers across diverse religions and ideologies in an effort to draw helpful ideas out of the many who encountered her. But she never lost sight of the goal of the Kingdom on Earth. She stated to an audience in 1953: "It is not only in the past that people have cried out for the coming of the Kingdom, and even if in our own day it has been perverted into the idea of a classless society, or laughed at as a Utopia, nevertheless I swear that in every honest human heart there is a hunger for a society which shall express the brotherhood, the love and unity which is the great inheritance of the world religions. And I do not believe that any human heart is completely blind or completely dead to the appeal of this Kingdom, of this brotherhood."[137] From that lecture to her death twenty-eight years later, Ward's horizons widened even more – from the developed and developing world to the very environment of the planet itself – in service of this vision. The tasks may be monumental but in the words of one of her book titles, *It Can Be Done*. In stressing the force of moral determination, Ward asked, in one of her last speeches prepared for the public, "can we dare to go further and ask from religious leaders everywhere the direction and the inspiration we must find if planetary unity not planetary destruction, is to be our fate? Perhaps the earth has never been looking so painfully and uneasily for a new sense of direction. To no one is the challenge greater than to the children of faith."[138]

Conclusion and Legacy

The four figures in this book were each presented in terms of a particular focus or theme. Julian Huxley was a purveyor of what was essentially a new religion, not based upon theism, which attempted to supply the world with a course correction consistent with the enhanced place of science as the source of explanation in modern life. From this radiated his multifarious activities. Bertrand Russell's efforts to defeat fear and promote reason and love were depicted as a conduit for a liberal rationalist outlook for the establishment of a better way of life based upon agnosticism and humanism. Malcolm Muggeridge, as a publicist first for his own conversion narrative, and then as a publicist for Mother Teresa, advocated traditional Christian belief in an afterlife as humanity's hope, which was part of his overall critique of a hostile, secularizing culture. Barbara Ward was the ultimate exponent of a fully mature and well-rounded social Christianity blended with social Catholicism. Collectively these four figures constituted important border markers in defining the parameters and architecture of public discourse about the application of moral philosophy to public life from the mid-twentieth century onward.

Huxley and Muggeridge tended to argue their underlying moral philosophies in a more overtly theoretical way before the public than did Ward or even Russell. But all exhibited strong underlying positions, based upon their respective ethical systems, which they attempted to sell to the public. The quality of arguments, together with their degree of mastery of the media, determined, in part at least, the results of their efforts in swaying opinion. They all wrote considerably, as the print medium (along with some platform oratory) was considered to be a prime way of disseminating views.

To our twenty-first century eyes Huxley, Russell, Muggeridge, and Ward all exhibit some attitudes that make them period pieces. While the age of television had arrived, as had the age of radio earlier, channel choices were more limited and the dictates of ratings were there but not yet supreme. It was not unrealistic to suppose that a sizeable portion of the audience would read a newspaper or occasionally tune in to the *Third Programme* for self-improvement – though as Peter Bowler has pointed out, for science at least the market for true self-education literature was already in decline.[1] The public were also less wary and cynical concerning the manipulations of the media than today. Timing, of course, was important and none could match Russell in that respect for the 1960s.

All four figures developed an international following in specific circles and sometimes on specific issues, especially in North America. In this respect Russell is again more of a period piece as a celebrity, with the diminished possibility of a nuclear Third World War now in the twenty-first century. Huxley has probably been reborn in the American and British versions of the new atheism, though ironically his name is less invoked by its leading figures than Russell's. Certainly there are some who would follow directly in his footsteps in relation to the adoration of science such as Carl Sagan[2] and E.O. Wilson. Along with figures such as Aldo Leopold, Huxley's view of ecology was probably the foundation for modern eco-centrism among environmentalists. Ward's position on the plight of the Third World and a more anthropocentric environmentalism is remembered, though in her late years she frequently had to confront the charge that her solutions were impractical. Impractical or not, Ward's words continue to resonate with those so concerned. In the latter case she might well be the direct inspiration for Al Gore's view of the prevention of global warming as a moral issue.[3] Certainly Ward is one of the iconic figures in the expanding ranks of Christian environmentalists, developing world advocates, and the diminishing fold of the Christian Left. Muggeridge has his conservative Christian following and, more broadly, is remembered as Mother Teresa's publicist throughout the world.

Generally the discourse in mid-twentieth-century Britain between theists and agnostics or atheists was polite and often focused on specific, practical issues. Co-operation between the latter group and

Christian modernists and liberals was often possible on a variety of issues, as seen in the careers of Ward and Russell – though the basic position of unbelievers remained unshakeable. Julian Huxley often resembled a diplomat in his sojourns among theists and atheists but, as in his 1959 Chicago speech and particularly in the fall-out from it, the division lines could quickly be laid bare again. Christian accommodationists such as John A.T. Robinson produced more discord among the ranks of believers than they did actually bridge any sort of gap with unbelievers. The suspicion of evangelicals and conservatives, such as Malcolm Muggeridge, was only reinforced. Was the mere defence of some minimal transcendent element enough to be classified as a Christian?

Christian intellectuals in this period of the long 60s, apart from the figures studied, and church leaders, never succeeded in inculcating an overall, renewed vision of a national culture informed by Christianity. Christopher Dawson, the cultural historian who had early on inspired Barbara Ward, appeared out of date in trying to heal the schism between religion and culture in the West, even by the 1940s. Though he lived until 1970, his major influence seemed to be through visiting professorships of religious studies in the United States. Fellow historian Herbert Butterfield, though more of a force amongst the British intelligentsia until his death in 1979, admitted that his commitment to Christianity did not derive from the historical discipline, just as the Whig interpretation of history, which he described, did not emanate initially from an analysis of history. Butterfield increasingly emphasized one's individual relationship with God.[4] Butterfield's observations on the workings of evil throughout history were based on his belief in original sin. Reasonably secular figures such as Rebecca West also had no doubt about the role of evil in human affairs but offered not much more than advocacy of a general sort of morality, presumably of Christian origin. For most of the intelligentsia a clear path back to a firmly Christian Britain seemed increasingly illusory.

Richard Weight has also described, in *Patriots*, the parallel ways in which the sense of Britishness declined in the twentieth century. As he sees it, in past generations Protestantism was a unifying principle in bringing the various constituent parts of the British Isles and the majority of the population together.[5] From the 1960s he states "Protestantism was no longer seen as one of the defining characteristics of the British. Opposition to papal visits or the building of mosques and temples was little more than the death throes of a national identity which had been diseased for half a century."[6] Also, by the late twentieth century such cultural attitudes might even seem racist with so many immigrants of different faiths now resident in the country.[7]

Socialist Humanism (Ethical Socialism) tended to reinforce the agnostic and atheistic dimensions of national dialogue. As noted in chapter 1, it was especially associated with two figures of the new Left, E.P. Thompson and Raymond Williams. Williams, in turn, shared many of the same views as Richard Hoggart. Hoggart, author of *The Uses of Literacy* (1957), sought to instill critical literacy in the underclass of modern Britain as a moral imperative. Earlier attempts to create a national culture – from the days of Matthew Arnold to the patriotism of the Second World War – were seen as measures of social control by the governing class. Critical literacy, as he defined it,[8] was induced by a level of literary awareness beyond straight literacy, which would ensure that the masses were not deceived by the holders of power. It was linked to the inculcation of intellectual imagination in this process of liberation from the oppression of the bourgeoisie. As Raymond Williams further developed it, truth and beauty, in the sense of Matthew Arnold's elite-directed cultural goals for the nation, would be democratized from below. As a corollary, there was also a traditional sense of social justice, but it was now released from the narrower, somewhat patronizing influence of the old Left which had included Christian figures such as William Temple.

The effects of all of this are very difficult to measure beyond common rooms and lecture halls of universities. A new appreciation of the legacy of the culture of common people was reasonably well spread through the social history publications of E.P. Thompson. But Thompson was to receive more public attention from his role by the 1980s as a leader of the revived movement for nuclear disarmament. In this Thompson obviously saw the pattern maintenance of nationalism and alliance of NATO to be the most immediate threat to the common well-being of the people. To this end Thompson became a leader of the revived movement for nuclear disarmament which focused on END – a nuclear free Europe. Hence, as Russell's heir in this respect, Thompson combated the formidable political appeal of Thatcher and Reagan in their heyday.

Before this, however, in his book *The Poverty of Theory* (1978), Thompson took on what he regarded as another set of dangers arising from the Marxist philosopher Louis Althusser, with the latter's removal of morality and individual agency in his interpretation of the workings of society. Against the later theories of some post-modernists, which would follow from Althusser and others, Thompson defended the authenticity and integrity of the discipline of history. Stefan Collini, in a commentary in the *TLS* (18 February 2005), saw him as a moralist at work. Thompson, in turn, had seen Williams as a moralist wearing "a literary habit."

Both Williams and Thompson also feared a new enslavement to the rich and powerful, a threat that was posed by consumerism. For Thompson, it was probably seen as a late twentieth-century equivalent of that earlier opiate of the people, religion. Williams early on became intensely interested in the negative effects of the media, especially television. Like Muggeridge he saw not only mass manipulation by malevolent forces (in Williams' case, the existing social order) but also the actual subversion of ethical questions, which should form part of the pursuit of truth and beauty.

By the 1980s the country witnessed another group, of a very different kind, which also opposed deleterious aspects of recent trends in national culture. Thatcherites viewed the social discord and weak economy of the 1970s as rooted in the permissive counter-culture of the 1960s. In a famous speech in 1976, Margaret Thatcher spoke of the erosion of faculties producing a moral crippling of people.[9] In this case, however, her reference was to the action of the state in limiting freedom of choice, thus hastening the disappearance of individual responsibility under the previous decades of the collectivist, welfare state. This led Thatcher's followers within the Conservative party to argue for a return to Victorian values of individualism, hard work, and sobriety. But many could also argue that Thatcher's political agenda resembled more the vision of nineteenth-century liberals than the somewhat paternalist ethic of her Tory ancestors, minus many of the moral restraints to the market mentality operating at the time.[10] Thatcherism was more a call for a return to a vision of laissez-faire than to the religious situation which originally inspired so-called Victorian values.

After 2000 a new wave of unbelief made its appearance. Richard Dawkins, an Oxford academic, in *The God Delusion*, as well as in his other publications and television programs, has become the leading figure in the so-called New Atheism, and one of the inspirations for their North American compatriots. Rejecting dialogue with liberal theists, and the tepid approach of many fence-sitting agnostics,[11] Dawkins has sought to dethrone God and elevate science to the vacancy so created. He has introduced some hypotheses such as memes (which should probably be classified as quasi-science) that have supplied some new reasons (through collective cultural inheritance in the case of memes) to believe that altruism can naturally exist within our beings without belief. He has been joined until recently by the shrill voice of the late Christopher Hitchens, in an intellectual war of liberation for the sake of humanity. This has produced not only a negative theistic response but charges of (almost irrational) scientific fundamentalism, even by some neutral observers. The fallout from reactions to fundamentalist extremism has seemingly radiated out on all sides since 9/11. Bowler's *Science and Religion* (2001) reminds us that the interaction of science and religion has gone through multiple phases, from the Victorian era of confrontation, to conciliation in the early twentieth century, to separation by the mid-twentieth century. Currently these interactions between science and religion seem to have returned to a mode of confrontation. Apart from a collection of combative responses, British Christians have had little of a positive nature to give to the general public of the order of impact of C.S. Lewis's *Mere Christianity* in past decades. There are a few scientists in the English-speaking world who have attempted to present a harmonious relationship between Christian belief and up-to-date science, such as Francis Collins, former head of the genome project, in his popular book, *The Language of God* (2006).

One might suppose that theism, or more specifically Christianity, has lost more ground in Britain since the time of Huxley, Russell, Muggeridge, and Ward in view of the dearth of effective advocates. A recent poll of 10,000 people conducted for the BBC[12] has indicated that the United Kingdom is one of the most secular-minded nations in the world. This included the lowest acceptance, among ten countries examined, of the belief that "God or a higher power made people better human beings." Yet it is interesting that this belief was still held by 56 per cent of those polled in the United Kingdom, almost statistically resting on an exact national line of dichotomy between belief and unbelief. Of course, today's Britain contains many theists other than Christians.

One can say that the cause of the New Atheists seemed boosted by recent scientific developments that have enormously increased our knowledge. The modern study of DNA through the human genome project is now uncovering the actual mechanisms which govern evolution in action, or natural selection. For human beings the number of genes for study has been vastly reduced to about 23,000 compared with earlier estimates, around 1990, of perhaps three times as many. How information is stored, how mutation works in relation to adaptive change, has been revealed with increasing accuracy through this more manageable scale of work.

Research on the ventromedial prefrontal cortex has located the decision-making area of the brain. Presumably here and in other places scientists will discover how moral behaviour is directed, and the mechanism involved, with precision. The primacy of the rational versus the emotional in moral decisions, an issue of debate between Kant and Hume, can perhaps more fully be determined. Researchers such as Joshua Greene at Harvard may supply more definitive answers based on moral judgment being a brain process. Such a position is generally in line, for example, with earlier work on human behaviour, including Julian Huxley's on the effects of hormones and the materialist implication that thought patterns were products of physical brain activity.[13]

The question of devising a moral system from a materialist base has certainly helped to motivate much of this scientific investigation. Dawkins believes that after abandoning religion humanity can move forward, employing science and logic, to a better future. The critic Chris Hedges believes such a faith in human perfectability to be inconsistent with the assumption that we are shaped by the laws of heredity and natural selection.[14] Nevertheless, Dawkins believes that there is a "broad liberal consensus of ethical principles" that has "no obvious connection with religion," though it extends to many, including religious people, "with notable exceptions such as the Afghan Taliban and the American Christian equivalent."[15] This moral Zeitgeist will continue in the right direction with better global leadership and education, Dawkins hopes.

Marilynne Robinson in *Absence of Mind* (2010), like Hedges, has vigorously criticized Dawkins and his disciples for their reductively materialist argument that such inwardness, or human consciousness, could be an accidental product of natural selection. Such "parascience" in her view makes such things as altruism inexplicable if one goes beyond the accumulated historical wisdom of humankind. Moreover the notion of human uniqueness cannot be explained, in the way that Dawkins (and Huxley) assert, that humans alone can rebel against the blind forces of nature and take control of their own destiny. Such a belief seems almost a restatement of the concept of free will that emanates from Judeo-Christian traditions – the very traditions which the new science-based atheists attack.

Sam Harris, a fellow new atheist from the American cohort and a neuroscientist, has recently published *The Moral Landscape* (2010) that would push this progressionism even further. As suggested in the subtitle, "How Science Can Determine Human Values," Harris has taken the struggle for unbelief to a new level (with clear support from Dawkins). Chastising most of his fellow scientists for their timidity, Harris argues that the time is ripe for the foundation of a proper science of morality. Rejecting the argument of culturalists that moral precepts are lodged in particular societal circumstances, Harris takes the position – not unlike the advocates of natural law – that common moral principles can be found within all peoples.[16] Unlike this classic Christian belief, however, he sees these moral principles as grounded in the physical world of facts rather than in some lofty, innate, God-given values. Values can be grouped around what he sees as conducive to human well-being.

Harris believes that the main contours of well-being can be determined by advancing neuroscience, with a dash of psychology. In this quest for a science of morals he rejects vehemently that there are no true answers to moral questions. Moral progress is already on the move as the world is advancing scientifically. Human well-being, happiness for individuals and society, can be found in a measured study of the facts of the real world. In pursing this goal of maximizing the greatest happiness for the greatest number, he duly acknowledges some debt of this consequentialism to its predecessor, the utilitarianism of Bentham, James Mill, and John Stuart Mill, but refines it much further.[17] In so doing Harris also denies the idea of free will (and with it sin), thus entering a general realm of determinism.

Russell might have shared many of these views if he were alive today. However, he also might have worried about some naïve aspects of Harris's thought, including the ready acceptance of scientific devices in determining our needs, proper behaviour, and deviance.[18] Do we once again enter the realm of possible new dystopias with such ready acceptance, in the fashion of Aldous Huxley?

In the establishment of a global, ethical system based upon fact, Harris collapses David Hume's distinction between the way the world is and the way we ought to behave.[19] Throughout this discussion moral relativism is assailed, thus finding some common ground with such unlikely bedfellows as Socialist humanists, Thatcherites, and traditional Christians. It follows from this attempted universalism of science.

However, on the side of unbelief, enormous problems still abound. British bioethicist John Harris, in *Enhancing Evolution: The Ethical Case for Making People Better* (2007), suggests that genetic engineering to make people stronger and smarter, in the tradition of Huxley's eugenics, has produced dilemmas concerning those who should first receive the benefits of technological breakthroughs. In general, as suggested in David Berlinski's *The Devil's Delusion*, science offers explanations and possibilities but little general direction and meaning. Again, this is the stuff of more dystopic novels to come.

Perhaps more scientific work may discover more physical evidence of altruism within our nature, and reinforce Huxley's and Russell's largely intuitive suggestions. In overcoming our "selfish" genes, perhaps scientific research may also uncover why some people are inclined to serve others more than themselves.[20] Also, is there truth to the current scientific investigation that our brains may be hard wired for religion, or conversely could atheists be missing something in the cranium?[21] Could this cover a sense of morality? Could the latter be another way of saying some of us do possess a soul, albeit a material one? Yet what is often missing in all of this is that sense that there could still be other intuitive ways of knowing. Such hope could be shared by believers and unbelievers alike, as with the sense of "joy" experienced by C.S. Lewis and the "transnatural awe" of Julian Huxley, or the surrender to the "infinite" in our nature which Russell noted earlier. The cold world of physical science lacks charm even for some confirmed atheists.

The recent state visit of Pope Benedict XVI to England and Scotland in September 2010 witnessed strong statements by his holiness against "aggressive forms of secularism," which marginalized Christian influence in the country. He mirrored a continued concern of some British Christians, for example earlier in the year, over media coverage (the BBC in this case) of religious matters.[22] Humanist organizations vigorously counterattacked through demonstrations protesting the papal visit. The Queen, cabinet, and Parliament showed polite attention to the Pope's words but the status quo appeared undisturbed. No doubt the Pope was also alarmed by the publicity successes of Dawkins and Hitchens, but here again E.R. Wickham's comment (in chapter 1) that the country was no more fertile ground for dogmatic atheism than for dogmatic religion might prove to be correct in the long run.

It is clear that contesting the moral high ground is not necessarily capturing it. By what authority does one render meaning to our world? In this, ethical humanists may have as many problems as believers have had in legitimizing a basis for taking the helm in plotting a course for humanity.

Notes

INTRODUCTION

1 Arthur Marwick, *The Sixties: Cultural Revolution in Britain, France, Italy, and the United States, c. 1958–c. 1974* (Oxford: Oxford University Press, 1998), 7.

2 Edward Royle, *Radical Politics 1790–1900 Religion and Unbelief* (London: Longman, 1971), 5; A.D. Gilbert, *Religion and Society in Industrial England: Church, Chapel and Social Change 1740–1914* (London: Longman, 1976), 184–7; and A.D. Gilbert, *The Making of Post-Christian Britain: A History of the Secularization of Modern Society* (London: Longman, 1980), 55–6.

3 Christine Davies, *Permissive Britain: Social Change in the Sixties and Seventies* (London: Pitman, 1975), 3.

4 Richard A. Posner, *Public Intellectuals: A Study of Decline* (Cambridge: Harvard University Press, 2003).

5 Jed Esty, *A Shrinking Island: Modernism and National Culture in England* (Princeton: Princeton University Press, 2004).

6 Ronald W. Clark, *Sir Julian Huxley, F.R.S.* (London: Phoenix House, 1960); Ronald W. Clark, *The Huxleys* (London: Heineman, 1968); and John R. Baker, *Julian Huxley, Scientist and World Citizen 1877 to 1975: A Biographical Memoir* (Paris: UNESCO, 1978).

7 Vassiliki Betty Smocovitis, *Unifying Biology: The Evolutionary Synthesis and Evolutionary Biology* (Princeton: Princeton University Press, 1996). See also Smocovitis, "The Unifying Vision: Julian Huxley, The Evolutionary Synthesis and Evolutionary Humanism," in Geert Somsen and Harmke Kamminga, eds, *Pursuing the Unity of Science: Ideology and Scientific Practice between the Great War and the Cold War* (Aldershot: Ashgate Publishing, 2009).

8 Roger Smith, "Biology and Values in Interwar Britain: C.S. Sherrington, Julian Huxley and the Vision of Progress," *Past and Present* 178, no. 1 (2003): 210–42; Michael Freeden, "Eugenics and Progressive Thought: A Study in Ideological Affinity," *Historical Journal* 22, no. 3 (1979): 645–71; Diane Paul, "Eugenics and the Left," *Journal of the History of Ideas* 45, no. 4 (1984): 567–90; John R. Durant "Evolution, Ideology and World View: Darwinian Religion in the Twentieth Century," in *History, Humanity and Evolution: Essays for John C. Greene*, ed. James R. Moore (Cambridge: Cambridge University Press, 1989), 355–74; Peter J. Bowler, "Julian Huxley: Religion without Revelation," in *Eminent Lives in Twentieth-Century Science and Religion*, ed. Nicolaas A. Rupke (Frankfurt am Main: Peter Lang, 2007), 139–56; Paul T. Phillips, "One World, One Faith: The Quest for Unity in Julian Huxley's Religion of Evolutionary Humanism," *Journal of the History of Ideas* 68, no. 4 (2007): 613–33; Marc Swetlitz, *Julian Huxley, George Gaylord Simpson and the Idea of Progress in Twentieth-Century Evolutionary Biology* (PhD Thesis, University of Chicago, 1991).

9 Ernest Mayr and William B. Provine, eds, *The Evolutionary Synthesis: Perspectives on the Unification of Biology* (Cambridge: Harvard University Press, 1980); Michael Ruse, *Monad to Man: The Concept of Progress in Evolutionary Biology* (Cambridge: Harvard University Press, 1996); Peter J. Bowler, *Reconciling Science and Religion: The Debate in Early Twentieth-Century Britain* (Chicago: University of Chicago Press, 2001); and Peter J. Bowler, *Science for All: The Popularization of Science in Early Twentieth-Century Britain* (Chicago: University of Chicago Press, 2009).

10 Jose Harris, "Political Thought and the Welfare State 1870–1940: An Intellectual Framework for British Social Policy," *Past and Present* 135, no. 1 (1992): 116–41.

11 Heavily influenced by Hegel, Idealism – or the idealist school of British philosophers – included F.H. Bradley, Bernard Bosanquet, and especially T.H. Green in England. It also included the Scottish brothers, John and Edward Caird.

12 Ronald Clark, *The Life of Bertrand Russell* (London: J. Cape, 1975); Caroline Moorehead, *Bertrand Russell: A Life* (London: Sinclair Stevenson, 1992); A.C. Grayling, *Russell* (Oxford: Oxford University Press, 1986); Ray Monk, *Bertrand Russell: The Spirit of Solitude*, vol. 1, 1872–1921, *Bertrand Russell: The Ghost of Madness,* vol. 2, 1921–70 (London: J. Cape, 1996 and 2000).

13 Philip Ironside, *The Social and Political Thought of Bertrand Russell: The Development of an Aristocratic Liberalism* (New York: Cambridge University Press, 1996).

14 Bart Schultz, ed., "The Social and Political Philosophy of Bertrand Russell, Parts I and II," *Philosophy of the Social Sciences* 27, no. 2 (1996): 157–256 and 27, no. 3 (1996): 317–416.

15 Charles R. Pigden, "Bertrand Russell: Moral Philosopher or Unphilosophical Moralist?," in *The Cambridge Companion to Bertrand Russell*, ed. Nicholas Griffin (Cambridge: Cambridge University Press, 2003), 475.

16 Gregory Wolfe, *Malcolm Muggeridge: A Biography* (Grand Rapids: William B. Eerdmans, 1997); Richard Ingrams, *Muggeridge: The Biography* (New York: Harper Collins, 1995); Ian Hunter, *Malcolm Muggeridge: A Life* (London: Collins, 1980).

17 Michael Walsh of Heythrop College, University of London is engaged in biographical work on Ward.

18 Kenneth LeRoy Gladish, *Barbara Ward Jackson and the Postwar World: The Ethic of Interdependence* (PhD Thesis, University of Virginia, 1985).

CHAPTER ONE

1 Callum G. Brown, *The Death of Christian Britain: Understanding Secularisation, 1800–2000*. Second Edition (London and New York: Routledge, 2009), 39.

2 E.R. Wickham, *Church and People in an Industrial City* (London: Lutterworth Press, 1957).

3 G. Kitson Clark, *Churchman and the Condition of England, 1832–1885: A Study in the Development of Social Ideas and Practice from the Old Regime to the Modern State* (London: Methuen, 1973); Desmond Bowen, *The Idea of the Victorian Church: A Story of the Church of England, 1833–1889* (Montreal: McGill University Press, 1968); and Owen Chadwick, *The Victorian Church*, Parts I and II (London: A. and C. Black, 1966 and 1970).

4 Charles Taylor, *A Secular Age* (Cambridge: Belknap Press of Harvard University Press, 2007), 25.

5 Ibid., 13.

6 Ibid., 146.

7 Ibid., 221–69.

8 Ibid.

9 K.S. Inglis, *Churches and the Working Classes in Victorian England* (London: Routledge and Kegan Paul, 1963), 326.

10 K.S. Inglis, "Patterns of Religious Worship in 1851," *Journal of Ecclesiastical History*, 11 (1960), 76–86.

11 For some urban, industrial areas, see Paul T. Phillips, *The Sectarian Spirit: Sectarianism, Society, and Politics in Victorian Cotton Towns* (Toronto: University of Toronto Press, 1982).

12 Gilbert, *Religion and Society in Industrial England*, 205.

13 See Walter L. Arnstein, *The Bradlaugh Case: Atheism, Sex and Politics among the Late Victorians* (Columbia: University of Missouri Press, 1983), 187–92. Many considered Gladstone's speech of 23 April 1883 to be the finest of his career.

14 Edward Norman, *The Victorian Christian Socialists* (Cambridge: Cambridge University Press, 1987), 34.

15 In Richard J. Helmstadter and Paul T. Phillips, eds, *Religion in Victorian Society: A Sourcebook of Documents* (Lanham: University Press of America, 1985), 452.

16 Ibid., 451.

17 Gilbert, *Religion and Society in Industrial England*, 113.

18 Jeffrey Cox, "Master Narratives of Long-term Religious Change," in *The Decline of Christendom in Western Europe, 1750–2000*, eds Hugh McLeod and Werner Ustorf (Cambridge: Cambridge University Press, 2003), 201.

19 Gilbert, *Religion and Society in Industrial England*, 206.

20 Ibid.

21 Jeremy Morris, "The Strange Death of Christian Britain: Another Look at the Secularization Debate," *The Historical Journal* 46, no. 4 (2003): 966.

22 W.R. Ward, *Religion and Society in England, 1790–1850* (London: Batsford, 1972).

23 Hugh McLeod, *Class and Religion in the Late Victorian City* (Hamden: Archon Books, 1974), 285.

24 E.R. Wickham, *Church and People in an Industrial City*, 15.

25 Taylor, *A Secular Age*, 395–6

26 Ibid., 395.

27 John Wolffe, *God and Greater Britain: Religion and National Life in Britain and Ireland, 1843–1945* (London: Routledge, 1994), 93.

28 Taylor, *A Secular Age*, 519.

29 E.R. Wickham, *Church and People in an Industrial City*, 188.

30 Ibid., 188.

31 Ibid.

32 Robert Currie, Alan D. Gilbert and Lee S. Horsley, *Churches and Churchgoers: Patterns of Church Growth in the British Isles since 1700* (Oxford: Clarendon Press, 1977), 64–74, 79–81; Gilbert, *The Making of Post-Christian Britain*, 78–9.

33 Gilbert, *The Making of Post-Christian Britain*, 85.

34 Morris, "The Strange Death of Christian Britain," 967.

35 Ibid., 967–8.

36 Ibid., 970.

37 Ibid., 971–6.

38 Keith Robbins, *History, Religion and Identity in Modern Britain* (London and Rio Grande: The Hambledon Press, 1993), 75.

39 I.D. McCalman, "Popular Irreligion in Early Victorian England: Infidel Preachers and Radical Theatricality in 1830s London," in *Religion and Irreligion in Victorian Society*, eds R.W. Davis and R.J. Helmstadter (London and New York: Routledge, 1992), 61.

40 Leonard W. Levy, *Blasphemy: Verbal Offense against the Sacred, From Moses to Salman Rushdie* (New York: Alfred A. Knopf, 1993), 454–7.

41 Peter J. Bowler, *Invention of Progress: The Victorians and the Past* (Oxford: Blackwell, 1989), 142.

42 Ibid., 157.

43 Ibid., 155.

44 Ibid., 195.

45 George Jacob Holyoake, "What Would Follow on the Effacement of Christianity," in *Religion in Victorian Society*, eds Helmstadter and Phillips, 405.

46 Gilbert, *The Making of Post-Christian Britain*, 56.

47 Ibid., 57.

48 Ibid., 60.

49 Taylor, *A Secular Age*, 59.

50 Keith Robbins, *History, Religion and Identity in Modern Britain*, 131. It is interesting that Hugh Price Hughes published, somewhat earlier, *Ethical Christianity: A Series of Sermons* (London: Sampson Low, 1892). Hughes attempted to respond to attacks from John Stuart Mill, among others, which described Christian morality in negative terms, 4.

51 Owen Chadwick, *The Victorian Church*, Part II, 121.

52 Ibid., Part II, 114.

53 Frank Turner, "The Victorian Crisis of Faith and the Faith That was Lost," in *Victorian Faith in Crisis: Essays on Continuity and Change in Nineteenth-Century Religions Belief*, eds Richard J. Helmstadter and Bernard Lightman (Stanford: Stanford University Press, 1990), 21–3.

54 Edward Royle, *Radical Politics, 1790–1900*, 79.

55 James R. Moore, "Theodicy and Society: The Crisis of the Intelligentsia," in *Victorian Faith in Crisis*, 153–86.

56 George Levine, "Scientific Discourse as an Alternative to Faith," in *Victorian Faith in Crisis*, 234–5.

57 Ibid., 253.

58 Quoted in Paul T. Phillips, *The Controversialist: An Intellectual Life of Goldwin Smith* (Westport: Praeger, 2002), 149.

59 Taylor, *A Secular Age*, 374.

60 Ibid., 369.

61 Beatrice Webb, "My Apprenticeship," 1926 selections in Helmstadter and Phillips, eds, *Religion in Victorian Society*, 406.

62 Ibid.

63 Ibid., 410.

64 Ibid., 411.

65 Ibid., 412.

66 Ibid., 406.

67 Ibid.

68 Ibid., 409.

69 Bowler, *Science for All*, 29.

70 Brown, *Death of Christian Britain*, 104.

71 J.M. Winter, "Spiritualism and the First World War," in *Religion and Irreligion in Victorian Society*, eds Davis and Helmstadter, 185–200.

72 Gilbert, *The Making of Post-Christian Britain*, 77.

73 Arthur Marwick, "Middle Opinion in the Thirties: Planning, Progress and Political Agreement," *English Historical Review* 79, no. 311 (April 1964): 285–98. It was argued here that there was a large area of political agreement in the 1930s which included the need to use science to solve social problems.

74 Gordon McOuat and Mary P. Winsor, "J.B.S. Haldane's Darwinism in its Religious Context," *British Journal for the History of Science* 28, no. 2 (June 1995): 231.

75 Bowler, *Science for All*, 23.

76 Adrian Hastings, *A History of English Christianity, 1920–1985* (London: Fount Paperback, Collins, 1987), 496.

77 Ibid., 495–6.

78 Ibid., 239.

79 Levy, *Blasphemy*, 570.

80 Quoted in Paul T. Phillips, *A Kingdom on Earth: Anglo-American Social Christianity, 1880–1940* (University Park: Pennsylvania State University Press, 1996), 277.

81 Ibid., 277–8.

82 Robbins, *History Religion and Identity in Modern Britain*, 116.

83 Hastings, *History of English Christianity, 1920–1985*, 496.

84 Ibid., 501.

85 Hugh McLeod, *The Religious Crisis of the 1960s* (Oxford: Oxford University Press, 2007), 1–5.

86 Taylor, *A Secular Age*, 1–4.

87 Richard Weight, *Patriots: National Identity in Britain, 1940–2000* (London: Macmillan, 2002), 224–5.

88 Stephen Toulmin, "On Remaining Agnostic," *The Listener* 58, no. 1490 (17 October 1957): 601.

89 Letter to the Editor, *The Listener* 58, no. 1492 (31 October 1957).

90 Brown, *Death of Christian Britain*, 176.

91 Geoffrey Robertson, "The Gamekeeper Had a Wife Also," in D.H. Lawrence, *Lady Chatterley's Lover*, fiftieth anniversary edition (London: Penguin Classics, 2010), 306–7.

92 Mark Roodhouse, "Lady Chatterley and the Monk: Anglican Radicals and the Lady Chatterley Trial of 1960," *Journal of Ecclesiastical History* 59, no. 3 (July 2008): 496.

93 Bryan R. Wilson, "The Functions of Religion: A Reappraisal," *Religion* 18, no. 3 (July 1988): 201.

94 Alister Chapman, "Secularisation and the Ministry of John R.W. Stott at All Souls, Langham Place, 1950–1970," *Journal of Ecclesiastical History* 56, no. 3 (July 2005): 510–11.

95 Austin Dacey, *The Secular Conscience: Why Belief Belongs in Public Life* (Amherst: Prometheus Books, 2008), 19.

96 Alasdair MacIntyre, "God and the Theologians," in *The Honest to God Debate: Some Reactions to the Book Honest to God*, ed. David L. Edwards (London: SCM Press, 1963), 216.

97 Ibid.

98 Ibid., John A.T. Robinson, "Why I Wrote It," 276.

99 Ibid., Alasdair MacIntyre, "God and the Theologians," 223.

100 G.I.T. Machin, *Churches and Social Issues in Twentieth-Century Britain* (Oxford: Clarendon Press, 1998), 209.

101 George L. Berstein, *Myth of Decline: The Rise of Britain since 1945* (London: Pimlico, 204), 451.

102 Richard Hoggart, *The Uses of Literacy: Aspects of Working-Class Life with Special Reference to Publications and Entertainments* (Harmondsworth: Penguin Books, 1954), 112.

103 Ibid., 113.

104 Ibid.

105 Ibid., 113, 114, 116.

106 Ibid., 119.

107 Ibid.

108 Ibid., 166.

109 Robert Towler, *A Sociological Study of Conventional Religion* (London: Routledge and Kegan Paul, 1984), 22–3.

110 Ibid., 20.

111 Ibid., 36–7.

112 Berstein, *Myth of Decline*, 455.

113 Quoted in Peter Clarke, *Hope and Glory, Britain 1900–2000* (London: Penguin Books, Second edition, 2004), 379.

114 Malcolm Muggeridge, "Thirteen Years Soft," *New Statesman* (16 October 1964): 571–2.

115 See Gertrude Himmelfarb, *The De-Moralization of Society: From Victorian Virtues to Modern Values* (New York: Alfred A. Knopf, 1995).

116 Eric James, *A Life of Bishop John A.T. Robinson: Scholar, Pastor, Prophet* (London: Fount Paperbacks, Collins, 1989), 115.

117 Paul Barker with John Henvey, "Facing Two Ways," *New Society* 14, no. 374 (27 November 1969): 849.

118 John Benson, *Affluence and Authority: A Social History of Twentieth-Century Britain* (London: Hodder Arnold, 2005), 172–6.

119 Keith Robbins, *England, Ireland Scotland, Wales: The Christian Church, 1900–2000,* (Oxford: Oxford University Press, 2008), 381.

120 Ibid.

121 Brown, *Death of Christian Britain*, 232.

122 Morris, "The Strange Death of Christian Britain," 975.

123 Ibid.

124 Taylor, *A Secular Age*, 371.

CHAPTER TWO

1 John Morley, quoted in Julian Huxley, *Religion without Revelation* (London: Ernest Benn, 1927), 127. The title of Morley's essay or volume is not named.

2 Ibid.

3 Julian Huxley, *What Dare I Think?* (London: Chatto and Windus, 1931), vi.

4 Houston Chronicle, 13 May 1916 in Julian Sorell Huxley papers, MS50, box 3, folder 14, Woodson Research Center, Fondren Library, Rice University.

5 Julian Huxley, *Memories* (London: George Allen and Unwin, 1970), 113.

6 Diaries February 1917, box 48, folder 5, diaries December 1917–March 1918, box 48, folder 8, Huxley Papers.

7 Huxley to Dean Iremonger, 2 February 1948, box 17, folder 9, Huxley Papers.

8 Huxley to William Temple, 18 July 1917, box 17, folder 15, Huxley Papers.

9 Huxley to Dean Iremonger, 2 February 1948.

10 Julian Huxley, *Essays of a Biologist* (New York: Alfred A. Knopf, 1923), 245.

11 Ibid., 300.

12 Huxley, *Religion without Revelation*, 50.

13 Ibid., 103.

14 Julian Huxley, "Evolutionary Ethics" in T.H. Huxley and Julian Huxley, *Evolution and Ethics* (London: The Pilot Press, 1947), 105.

15 See Jose Harris, "Political Thought and the Welfare State 1870–1940: An Intellectual Framework for British Social Policy," *Past and Present* 135, no. 1 (1992): 116–41.

16 Huxley, *Religion without Revelation*, 105.

17 Huxley to Professor U. Campagnolo, 2 December 1955, box 26, folder 6, Huxley Papers.

18 Julian Huxley, *Evolution in Action* (New York: New American Library, 1961), 119.

19 Vassiliki Betty Smocovitis, *Unifying Biology: The Evolutionary Synthesis and Evolutionary Biology* (Princeton: Princeton University Press, 1996), 138.

20 Roger Smith, "Biology and Values in Interwar Britain: C.S. Sherrington, Julian Huxley and the Vision of Progress," *Past and Present* 178, no. 1 (2003): 213.

21 Marc Swetlitz, "Julian Huxley, George Gaylord Simpson and the Idea of Progress in Twentieth-century Evolutionary Biology" (PhD Thesis, University of Chicago, 1991), 39.

22 Michael Ruse, *Monad to Man: The Concept of Progress in Evolutionary Biology* (Cambridge: Harvard University Press, 1996), 338.

23 Smocovitis, *Unifying Biology*, 99–100.

24 John C. Greene, "The Interaction of Science and World View in Sir Julian Huxley's Evolutionary Biology," *Journal of the History of Biology* 23, no. 1 (Spring 1990): 51.

25 Bowler, *Science for All*, 211.

26 Ibid., 222.

27 Daniel. L. LeMahieu, "The Ambiguity of Popularization," in *Julian Huxley: Biologist and Statesman of Science*, eds C. Kenneth Waters and Alvert Van Holden (Houston: Rice University Press, 1992), 256.

28 Peter J. Bowler, "Julian Huxley: Religion without Revelation," in *Eminent Lives in Twentieth-Century Science and Religion*, ed. Nicholaas A. Rupke (Frankfurt am Main: Peter Lang, 2007), 147.

29 Ibid., 154.

30 Greene, "The Interaction of Science and World View," 46.

31 Huxley, *Religion without Revelation*, 12.

32 Ibid., 24.

33 Ibid., 29.

34 Ibid., 30, 31, 32.

35 Ibid., 240.

36 Ibid., 63.

37 Ibid., 179.

38 Ibid., 305.

39 Ibid., 73

40 Ibid., 74.

41 Ibid., 77 and 334.

42 Ibid., 376.

43 Ibid., 328

44 Ibid., 331.

45 Ibid., 58.

46 Ibid., 127.

47 Ibid., 125.

48 Huxley, *Essays of a Biologist*, 162.

49 Julian Huxley, "The Evolutionary Vision," in *Evolution after Darwin, vol. III: Issues in Evolution*, eds Sol Tax and Charles Callender (Chicago: University of Chicago Press, 1960), 253.

50 Huxley, *Religion without Revelation*, 108.

51 Ibid., 161.

52 One of Huxley's few direct references to Idealism was to disparage "the philosophical idealist superstition" when taken to the extreme, just as he does for the other extreme of the "pseudo-scientific behaviourist superstition." Julian Huxley, "The Humanist Frame," in *The Humanist Frame*, ed. Julian Huxley (London: George Allen and Unwin, 1961), 25, footnote.

53 Huxley, *Religion without Revelation*, 190.

54 Julian Huxley, "The Vindication of Darwinism," in T.H. Huxley and Julian Huxley, *Evolution and Ethics*, 175.

55 Huxley, *Religion without Revelation*, 1957 ed., 140–2.

56 Ibid., 150.

57 Ibid., 145.

58 Ibid., 201.

59 Ibid., 208.

60 Ibid., 181.

61 Ibid., 183.

62 Julian Huxley, "Introduction" in T.H. Huxley and Julian Huxley, *Evolution and Ethics*, 9.

63 Julian Huxley, "Conclusion" in T.H. Huxley and Julian Huxley, *Evolution and Ethics*, 198.

64 Huxley, "Evolutionary Ethics," 109.

65 Ibid., 119.

66 Julian Huxley, *Evolution: The Modern Synthesis* (New York: Harper and Brothers, 1942), 576. See also William B. Provine, "Progress in Evolution and Meaning in Life," 167.

67 John C. Greene, "The Interaction of Science and World View," 40.

68 Peter J. Bowler, *Science for All*, 48.

69 Julian Huxley, *If I Were Dictator* (London: Methuen and Co., 1934), 7.

70 William B. Provine, "Progress in Evolution and Meaning in Life," in *Julian Huxley: Biologist and Statesman of Science*, 178.

71 John C. Greene, *Science, Ideology and World View: Essays in the History of Evolutionary Ideas* (Berkeley: University of California Press, 1981), 166–7.

72 Huxley, "Evolutionary Ethics," 137.

73 For more on PEP see Arthur Marwick, "Middle Opinion in the Thirties: Planning, Progress and Political 'Agreement'" *English Historical Review* 79, no. 311 (1964): 285–98.

74 Huxley, *If I Were Dictator*, 75.

75 Ibid., 64.

76 Ibid., 19.

77 *Gemeinschaft*, or community, and *Gesellschaft*, or society, were terms originally introduced by the sociologist Ferdinand Tönnies for two types of social organizations. The former was characteristic of associations bound by common values and the loyalty of individuals to each other. The latter was seen in modern societies where large numbers of individuals were brought together and governed largely by impersonal relationships.

78 Huxley, *If I Were Dictator*, 50.

79 Ibid., 97.

80 Ibid., 116.

81 Ibid., 94.

82 Ibid., 30.

83 Ibid., 79.

84 Ibid., 91.

85 Ibid., 80.

86 Ibid., 119.

87 Ibid., 122.

88 Ibid., 50.

89 Ibid., 121–2.

90 Julian Huxley, "Marriage and Eugenics," in *Love, Marriage, Jealousy* (London: Pallas Publishing Co., 1938), 318.

91 Huxley, *What Dare I Think?*, 98.

92 Ibid., 93.

93 Huxley, "Marriage and Eugenics," 320.

94 Ibid., 319.

95 Julian Huxley, "'Race' in Europe," in *Oxford Pamphlets on World Affairs*, no. 5 (Oxford: Clarendon Press, 1939).

96 Elazar Barkan, *The Retreat of Scientific Racism: Changing Concepts of Race in Britain and the United States between the World Wars* (Cambridge: Cambridge University Press, 1992), 178.

97 Julian Huxley, *Africa View* (New York and London: Harper and Brothers, 1931), 395.

98 Ibid., 397.

99 Ibid., 410.

100 Ibid., 317.

101 Ibid., 358.

102 Julian Huxley, "Why is the White Man in Africa?," *Fortnightly Review*, 131, New Series, (January–June 1932): 60.

103 Ibid., 65.

104 Barkan, *The Retreat of Scientific Racism*, 241.

105 Huxley, *Africa View*, 405–6.

106 Tony Kushner, *We Europeans? Mass Observation, Race and British Identify in the Twentieth Century*, Studies in European Cultural Transition, vol. 25 (Aldershot: Ashgate, 1988), 48.

107 Huxley, "Why is The White Man in Africa?," 68.

108 Julian Huxley and Phyllis Deane, "The Future of the Colonies," *Target for Tomorrow*, no. 8 (London: Pilot Press, 1944), 8.

109 Michelle Brattain, "Race, Racism, and Antiracism: UNESCO and the Politics of Presenting Science to the Postwar Public," *American Historical Review* 112, no. 5 (Dec. 2007): 1400.

110 Ibid., 1397.

111 Barkan, *The Retreat of Scientific Racism*, 247.

112 Kushner, *We Europeans?*, 49.

113 Michael Freeden, "Eugenics and Progressive Thought: A Study in Ideological Affinity," *Historical Journal* 22 (September 1979): 669.

114 Diane Paul, "Eugenics and the Left," *JHI* 45, no. 4 (October–December 1984): 589.

115 Julian Huxley, "Religion as an Objective Problem," *The Thinker's Forum*, no. 38 (London: Watts and Co., 1946), 13–14.

116 Huxley, *Evolution in Action*, 119.

117 Huxley, "Conclusion," *Evolution and Ethics*, 190.

118 Julian Huxley, *Education and the Humanist Revolution* (Southampton: University of Southampton, 1962), 6–7.

119 "Interim Report," 5 March 1951, 1, box 113, folder 4, Huxley Papers.

120 Huxley, *Education and the Humanist Revolution*, 9.

121 Ibid., 15.

122 Julian Huxley, *Essays of a Humanist* (London: Chatto and Windus, 1964), 243.

123 Ibid.

124 Ibid., 244.

125 Bowler, "Julian Huxley: Religion without Revelation," 153.

126 Julian Huxley, "The Ecological Idea," Box 113, folder 4, Huxley Papers.

127 Transcript of interview, page 1, Books and Writers, Box 138, folder 7, Huxley Papers.

128 Huxley, *Africa View*, 255.

129 Julian Huxley, *Man Stands Alone* (New York: Harper, 1941), 128.

130 Ibid., 189.

131 Huxley, *Africa View*, 238–9.

132 Krishna R. Dronamraju, *If I Am To Be Remembered: The Life and Work of Julian Huxley with Selected Correspondence* (Singapore: World Scientific Publishing Co., 1993), 162.

133 Julian Huxley, *Memories*, vol. 2 (London: George Allen and Unwin, 1973), 79.

134 Krishna R. Dronamraju, *If I Am To Be Remembered*, 162.

135 Huxley, *Man Stands Alone*, 182.

136 Huxley, "The Ecological Idea," 8.

137 Ibid.

138 Huxley, "Conclusion," Evolution and Ethics, 181.

139 Julian Huxley, *Evolutionary Humanism*, Presidential Address to the first International Congress on Humanism and Ethical Culture, 22 August 1952, 2b, in box 106, folder 15, Huxley Papers.

140 John Ardagh, "Brave New World of Julian Huxley," *Observer*, 10 June 1962.

141 Huxley, *Education and the Humanist Revolution*, 23.

142 Huxley, *Evolution in Action*, 133.

143 Ibid., 134.

144 Bertrand Russell to Julian Huxley, 10 March 1963, in *Autobiography of Bertrand Russell*, 1944–1969 (New York: Simon and Schuster, 1969), 249.

145 John Beatty, "Julian Huxley and the Evolutionary Synthesis," *Julian Huxley: Biologist and Statesman of Science*, 189.

146 Julian Huxley, UNESCO: *Its Purpose and Its Philosophy* (Washington: Public Affairs Press, 1948), 6.

147 Ibid., 73.

148 Julian Huxley, *Memories*, vol. 2 (London: George Allen and Unwin, 1973), 16.

149 Bertrand Russell to Julian Huxley, 10 March 1963, in *Autobiography of Bertrand Russell, 1944–1969*, 249.

150 Huxley, "Evolutionary Ethics," 133.

151 Huxley, *Essays of a Humanist*, 222.

152 Eric Fenn to Director of Talks (G.R. Barnes), 5 November 1943, BBC. Written Archives Centre [WAC], RCONT 1, Julian Huxley Talks, File 2, 1943–1949.

153 L. Holme, Head of Religious Broadcasting to CT, 21 December 1951, WAC, RCONT 1, Julian Huxley Talks, File 3, 1950–1962.

154 See Preface, C.H. Douglas Clark, *The Scientist and the Supernatural: A Systematic Examination of the Relation between Christianity and Humanism, with Special Reference to the Work Religion without Revelation, by J.S. Huxley, and Other Agnostic Writings* (London: Epworth Press, 1966).

155 Huxley, "The Evolutionary Vision," 255.

156 Ibid., 252.

157 Vassiliki Betty Smocovitis, "The 1959 Darwin Centennial Celebration in America," *Osiris*, 2nd Series, 14, "Commemorative Practices in Science: Historical Perspectives on the Politics of Collective Memory" (1999): 322.

158 Huxley, "The Evolutionary Vision," 256.

159 Huxley, *Essays of a Humanist*, 223.

160 Huxley, *Evolution in Action*, 132.

161 Andrew Wernick, *Auguste Comte and the Religion of Humanity: The Post-Theistic Program of French Social Theory* (Cambridge: Cambridge University Press, 2001), 266.

162 Provine, "Progress in Evolution and Meaning in Life," 179–80.

163 Hugh Trevor-Roper, "The Tertiary Humanists," *Sunday Times*, 11/9/61, box 138, folder 2, Huxley Papers.

164 Callum G. Brown, *The Death of Christian Britain: Understanding Secularisation 1800–2000* (London: Ron Hedge, 2001), 176.

165 Philip Toynbee, "How to Give a Word a Bad Name," *Observer Weekend Review*, 22 March 1964, box 138, folder 3, Huxley Papers.

166 Quincy Wright to Julian Huxley, 22 July 1955, box 23, folder 4, Huxley Papers.

167 Toynbee, "How to Give a Word a Bad Name."

CHAPTER THREE

1 Bertrand Russell, "The Essence of Religion," 1912, reprinted in Louis Greenspan and Stefan Andersson, eds, *Russell on Religion: Selections from the Writings of Bertrand Russell* (London: Routledge, 1999), 57.

2 Russell to Gilbert Murray, 18 June 1941, reproduced in Bertrand Russell, *Autobiography of Bertrand Russell, vol. 2, 1914–1944* (Boston: Atlantic-Little, Brown, 1968), 385.

3 Terry Eagleton, *Reason, Faith and Revolution: Reflections on the God Debate* (New Haven and London: Yale University Press, 2009), 95.

4 Ibid.

5 Russell, "The Essence and Effect of Religion," 1921, reprinted in Greenspan and Andersson, eds, *Russell on Religion*, 74.

6 Russell, "Mysticism and Logic," 1914, in *Russell on Religion*, 130.

7 Russell, "The Essence of Religion," 58.

8 Ibid.

9 Ibid., 59.

10 Ibid, 67.

11 Ibid., 69.

12 Taylor, *A Secular Age*, 252.

13 Ibid., 254.

14 Russell, "The Essence of Religion," 58, also quoted in Taylor, *A Secular Age*, 251.

15 Taylor, *A Secular Age*, 255.

16 Ibid., 576.

17 Bertrand Russell, *Unpopular Essays* (London: Allen and Unwin, 1950), 33, 35–7, 39, 41–3.

18 Russell, "What is an Agnostic?," 1953, in *Russell on Religion*, 48.

19 Quote from Russell, *The Impact of Science on Society* (London: Allen and Unwin, 1952), in Louis Greenspan and Stefan Andersson, *Russell on Religion*, "Introduction," 17.

20 Stephen Patrick to Christopher Farley, October 1966, in reply to letter of 18 October 1966, archives II, box 10:32, 410 publishing correspondence, file BBC 1966-8, 141231, Russell Papers, Bertrand Russell Collection, Bertrand Russell Research Centre, William Ready Division of Archives and Research Collections, Mills Memorial Library, McMaster University, Hamilton, Ontario, Canada.

21 Bertrand Russell, *Autobiography, vol. 1, 1872–1914* (London: Allen and Unwin, 1967), 22.

22 Russell, "How I Came by My Creed [1929]," in *The Collected Papers of Bertrand Russell, vol. 10: A Fresh Look at Empiricism, 1927–42*, ed. John G. Slater (London and New York: Routledge, 1996), 11.

23 Russell, *Autobiography, vol. 1*, "Adolescence," Appendix "Greek Exercises," 20 July 1888, 55.

24 Russell "Has Religion Made Useful Contributions to Civilization?," 1930, reproduced in *Why I Am Not a Christian and Other Essays on Religion and Related Subjects*, ed. Paul Edwards (New York: Touchstone Books, Simon and Schuster), 39.

25 A.J. Ayer, *Bertrand Russell* (Chicago: University of Chicago Press, 1972), 117.

26 See Charles R. Pigden, "Bertrand Russell: Moral Philosopher or Unphilosophical Moralist?," in *The Cambridge Companion to Bertrand Russell*, ed. Nicholas Griffin (Cambridge: Cambridge University Press, 2003), 475–506.

27 Michael K. Potter, *Bertrand Russell's Ethics* (London: Continuum, 2006), chapter 3.

28 Ibid., 152.

29 Quoted in Pigden, "Bertrand Russell: Moral Philosopher or Unphilosophical Moralist?," 475.

30 Ayer, *Bertrand Russell*, 130.

31 Russell, *What I Believe* (New York: E.P. Dutton and Co., 1925), 70–1.

32 Russell, *Freedom and Organization, 1814–1914* (London: George Allen and Unwin, 1934), 509.

33 Russell, *Autobiography, vol. 2, 1914–1944*, 3.

34 Ved Mehta, *Fly and the Fly-Bottle: Encounters with British Intellectuals* (Boston: Atlanta Monthly Press Book, Little, Brown, 1963), 44.

35 Bowler, *Science for All*, 99, 256.

36 Russell, *Portraits from Memory and Other Essays* (London: Allen and Unwin, 1956), 22.

37 Richard A. Rempel, Louis Greenspan, Beryl Haslam, Albert C. Lewis, and Mark Lippincott, eds, "General Headnote to Part X," *The Collected Papers of Bertrand Russell, vol. 14: Pacifism and Revolution, 1916–18* (London and New York: Routledge, 1995), 415.

38 Russell, "A Free Man's Worship," 1903 reproduced in *Why I Am Not a Christian and Other Essays on Religion and Related Subjects*, 116.

39 Ibid., 109.

40 Russell, "On Catholic and Protestant Skeptics," 1928, reproduced in *Why I Am Not a Christian and Other Essays on Religion and Related Subjects*, 118.

41 John G. Slater, ed., "Introduction," "Why I Am Not a Christian [1927]," *The Collected Papers of Bertrand Russell, vol. 10*, 178.

42 R.J. Helmstadter, ed., "Introduction," *Freedom and Religion in the Nineteenth Century* (Stanford: Stanford University Press, 1997), 6–8.

43 Russell, "The Reformation and Counter-Reformation," reproduced from the *History of Western Philosophy*, 1945, in *Russell on Religion*, 240.

44 Greenspan and Andersson, "Religion and History," in *Russell on Religion*, 197.

45 Christopher Hitchens, *God Is Not Great: How Religion Poisons Everything* (Toronto: McClelland and Stewart, 2007), 11.

46 Russell, "On Catholic and Protestant Skeptics," 119.

47 Taylor, *A Secular Age*, 402.

48 Russell, *What I Believe*, 12.

49 Russell, "Has Religion Made Useful Contributions to Civilization?," *Why I Am Not a Christian and Other Essays on Religion and Related Subjects*, 24.

50 Russell, "Why I Am Not a Christian," 1927, reproduced in *Why I Am Not a Christian and Other Essays on Religion and Related Subjects*, 22.

51 Russell, *Principles of Social Reconstruction* (London: George Allen and Unwin, reprinted, 1927), 166–7.

52 Russell, "How I Came by My Creed," *The Collected Papers of Bertrand Russell, vol. 10*, 13.

53 Richard A. Rempel, ed., "Introduction," "Syllabuses for Eight Lectures on Social Reconstruction," *The Collected Papers of Bertrand Russell, vol. 13: Prophecy and Dissent, 1914–16* (London: Unwin Hyman, 1988), 283.

54 Russell, *Principles of Social Reconstruction*, 6.

55 Ibid., 228.

56 Edwin T. Buehrer to Russell, 21 September 1964, archives II, box 10.33, 410 Publishing Correspondence, 141321, Russell Archives.

57 Russell, *Freedom and Organization, 1814–1914*, 252.

58 Russell, *Power: A New Social Analysis* (London: George Allen and Unwin, 1948), 273.

59 H. Laski to Russell, 29 August 1919, archives I, 5.27, 710.051996, Russell Papers.

60 Russell, *What I Believe*, 70.

61 Russell, "How Will Science Change Morals? [1928]," *Collected Papers of Bertrand Russell, vol. 10*, 388.

62 Russell, "The Existence and Nature of God [1939]," *The Collected Papers of Bertrand Russell, vol. 10*, 261.

63 Russell, *The Scientific Outlook* (London: George Allen and Unwin, 1931), 269.

64 Ibid., 224, 241.

65 Ibid., 244.

66 Ibid., 233.

67 Ibid., 243.

68 Ibid., 253.

69 Ibid., 249.

70 Ibid., 256–7.

71 Ibid., 261, 263.

72 Ibid., 165–6.

73 Ibid., 267.

74 Ibid., 270.

75 Ibid., 273.

76 Ibid., 279.

77 Slater, ed., "Introduction," *The Collected Papers of Bertrand Russell,* *vol. 10*, xii.

78 Russell, *Principles of Social Reconstruction*, 164.

79 Russell, *What I Believe*, 74.

80 Russell to H.G. Wells, 24 May 1928, archives I, box 5.53, 710.056280, Russell Papers. Reprinted in *Autobiography, vol. 2, 1914–1944*, 265–7.

81 Russell, *On Education, Especially in Early Childhood* (London: George Allen and Unwin, 1966), 22–3.

82 Taylor, *A Secular Age*, 398.

83 Russell, *On Education*, 25.

84 Ibid., 87.

85 Ibid., 171.

86 Russell, *Power*, 311.

87 Russell, *Marriage and Morals* (London: Unwin Paperbacks, George Allen and Unwin, 1976), 178.

88 Ibid., 62.

89 Russell, *Autobiography, vol. 2, 1914–1944*, 227.

90 Russell, *Marriage and Morals*, ch. 18, "Eugenics," 167.

91 Ibid.

92 Stephen Heathorn, "Explaining Russell's Eugenic Discourse in the 1920s," *Russell: The Journal of Bertrand Russell Studies* 25, no. 2 (2006): 107–40.

93 Russell, *Marriage and Morals*, 168.

94 Ibid., 175.

95 Russell, *Autobiography, vol. 2, 1914–1944*, 287.

96 Russell, "Is Religion Desirable? [1929]," *The Collected Papers of Bertrand Russell, vol. 10*, 232.

97 Bertrand Russell, *Human Society in Ethics and Politics* (London: George Allen and Unwin, 1954), 219–220.

98 Bertrand Russell, *The Impact of Science on Society* (New York: Columbia University Press, 1951), 57.

99 Russell, *Human Society in Ethics and Politics*, 221.

100 Russell, "Is the Notion of Progress an Illusion? [1957]," "London Forum" Radio Discussion, in *The Collected Papers of Bertrand Russell, vol. 29: Détente or Destruction, 1955–57*, ed. Andrew G. Bone (London and New York: Routledge, 2005), 235.

101 Russell, *Philosophy and Politics* (London: National Book League, published by Cambridge University Press, 1947), 20.

102 Ibid., 27.

103 Russell, *Religion and Science* (New York: A Galaxy Book, Oxford University Press, 1961), 243.

104 Russell, "Why I Am Not a Christian," *Why I Am Not a Christian and Other Essays on Religion and Related Subjects*, 22.

105 Russell, "How Will Science Change Morals? [1928]," *The Collected Papers of Bertrand Russell, vol. 10*, 383.

106 Russell, *Religion and Science*, 242.

107 Russell, "Religion and the Training of the Young," 1955, "London Forum" Discussion, in *The Collected Papers of Bertrand Russell, vol. 28: Man's Peril, 1954–55*, ed. Andrew G. Bone (London and New York: Routledge, 2003), 233.

108 Russell, *Human Society in Ethics and Politics*, 172.

109 Ibid., 139.

110 For a guide to Russell's definition of "right" see Russell, *Human Society in Ethics and Politics*, 115–18.

111 Taylor, *A Secular Age*, 395.

112 Russell, *Human Society in Ethics and Politics*, 221.

113 Russell, "Is the Notion of Progress an Illusion? [1957]," *The Collected Papers of Bertrand Russell, vol. 29*, 237.

114 Malcolm Muggeridge, *Chronicles of Wasted Time, vol. 1: The Green Stick* (London: Collins, 1972), 175.

115 Russell, "How Will Science Change Morals? [1928]," *The Collected Papers of Bertrand Russell, vol. 10*, 386.

116 Russell, *What I Believe*, 73.

117 Russell, "Symptoms of George Orwell's 1984 [1956]," *The Collected Papers of Bertrand Russell, vol. 29*, 160.

118 Russell, *Human Society in Ethics and Politics*, 213.

119 Bertrand Russell, *The Conquest of Happiness* (New York: Bantam Book edition, 1968), 96.

120 Russell, "Man's Peril [1954]," *The Collected Papers of Bertrand Russell,* vol. 28, 88.

121 Russell, *Human Society in Ethics and Politics,* 157.

122 Russell, *Has Man a Future?* (London: George Allen and Unwin, 1961), 103.

123 Russell to Kay Fuller, 8 September 1960, archives III, file RA 3, folder 1351c, Russell Papers.

124 Russell to J. Newall, 28 March 1962, archives I, Box 5:28, 710.051.277, Russell Papers.

125 Richard Weight, *Patriots,* 289. For a full account see Paul Byrne, *The Campaign for Nuclear Disarmament* (London: Croom Helm Routledge, 1988).

126 Russell, *Autobiography, vol. 3, 1944–1969,* 139.

127 Canon John Collins Papers, rol. 3301, 110–26, Lambeth Palace Library.

128 Haddon Willmer, "John Collins, Gadfly of the Resurrection," in *Modern Religious Rebels: Presented to John Kent,* ed. Stuart Mews (London: Epworth Press, 1993), 255.

129 Text found in MS 3308, Collins Papers.

130 John L. Collins, *A Theology of Christian Action: The Lichfield Cathedral Divinity Lectures, 1948* (London: Hodder and Stoughton, 1949), 25.

131 Russell to John Gollin, 20 November 1962, archives I, 5.9, 710.048487, Russell Papers.

132 Russell, *Human Society in Ethics and Politics,* 170.

133 Russell, *Common Sense and Nuclear Warfare* (New York: Simon and Schuster, 1959), 51–2.

134 Bertrand Russell, *Authority and The Individual: Reith Lectures for 1948–9* (London: George Allen and Unwin, 1949), 93.

135 Ibid., 82.

136 Ibid., 83–4.

137 See Bertrand Russell, *War Crimes in Vietnam* (London: George Allen and Unwin, 1967).

138 Russell, "Have Liberal Ideals a Future? [1954]," *The Collected Papers of Bertrand Russell, vol. 28,* 148.

139 Russell, "Is the Notion of Progress an Illusion? [1957]," *The Collected Papers of Bertrand Russell, vol. 29,* 235.

140 Russell to R.C. Marsh, 3 December 1955, Bertrand Russell Letters to Robert Charles Marsh, MS Eng 1282, Houghton Library, Harvard College Library, Harvard University.

141 Russell, "*The Brains Trust* no. 89, 19 May 1957," *The Collected Papers of Bertrand Russell, vol.* 29, 436.

142 Statement, 31 December 1966, Allen and Unwin, archives I, Publisher's Correspondence, Box 5, Royalty Statements, file A-17, Russell Papers.

143 Russell to Julian Huxley, 10 March 1963, archives I, 5.24, 710.051356, Reprinted in *Autobiography, vol. 3,* 249.

144 Maurice Chittenden, "Sir Paul McCartney: I was the Anti-war Beatle," *Sunday Times,* 14 December 2008.

145 Russell, *Autobiography, volume 1, 1872–1914,* 13.

146 Russell, *The Conquest of Happiness,* 73–4.

147 Russell, "*The Brains Trust,* no. 74, 3 February 1957," *The Collected Papers of Bertrand Russell, vol.* 29, 432.

148 Russell, *Human Society in Ethics and Politics,* 219.

149 Russell, *Autobiography, vol. 2, 1914–1944,* 229–30.

150 Mehta, *Fly and the Fly-Bottle,* 44.

151 Russell's probated will indicated his wealth was £69,243 at his death in 1970. Ray Monk, "Russell, Arthur William, third Earl Russell, 1872–1970," in *Dictionary of National Biography,* vol. 48 (Oxford: Oxford University Press, 2004), 219.

152 Greenspan and Andersson, eds, *Russell on Religion,* 197.

153 Ibid., 11.

CHAPTER FOUR

1 Muggeridge, *Jesus Rediscovered* (London: Fontana Books, 1969), 154.

2 Frank M. Turner, *John Henry Newman: The Challenge to Evangelical Religion* (New Haven and London: Yale University Press, 2002), 294.

3 Muggeridge, *Jesus Rediscovered,* 195.

4 Charles Taylor, *A Secular Age,* 734.

5 Quoted in Ian Hunter, *Malcolm Muggeridge: A Life* (London: Collins, 1980), 188.

6 "Buckley Remembering Muggeridge (2003)," *The Gargoyle: The Journal of the Malcolm Muggeridge Society* 18 (April 2008): 12.

7 Julia Stapleton, *Political Intellectuals and Public Identities in Britain since 1850* (Manchester: Manchester University Press, 2001), 167.

8 Noel Annan, *Our Age: English Intellectuals Between the Wars – A Group Portrait* (New York: Random House, 1990), 167.

9 Hunter, *Malcolm Muggeridge,* 197.

10 Muggeridge, January 18 1937, in *Like It Was: The Diaries of Malcolm Muggeridge*, selected and edited by John Bright-Holmes (London: Collins, 1981), 162.

11 Muggeridge, *Jesus Rediscovered*, 154.

12 Muggeridge, "A Kingdom Not of This World [1975]," in *Things Past: Malcolm Muggeridge*, ed. Ian Hunter (London: Collins, 1978), 239.

13 Muggeridge to Alec Vidler, November 1921 [dated by Vidler on original held by Vidler, photocopies in Muggeridge Papers], Box 1A:1, Correspondence with Vidler folder, Malcolm Muggeridge Papers, SC-4, Archives and Special Collections, Buswell Memorial Library, Wheaton College, Wheaton, Illinois.

14 Ibid., Muggeridge to Vidler, 15 March 1921, emphasis in original.

15 Ibid, Muggeridge to Vidler, 3 September 1921.

16 See Muggeridge, "By Law Established," in *Jesus Rediscovered*, 145.

17 M. Gandhi to Muggeridge, 12 September 1926, Box 1B,1:18, folder "India letters," Muggeridge papers.

18 Muggeridge, *Winter in Moscow* (London: Eyre and Spottiswoode, 1934), 228.

19 George Orwell to Malcolm Muggeridge, 4 December 1948, Box 1B, 1:27, "O" folder, Muggeridge Papers.

20 Muggeridge, "To the Friends of the Soviet Union," *English Review* 1 (January 1934): 46.

21 Ibid., 47.

22 Ibid., 49.

23 Ibid., 50.

24 Ibid., 54.

25 Ibid., 52.

26 Ibid., 53.

27 Ibid., 51.

28 Muggeridge, "Thirteen Years Soft," *New Statesman*, 16 October 1964, 572.

29 Muggeridge to Archbishop of Canterbury, 16 March 1951, Box 1A, Correspondence 1951–60, Muggeridge Papers.

30 On a visit to Pittsburg, November 19, 1962 in *Like It Was*, 516.

31 Muggeridge, "Words for Communicating through Television," 75, session IV, *Consultation on Religious Television*, held at William Temple College, Rugby, 14–17 March 1962, Box V:2, Speeches and Addresses, Muggeridge Papers.

32 Muggeridge, April 11 1961 in *Like it Was*, 522.

33 Noel Annan, *Our Age*, 168.

34 Muggeridge, *A Third Testament* (Farmington: Plough Publishing House, 1983), xii, 6.
35 Muggeridge, *Chronicles of Wasted Time, vol. 1: The Green Stick* (London: Collins, 1972), 19.
36 Muggeridge, February 17, 1962, March 14, 1962 in *Like It Was*, 533, 536.
37 Muggeridge, *A Third Testament*, 4.
38 Ibid., 33.
39 Ibid., 81.
40 For a discussion of Pascal, Tolstoy, Blake, and Kierkegaard, as well as Bonhoeffer, Dostoevsky, and always St Augustine by Muggeridge, see *A Third Testament*, passim.
41 Donald Soper, Baron (1903–1998), Methodist minister and social activist, especially in the peace movement. See Donald Soper, *Calling For Action: An Autobiographical Enquiry* (London: Robson Books, 1984).
42 Gauri Viswanathan, *Outside the Fold: Conversion, Modernity and Belief* (Princeton: Princeton University Press, 1998), 44.
43 Muggeridge, *The End of Christendom* (Grand Rapids: William B. Eerdmans, 1980), 28–9.
44 Ibid., 29.
45 Paul Johnson, "Mugg Waits for Godot," *New Statesman* 77, no. 1996 (13 June 1969): 838.
46 Muggeridge, *Conversion: A Spiritual Journey* (London: Collins, 1988), 14.
47 "Pilgrims to Lourdes," 1965, narration transcript file copy, 2, Box II, G5, Muggeridge Papers.
48 Ibid., 1.
49 Ibid., 6–7.
50 Ibid., 10.
51 Raymond Williams, *Culture and Society, 1780–1950* (London: Chatto and Windus, 1958), 205.
52 Muggeridge, "A Socialist Childhood": Malcolm Muggeridge remembers scenes, people, and places from his formative years, first transmission, BBC 1, 13 October 1966, post-production script (5115/7567), folder Talks T56/251/1, TX 66.10.13, BBC Written Archives Centre [WAC], 19.
53 Ibid., 17.
54 Ibid., 26.
55 Kathleen Burk, *Troublemaker: The Life and History of A.J.P. Taylor* (New Haven and London: Yale University Press, 2000), 120.
56 "A Socialist Childhood," post-production script, 7.
57 Raymond Williams, *Culture and Society*, 217.

58 John Worthen, *D.H. Lawrence, The Life of an Outsider* (London: Allen Lane, 2005).

59 Raymond Williams, *Culture and Society*, 205.

60 An Audience Research Report on "A Socialist Childhood" recalled by Malcolm Muggeridge, produced and directed by Kevin Billington, 13 October 1966, T. Doc, VR/66/559, 4 November, 1966, File R9/7/83, WAC, 1.

61 An Audience Research Report on Muggeridge, "Pilgrims to Lourdes," produced and directed by Michael Tuchner, 7 September 1965, TDoc. VR/65/485, 7 October 1965, File R9/7/77, WAC, 1.

62 An Audience Research Report on Muggeridge "The American Way of Sex," produced and directed by Michael Tuchner, 21 October 1965, R9/7/77, WAC, 1.

63 An Audience Research Report on Muggeridge, Three Films on "A Life of Christ," produced by Christopher Martin, 10–12 April 1968, VR/68/222, 8 May 1968, R9/7/92, WAC, 1-2.

64 Muggeridge, *Chronicles of Wasted Time, vol. 1: The Green Stick*, 11.

65 See Muggeridge, "The Great Liberal Death Wish," 1970 in *Things Past* (London: Collins, 1978), ed. Ian Hunter, 220–38. Also in a shorter lecture given in March 1979, at Hillsdale College also entitled "The Great Liberal Death Wish," reprinted in *The Gargoyle: The Journal of the Malcolm Muggeridge Society* 4 (October 2004): 7–11.

66 Muggeridge to Archbishop of Canterbury, 21 September 1971, Box 1A, Correspondence, Muggeridge Papers.

67 Muggeridge, *Jesus Rediscovered*, 143.

68 Ibid., 197.

69 Television interview with William Buckley, "The Culture of the Left," *Firing Line*, 26 February 1968.

70 Muggeridge, "The Great Liberal Death Wish," in *Things Past*, 237.

71 Muggeridge, "Another Opinion: The Mumbo-Jumbo of Education," *New York Times*, 19 February 1967.

72 Taylor, *A Secular Age*, 395.

73 Muggeridge, *Another King: A Sermon*, delivered at the University of Edinburgh service at the High Kirk of St Giles, 14 January 1968 (Edinburgh: The St Andrews Press, 1968), 10.

74 Muggeridge to Dr Michie, Department of Machine Intelligence and Perception, Edinburgh University, 2 January 1968, Box 1A, file "Edinburgh University 1967–1972," Muggeridge Papers.

75 Noel Annan, *Our Age*, 166.

76 Frank Turner, *John Henry Newman*, 425.

77 Northrop Frye, *The Great Code: The Bible and Literature* (New York: Harcourt, Brace, Jovanovich, 1981), 169.

78 Paul Johnson, "Mugg Waits for Godot," *New Statesman*, 13 June 1969, 838.

79 Muggeridge, *Christ and the Media*, (Grand Rapids: William B. Eerdmans, 1978), 23.

80 Muggeridge to Charles Curran, 5 February 1974, R78/1/80, WAC.

81 Muggeridge, *Jesus Rediscovered*, 159.

82 Muggeridge, *Christ and the Media*, 52.

83 Muggeridge in "The Mystery," in *In Search of C.S. Lewis* (South Plainfield: Bridge Publishing, 1983), ed. Stephen Schofield, 130.

84 Justin Phillips, *C.S. Lewis at the B.B.C.: Messages of Hope in the Darkness of War* (London: Harper Collins, 2003), 275–6.

85 Muggeridge, *Christ and the Media*, 84.

86 Ibid., 107.

87 Margaret Somerville, *The Ethical Imagination: Journeys of the Human Spirit* (Toronto: House of Anansi Press, 2006), 9–10.

88 Muggeridge, *Christ and the Media*, 30.

89 "Lord Reith Looks Back" with Malcolm Muggeridge, transcription from a recording by Radio Direction Telediphone Unit, Producer George Angell, Radio 4, tape no. T1 NO1/TK 759/H, transmission, 4 January 1968, a selected sixty minutes from three programmes broadcast on BBC 1, November/December 1967, 2, Box II, G:5, Muggeridge Papers.

90 "Lord Reith Looks Back," the second of three programmes of Malcolm Muggeridge interviewing Lord Reith, produced and directed by Stephen Peet, BBC 1, filmed February 1967, 2, Box II, G:5, Muggeridge Papers.

91 "Lord Reith Looks Back," the third of three programmes of Malcolm Muggeridge interviewing Lord Reith, produced and directed by Stephen Peet, BBC 1, filmed February 1967, 21, Box II, G:5, Muggeridge Papers.

92 Muggeridge, *Christ and the Media*, 70–1.

93 Ibid., 70.

94 Muggeridge, *Conversion*, 140–1.

95 There is a thick folder of "Correspondence about Nomination for Nobel Peace Prize" for Mother Teresa, including many letters soliciting support, an exchange with Barbara Ward, and his own four page statement in 1975, Box 1B 1:37, Muggeridge Papers.

96 C.E.M. Joad (1891–1953) was a popular philosopher and broadcaster, especially as a regular participant on the radio programme, *The Brains Trust* during the Second World War. He was also a well-known atheist. In the

late 1940s he was disgraced by being arrested as a fare dodger on the railway and was dismissed by the BBC. His return to theism announced by the publication of his *The Recovery of Belief: A Restatement of Christian Philosophy* (London: Faber and Faber, 1952), shortly before his death, was treated with suspicion by many.

97 Christopher Booker, "Muggeridge at Seventy-five," *New Statesman* 95, no. 2453 (24 March 1978): 394.

98 Paul Johnson, "Mugg Waits for Godot," 839.

99 David Mills, "Years the Locusts Have Eaten: Malcolm Muggeridge's Chronicles of Wasted Time as an Apology of Love," *Touchstone: A Journal of Mere Christianity* 16, no. 10 (December 2003): 35.

100 See "The Destroyer of Civilization," where Muggeridge joins the Canadian historian George Woodcock, in suggesting that McLuhan's alleged statements on the demise of the book could aid in the destruction of our civilization. CBC broadcast, Vancouver, 8 July 1974, CBC Digital Archives. Rebecca West, in *McLuhan and the Future of Literature* (London: The English Association, 1969) makes more or less the same point.

101 Patricia Beer, "Spotlights and Haloes: Something Beautiful for God," *Listener* 85, no. 2199 (20 May 1971): 656.

102 Vijay Prashad, "Mother Teresa: Mirror of Bourgeois Guilt," *Economic and Political Weekly* 32, no. 44/45 (8 November 1997): 2856–8.

103 Muggeridge, "Importance of Being Beveridge," *Punch*, 6 January 1954, 74.

104 Muggeridge, *Something Beautiful for God: Mother Teresa of Calcutta*, (London: Collins, 1971), 118.

105 Ibid., 28.

106 Ibid., 118.

107 Ibid., 132.

108 Muggeridge, "Why Poverty?," *The Question Why: Poverty*, introduced by Malcolm Muggeridge, transmission 13 February 1972, BBC-1, Box II, G:5, Muggeridge Papers.

109 Muggeridge, *The Question Why: Majority Rule*, introduced by Malcolm Muggeridge, transmission, 30 January 1972, BBC-1, Box II, G:5, Muggeridge Papers, 3.

110 Ibid., 4.

111 Ibid., 3.

112 Muggeridge, *The Question Why: Racialism*, introduced by Malcolm Muggeridge, transmission 14 July 1968, BBC-1, Box II, G:5, Muggeridge Papers, 2.

113 Muggeridge, *The Question Why: Freedom of Speech*, introduced by Malcolm Muggeridge, transmission 9 January 1972, BBC-1, Box II, G:5, Muggeridge Papers, 4.

114 Muggeridge, *The Question Why: Breakdown of Society*, introduced by Malcolm Muggeridge, transmission 20 February 1972, BBC-1, Box II, G:5, Muggeridge Papers, introductory page.

115 Taylor, *A Secular Age*, 734.

116 See endnote 95. Barbara Ward wrote to Muggeridge on the subject on 31 August 1975, 4 December 1977, and 12 May 1980, all supporting Mother Teresa.

117 Ian Hunter, *Malcolm Muggeridge*, 193.

118 Muggeridge, "Humour, Humility and Faith," Convocation Address, St Francis Xavier University, 6 May 1979, Public Relations Records, RG 44/3/519, University Archives, Angus L. MacDonald Library, St Francis Xavier University, Antigonish, Nova Scotia.

119 Muggeridge, *Chronicles of Wasted Time, vol. 1: The Green Stick*, 18.

CHAPTER FIVE

1 Hastings, *A History of English Christianity 1920–1985*, 659.

2 E.R. Norman, *Christianity and the World Order* (Oxford: Oxford University Press, 1976), 10.

3 Pauline Adams, *Somerville for Women: An Oxford College, 1879–1993* (New York: Oxford University Press, 1996), 155.

4 Ward, "Women Students at Oxford," n.d., 4 pages, Manuscripts – Articles series, Box 9, folder 17, Barbara Ward (Baroness Jackson) Papers, Special Collections, Georgetown University Library.

5 Ward, "Full Circle," n.d., Manuscripts – Fiction series, Box 7, folder 27, Barbara Ward Papers.

6 Ward, *Hitler's Route to Baghdad, Prepared for the International Research Section of the Fabian Society by Barbara Ward, the Hon. Barbara Buckmaster, Clare Hollingworth, Vandeleur Robinson, Lilo Linke* (Freeport: Books for Libraries Press, 1971, first published in 1939), 94.

7 Ibid., 13.

8 See John C. Heenan, *Cardinal Hinsley* (London: Burns Oates and Washbourne, 1944).

9 His Grace the Archbishop of Westminster [Arthur Hinsley], "Sermons For the Times LXXIII – The Italian – Abyssinian Situation." *The Tablet* 166, no. 4980 (19 October 1935): 500.

10 See Christina Scott, *A Historian and His World: A Life of Christopher Dawson, 1889–1970* (London: Sheed and Ward, 1984).

11 See Keith Robbins, chapter 14, "Britain, 1940 and Christian Civilization," in *History, Religion and Identity in Modern Britain* (London: Hambledon Press, 1993), 195–213.

12 Ward to parents, 9 August, 1937, Box 1, folder 9, Family Correspondence 1937, Barbara Ward Papers.

13 Ward, Personal Diary, travels in Germany, 27 January 1937, 10, Box 11, folder 19, Barbara Ward Papers.

14 Ward, "Ignaz Seipel and the Anschluss," *Dublin Review* 203, nos 406–7 (July 1938): 33.

15 Ward, "The Condition of the Church in Germany," 32–3, n.d. Box 8, Manuscripts, speeches, folder 108, Barbara Ward Papers.

16 For the private, rather complicated communications amongst Hinsley, the Vatican, and the British Government see Thomas Moloney, *Westminster, Whitehall and the Vatican: The Role of Cardinal Hinsley, 1935–43* (London: Burns and Oates, 1985).

17 Alan Wilkinson, *Dissent or Conform? War, Peace and the English Churches, 1900–1945* (London: SCM Press, 1986), 256.

18 Keith Robbins, *History, Religion and Identity in Modern Britain*, 223.

19 Christopher Dawson to Dr Hinsley, 17 July 1940, Sword of the Spirit records box, Cardinal Hinsley Papers, Westminster Diocesan Archives, London.

20 Ward and Professor A.C.F. Beales believed that the membership should be open to all who accepted the ten points of December 1940 with aims based upon the principles of natural law. Ward to Cardinal Hinsley, 23 November 1941, Sword of the Spirit records box, Hinsley Papers.

21 Ward agreed that the aim of the Sword of the Spirit was spiritual but it was difficult to separate spiritual issues from political. Ward to Cardinal Hinsley, 5 September 1940, Sword of the Spirit records box, Hinsley Papers.

22 Barbara Ward, "Peace at any Price?," *Sword of the Spirit Bulletin* 21, 29 May 1941.

23 Ian McLaine, *Ministry of Morale: Home Front Moral and the Ministry of Information in World War II* (London: George Allen and Unwin, 1979), 152.

24 Ward to parents, 12 January 1941, box 1 folder 13 Family Correspondence 1941, Barbara Ward Papers.

25 It has been noted how much of the British intelligentsia was absorbed by both the BBC and the Ministry of Information at the time in Richard Weight, *Patriots*, 46–7.

26 Ward, *The Defence of the West* (London: Sword of the Spirit pamphlet, reproduced from *The Listener*, Sands, 1942), 3.

27 Ibid., 7.

28 Ibid., 11.

29 Hinsley, Westminster Cathedral address, 8 December 1942, Sword of the Spirit records box, Hinsley Papers.

30 Index cards of scripts for talks, 1941–43. "The Position of Women under the Nazi Regime," 18–19 November 1941, RCONT 1, (Miss) Barbara Ward's Talks, file 1, 1940–1943, WAC.

31 Miss Janet Quigley to the Directory of Talks, 19 March 1942, BBC Internal Circulating Memo, Barbara Ward Talks, file 1, 1940–1943, WAC.

32 G.R. Barnes, Director of Talks to Miss Janet Quigley, 9 April 1942, BBC Internal Circulating Memo. Also H.V. Usill, Ministry of Information to G.R. Barnes, 4.3.42, R Cont 1, Barbara Ward Talks, file 1, 1940–1943, WAC.

33 This was evident in a conversation with an evangelical pastor. She noted that "the frightening thing was that the young pastor was in many ways a genuinely Christian man." Diary, Thursday 21 March 1946, 28, Box 11, folder 28, Barbara Ward Papers.

34 Ward, "Unsordid Act," *The Economist*, 10 April 1948, 569.

35 Marion Barker to Ward, 28 February 1945, Box 3, folder 14, Fan Mail February–March 1945, Barbara Ward Papers.

36 Ward, "Note on the Director of Religious Broadcasting," 1, Board of Governors Papers, 1946, file 2, R1/82/2. The note was discussed at the Board meeting of 28 November 1946, Minutes of Board of Governors, 1946, 2, R1/14/1, WAC.

37 Ward, *The West at Bay* (London: Allen and Unwin, 1948), 54.

38 Ibid., 55.

39 Ibid., 226.

40 Ibid., 227.

41 Ibid., 107.

42 Ibid., 228–9.

43 Ibid., 229.

44 Ibid.

45 Ward to parents, 18 July 1953, box 1, folder 16 Family Correspondence July–August 1953, Barbara Ward Papers.

46 Ward to Jack Kennedy, 4 August 1959, box 2, folder 43, correspondence with John F. Kennedy, Barbara Ward Papers.

47 "Oral History Interview with Barbara Ward" by Walter and Elspeth Rostow for John F. Kennedy Library, 28 June 1964, Box 9, folder 39, Barbara Ward Papers.

48 Barbara Ward, *Faith and Freedom* (New York: W.W. Norton, 1954), 265–6.

49 Barbara Ward, *My Brother's Keeper* (London: Sword of the Spirit, new edition, 1959), 1.

50 Barbara Ward, *The Interplay of East and West: Elements of Contrast and Co-operation* (London: Allen and Unwin, 1957), 93.

51 Ward, "The Quest for Christian Unity," *The Atlantic Monthly*, August 1962, 126.

52 Ward, "Are Today's Basic Problems Religious? Moral Order In An Uncertain World," *The Mott Foundation Lectures*, 3–5 March 1953, University of Michigan, Ann Arbor, 9.

53 Ibid., 16.

54 Ward, "The Quest for Christian Unity," 124.

55 Ibid., 126.

56 Ibid., 125.

57 Ibid.

58 Ibid., 126.

59 Ward, "*Are Today's Basic Problems Religions?*," 8.

60 Ward, *Faith and Freedom*, 60.

61 Ibid., 79.

62 Ibid.

63 Ibid., 64.

64 Ibid., 61.

65 Ibid., 49.

66 Ibid., 51.

67 Ward, *Spaceship Earth* (New York: Columbia University Press, 1966), 113.

68 Ibid., emphasis in original.

69 Ibid.

70 Ward, *It Can be Done: An Approach to the Problem of World Poverty* (London, Dublin: Geoffrey Chapman, 1965), 19.

71 Ward, "The Moral Challenge of Communism," *The Atlantic Monthly*, December 1951, 39–40.

72 Ward, *Policy for the West* (London: Allen and Unwin, 1951), 305.

73 Ward, *Spaceship Earth*, 112.

74 Ibid.

75 Ward, *The Interplay of East and West*, 139.

76 Ward, *Faith and Freedom*, 60.

77 Ward, *Poverty and Politics* (London: Catholic Institute for International Relations, 1968), 2.

78 Ward, *Five Ideas That Change the World* (New York: W.W. Norton, 1959), 187.

79 See Kenneth LeRoy Gladish, *Barbara Ward Jackson And The Postwar World: The Ethic Of Interdependence* (PhD Thesis, Government and Foreign Affairs, University of Virginia, 1985), 357–70.

80 Ward, "Moral Challenge of Communism," 38.

81 Ibid.

82 Ward, *Policy for the West*, 270.

83 Ward, *The Moral Challenge of Communism,*" 40.

84 Ward, *The Interplay of East and West*, 137.

85 Ward, *The Rich Nations and the Poor Nations* (Toronto: Canadian Broadcasting Corporation, 1965), 96.

86 Ibid., 96–7.

87 Ward, *India and the West*, (New York: Norton, 1961), 238–9.

88 Ibid., 238.

89 Ward, *The Home of Man* (Toronto: McClelland and Stewart, 1976), 126.

90 Ibid.., 140.

91 Ibid., 122.

92 Ibid., 130.

93 Ward, *India and the West*, 46.

94 Ward, *The Rich Nations and the Poor Nations*, 90.

95 Ward, *India and the West*, 239.

96 Ward, *The Home of Man*, 263.

97 Ward, *India and the West*, 239.

98 Ward, *The Rich Nations and the Poor Nations*, 93.

99 Ward, *The Lopsided World* (New York: Norton, 1968), 98.

100 Ward, *The International Share-out* (London: Thomas Nelson, 1938), 166–7.

101 Ibid., 167.

102 Ibid.

103 Letter to the Editor, "Foundations of Peace, A Christian Basis. Agreement Among the Churches," *The Times*, 21 December 1940.

104 See Craig N. Murphy, *The United Nations Development Programme. A Better Way?* (Cambridge: Cambridge University Press, 2006), chs 5, 6.

105 Barbara Ward, "The Decade of Development – A Study in Frustration," in Barbara Ward and P.T. Bauer, *Two Views on Aid to Developing Countries* (London: Institute of Economic Affairs, 1966), 20–1.

106 Ward, *Poverty and Politics*, 18.

107 Ibid., 20.

108 Ward, *Spaceship Earth*, 126.

109 Quoted in Murphy, *The United Nations Development Programme*, 166.

110 Shirley Williams to Barbara Ward, 21 October 1975, Box 3 folder 3, Correspondence with Shirley Williams, Barbara Ward Papers.

111 Ward to Shirley Williams, 30 December 1976, Box 3, folder 3, Barbara Ward Papers.

112 Ward, "The Quest for Christian Unity," 126.

113 Ward, "The Breakthrough to Modernity," in *Education in World Perspective: The International Conference on World Educational Problems*, ed. Emmet John Hughes (New York: Harper and Row, 1962), 132–3.

114 See *The Churches Survey Their Task: The Report of the Conference at Oxford, July, 1937, on Church, Community and State* (London: George Allen and Unwin, 1937), 117. For the Reverend V.A. Demant, see also V.A. Demant, "Respect for the Earth, or Fulfilment of Agronomic Responsibilities" in *Malvern, 1941: The Life of the Church and the Order of Society* (London: Longmans, Green and Co., 1941), 145. For Archbishop William Temple, see William Temple, *Christianity and Social Order* (London: Shepheard-Walwyn, reprinted 1987 from 1942 publication), Appendix: A Suggested Programme, 111–12.

115 Ward, *Faith and Freedom*, 50–1.

116 Ward and René Dubos, *Only One Earth: The Care and Maintenance of a Small Planet* (New York: W.W. Norton, 1972), 219.

117 Ibid., 217.

118 Ward, *A New Creation? Reflections on the Environmental Issue* (Vatican City: Pontifical Commission on Justice and Peace, 1973), 36.

119 Ibid., 56.

120 Ibid., 59.

121 Ibid., 61.

122 Ibid., 66.

123 Ibid., 65.

124 Ward to Archbishop J. Benelli, Secretariat of State, Vatican, 15 April 1975, box 2, folder 39, Barbara Ward Papers.

125 Ward to Cardinal Gantin, Pontifical Commission on Justice and Peace, Vatican, 27 June 1978, box 3, folder 33, Barbara Ward Papers.

126 *Summary of Address by Lady Jackson at Midhurst Catholic Church*, "Women's World Day of Prayer, 7 March 1975," Box 8, Manuscripts, Speeches Series, folder 92, Barbara Ward Papers.

127 Ward, *The Home of Man*, 99.

128 Ward, "The Conserving Society," 5 outlines for programmes, undated, Box 9, folder 37, Barbara Ward Papers.

129 Ward, *The Home of Man*, 294.

130 Gladwin Hill, "Trenchant Ecology Treatise," *New York Times*, 24 April 1976.

131 Ward, *Progress for a Small Planet* (London: Earthscan Publications, 1988), 265.

132 John Kenneth Galbraith, "Our World Can Be Saved," *Washington Post*, 2 September 1979.

133 Ward, *Are Today's Basic Problems Religious?*, 19.

134 Ibid., 20.

135 Ibid., 21.

136 Barbara Ward, *A New History*, (Cape Town: University of Cape Town, 1969), 7.

137 Ward, *Are Today's Basic Problems Religious?*, 56.

138 Ward, "Solutions to the Problems of Development: A Futuristic Outlook," September 1978, for the fiftieth anniversary of the St Francis Xavier University Extension Department. Prepared but not delivered in person due to illness, Malcolm McClelland Papers, MG 53/5/144, University Archives, Angus L. MacDonald Library, St Francis Xavier University, Antigonish, Nova Scotia, Canada.

CONCLUSION AND LEGACY

1 Bowler, *Science for All*, 274.

2 See Carl Sagan, *The Varieties of Scientific Experience: A Personal View of the Search for God*, ed. Ann Dryan (New York: Penguin Press, 2006).

3 See Al Gore, *An Inconvenient Truth: The Planetary Emergency of Global Warming and What We Can Do about It* (New York: Rodale Press, 2006); and *Our Purpose: The Nobel Peace Prize Lecture 2007* (New York: Rodale Press, 2008).

4 C.T. McIntire, *Herbert Butterfield: Historian as Dissenter* (New Haven and London: Yale University Press, 2004), 298–9.

5 Richard Weight, *Patriots*, 6.

6 Ibid., 451.

7 Ibid., 446.

8 See Richard Hoggart, "Adult Education: The Legacy and the Future," *Lecture given to celebrate the 50th Anniversary of the University of Glasgow's Department of Adult and Continuing Education*, 18 October 2001, 4–5.

9 Peter Jenkins, *Mrs. Thatcher's Revolution: The Ending of the Socialist Era* (Cambridge, MA: Harvard University Press, 1988), 66.

10 Eric J. Evans, *Thatcher and Thatcherism* (London and New York: Routledge, second edition, 1997), 144–5.

11 Richard Dawkins, *The God Delusion* (Boston: Houghton Mifflin, 2006), 46–54.

12 Can be found on BBC website, "UK among most secular nations," 26 February 2004. Ten thousand people questioned in a poll by research company ICM for BBC programme, *What the World Thinks of God.*

13 Bowler, *Science for All*, 50.
14 Chris Hedges, *I Don't Believe in Atheists* (New York: Free Press, 2008), 53.
15 Dawkins, *The God Delusion*, 262–3.
16 Sam Harris, *The Moral Landscape: How Science Can Determine Human Values* (New York: Free Press, 2010), ch. 1, "Moral Truth," 27–51.
17 Ibid., 207, n. 12.
18 Ibid., 135.
19 Ibid., 10.
20 See Joan Roughgarden, *The Genial Gene: Deconstructing Darwinian Selfishness* (Berkeley: University of California Press, 2009).
21 See Lionel Tiger and Michael McGuire, *God's Brain* (Amherst: Prometheus Books, 2010).
22 The Pope made his comments in his opening address to the Queen at the Holyroodhouse, Edinburgh, 16 September 2010. See also John Plunkett, "BBC should have a religion editor, says Church of England," *The Guardian* 23 August 2010, and Alan Wilson, "The Media's Trouble with Religion," *The Guardian* 19 January 2010.

Sources

ARCHIVAL MATERIALS

The Julian Huxley papers are located at the Woodson Research Centre, Fondren Library of Rice University in Houston, Texas. The collection is 91 linear feet, and about one third is correspondence while the remaining materials are diaries, log books, professional records, and drafts of works. There is also a Julian Huxley file in the archives of the Family Planning Association at the Wellcome Library in London. The Bertrand Russell Collection at the Bertrand Russell Research Centre, Mills Memorial Library of McMaster University in Hamilton, Ontario contains about 1,008 boxes, including about 100,000 letters. The Centre has undertaken a massive program to publish the *Collected Papers of Bertrand Russell* producing about twenty volumes to date. A small amount of correspondence can be found at the Houghton Library of Harvard University. The papers of Canon John Collins at the Lambeth Palace Library, London contain some items pertaining to Russell's peace advocacy. The Malcolm Muggeridge Collection at the Buswell Memorial Library Archives and Special Collections section of Wheaton College is very extensive and includes correspondence, journals, speeches, manuscript drafts, scripts, and reviews by Muggeridge. The Barbara Ward papers are found at the Georgetown University Library in Washington, DC. They contain correspondence, manuscripts, and journals. There is also important information in the Sword of the Spirit material within the Cardinal Hinsley Papers held at the Westminster Diocesan Archives, London. The BBC Written Archives at Caversham Park in Reading contains important files pertaining to the broadcasting activities of these figures – useful when not located in their own papers. Periodical sources, including articles and reviews by or about these figures, were also researched. Copies and clippings were usually found within the paper collections of these figures, supplemented by reading issues of leading journals and newspapers, especially for the long sixties, such as the *New Statesman*, *The Listener*, *The Tablet*, *The Dublin Review*, *The Economist*, *The Observer*, and *The Times*. Lastly, one paper by Barbara Ward and one by Malcolm Muggeridge prepared for separate visits to St Francis Xavier University in Antigonish, Nova Scotia were found in the university archives located in the Angus L. MacDonald Library on campus.

SELECTED CHRONOLOGICAL LISTS OF IMPORTANT BOOKS BY JULIAN HUXLEY, BERTRAND RUSSELL, MALCOLM MUGGERIDGE, AND BARBARA WARD

Julian Huxley

The Individual in the Animal Kingdom. Cambridge: Cambridge University Press, 1912.

Essays of a Biologist. London: Chatto and Windus, 1923.

Essays in Popular Science. London: Chatto and Windus, 1926.

Religion without Revelation. London: Ernest Benn, 1927. Revised Edition, New York: New American Library, 1957.

With H.G. Wells and G.P. Wells. *The Science of Life*. Garden City: Doubleday, Doran, 1931. See also below in Selected Bibliography.

What Dare I Think? The Challenge of Modern Science to Human Action and Belief. London: Chatto and Windus, 1931.

Africa View. New York: Harper and Brothers, 1931.

Scientific Research and Social Needs. London: Watts, 1934.

If I Were Dictator. London: Methuen, 1934.

With A.C. Haddon. *We Europeans: A Survey of "Racial" Problems*. London: Cape, 1936.

Race in Europe. Oxford: Claredon Press, 1939.

Man Stands Alone. New York: Harper, 1941.

Democracy Marches. New York: Harper and Brothers, 1941.

Evolution: The Modern Synthesis. London: Allen and Unwin, 1942.

On Living in a Revolution. London: Chatto and Windus, 1944.

Evolution in Action. New York: Harper and Row, 1953.

Essays of a Humanist. London: Chatto and Windus, 1964.

Memories. 2 volumes. London: George Allen and Unwin, 1970 and 1973.

Bertrand Russell

The Principles of Mathematics. Cambridge: Cambridge University Press, 1903.

Philosophical Essays. London: Longmans, Green, 1910.

With Alfred North Whitehead. *Principia Mathematica*. 3 volumes. Cambridge: Cambridge University Press, 1910–1913.

Principles of Social Reconstruction. London: George Allen and Unwin, 1916.

Mysticism and Logic and Other Essays. London: Longmans, Green, 1918.

The ABC of Atoms. London: Kegan Paul, 1923.

The ABC of Relativity. London: Kegan Paul, 1925.

On Education, Especially in Early Childhood. London: George Allen and Unwin, 1926.

Why I Am Not a Christian. London: Watts, 1927. Also in *Why I Am Not a Christian and Other Essays on Religion and Related Subjects*, edited by Paul Edwards. London: George Allen and Unwin, 1957.

Marriage and Morals. London: George Allen and Unwin, 1929.

The Conquest of Happiness. London: George Allen and Unwin, 1930.

The Scientific Outlook. London: George Allen and Unwin, 1931.

Education and Social Order. London: George Allen and Unwin, 1932.

Freedom and Organization, 1814–1914. London: George Allen and Unwin, 1934.

Religion and Science. London: Thornton Butterworth, 1935.

Power: A New Social Analysis. London: George Allen and Unwin, 1938.

A History of Western Philosophy and Its Connection with Political and Social Circumstances from the Earliest Times to the Present Day. New York: Simon and Schuster, 1945.

Authority and the Individual. London: George Allen and Unwin, 1949.

New Hopes for a Changing World. London: George Allen and Unwin, 1951.

Human Society in Ethics and Politics. London: George Allen and Unwin, 1954.

Common Sense and Nuclear Warfare. London: George Allen and Unwin, 1959.

My Philosophical Development. George Allen and Unwin, 1959.

Has Man a Future? London: George Allen and Unwin, 1961.

War Crimes in Vietnam. London: George Allen and Unwin, 1967.

The Autobiography of Bertrand Russell. 3 volumes. London: George Allen and Unwin, 1967–69.

Malcolm Muggeridge

Winter in Moscow. London: Eyre and Spottiswoode, 1934.

The Earnest Atheist: A Study of Samuel Butler. London: Eyre and Spottiswoode, 1936.

In A Valley of This Restless Mind. London: Routledge and Son, 1938. Reissued by London: Collins, 1978.

The Thirties, 1930–1940 in Great Britain. London: H. Hamilton, 1940.

Tread Softly for You Tread in My Jokes. London: Collins, 1966.

Jesus Rediscovered. London: Collins, 1969.

Something Beautiful for God: Mother Teresa of Calcutta. London: Collins, 1971.

With Alec Vidler. *Paul: Envoy Extraordinary*. London: Collins, 1972.

Chronicles of Wasted Time I: The Green Stick. London: Collins, 1972.

Chronicles of Wasted Time II: The Infernal Grove. London: Collins, 1975.

Jesus, the Man Who Lives. London: Collins, 1975.

Christ and the Media. Grand Rapids: W.B. Eerdmans, 1976.

A Third Testament. New York: Little Brown, 1976. Second edition and new foreword by Malcolm Muggeridge, Farmington: Plough Publishing House, 1983.

Like It Was: The Diaries of Malcolm Muggeridge. Selected and edited by John Bright-Holmes. London: Collins, 1981.

Conversion: A Spiritual Journey. London: Collins, 1988.

Barbara Ward

The International Share-out. London: T. Nelson, 1938.

The Defence of the West. London: Sands, Sword of the Spirit, 1942.

The West at Bay. London: Allen and Unwin, 1948.

Policy for the West. London: Allen and Unwin, 1951.

Faith and Freedom. New York: Norton, 1954.

The Interplay of East and West: Elements of Contrast and Co-operation. London: Allen and Unwin, 1957.

My Brother's Keeper. London: Sword of the Spirit, 1959.

Five Ideas that Change the World. New York: Published for the University College of Ghana by Norton, 1959.

The Rich Nations and the Poor Nations. Toronto: Canadian Broadcasting Corporation, 1961. New York: Norton, New edition, 1962.

India and the West. London: H. Hamilton, 1961. New York: Norton, Revised edition, 1964.

It Can Be Done: An Approach to World Poverty. London: Geoffrey
  Chapman, 1965.
Nationalism and Ideology. New York: Norton, 1966.
Spaceship Earth. New York: Columbia University Press, 1966.
The Lopsided World. New York: Norton, 1968.
With René Dubos. *Only One Earth: The Care and Maintenance of a Small
  Planet*. Harmondsworth: Penguin, 1972.
With Maurice F. Strong. *Who Speaks for Earth?* New York: Norton,
  1973.
A New Creation? Reflections on the Environmental Issue. Vatican City:
  Pontifical Commission on Justice and Peace, 1973.
The Home of Man. New York: Norton, 1976.
Progress for a Small Planet. New York: Norton, 1979.

SELECTED BIBLIOGRAPHY

Adams, Pauline. *Somerville for Women: An Oxford College, 1879–1993*.
  New York: Oxford University Press, 1996.
Addison, Paul. *The Road to 1945: British Politics and the Second World
  War*. London: Cape, 1975.
Allen, Peter. "Mark Rutherford: The Anatomy of a Failure." In *The View
  from the Pulpit: Victorian Ministers and Society*, edited by Paul T.
  Phillips, 143–59. Toronto: Macmillan of Canada, 1978.
Allitt, Patrick. *Catholic Converts: British and American Intellectuals Turn
  to Rome*. Ithaca and London: Cornell University Press, 1997.
Amberley, John Russell, Viscount. *An Analysis of Religious Belief*. New
  York: Bennett, 1877.
Annan, Noel. *Leslie Stephen: The Godless Victorian*. London: Werdenfeld
  and Nicolson, 1984.
– *Our Age: English Intellectuals between the Wars – A Group Portrait*.
  New York: Random House, 1990.
Arnstein, Water L. *The Bradlaugh Case: Atheism, Sex, and Politics among
  the Late Victorians*. Columbia: University of Missouri Press, 1983.
Ayer, A.J. *Bertrand Russell*. Chicago and London: University of Chicago
  Press, 1972.
Bachelor, John. *H.G. Wells*. Cambridge: Cambridge University Press, 1984.
Bailkin, Jordanna. *The Culture of Property: The Crisis of Liberalism in
  Modern Britain*. Chicago: University of Chicago Press, 2004.
Baker, J.R. *Julian Huxley, Scientist and World Citizen 1887 to 1975: A
  Biographical Memoir*. Paris: UNESCO, 1978.

Barkan, Elazar. *The Retreat of Scientific Racism: Changing Concepts of Race in Britain and the United States between the World Wars.* New York: Cambridge University Press, 1992.

Barker, Eileen, James A. Beckford and Karel Dobbelaere, eds. *Secularization, Rationalism and Sectarianism: Essays in Honour of Bryan R. Wilson.* Oxford: Clarendon Press, 1993.

Benson, John. *Affluence and Authority: A Social History of Twentieth-Century Britain.* London: Hodder Arnold, 2005.

Berg, Maxine. "The First Women Economic Historians." *Economic History Review* 45, no. 2 (May 1992): 308–29.

– *A Woman in History, Eileen Power, 1889–1940.* Cambridge: Cambridge University Press, 1996.

Berlinski, David. *The Devil's Delusion: Atheism and its Scientific Pretensions.* New York: Crown Forum, 2008.

Berstein, George L. *The Myth of Decline: The Rise of Britain since 1945.* London: Pimlico, 2004.

Bevir, Mark and Frank Trentmann. *Marets in Historical Contexts: Ideas and Politics in the Modern World.* Cambridge: Cambridge University Press, 2004.

Binde, Per. "Nature in Roman Catholic Tradition." *Anthropological Quarterly* 74, no. 1 (January 2001): 15–27.

Bingham, Adrian. *Family Newspapers? Sex, Private Life, and the British Popular Press, 1918–1978.* Oxford and New York: Oxford University Press, 2009.

Black, Lawrence. *The Political Culture of the Left in Affluent Britain, 1951–64.* Houndmills, Basingstoke: Palgrave Macmillan, 2003.

Bowler, Peter J. *Evolution: The History of an Idea.* Berkeley: University of California Press, 1984.

– *The Invention of Progress: The Victorians and the Past.* Oxford: Blackwell, 1989.

– *Reconciling Science and Religion: The Debate in Early Twentieth-Century Britain.* Chicago: University of Chicago Press, 2001.

– *Science for All: The Popularization of Science in Early Twentieth-Century Britain.* Chicago: University of Chicago Press, 2009.

Briggs, Asa. *The BBC: The First Fifty Years.* Oxford: Oxford University Press, 1985.

– *The History of Broadcasting in the United Kingdom.* 5 volumes. London and New York: Oxford University Press, 1961–1995.

Brocklehurst, Helen and Robert Phillips, eds. *History, Nationhood and the Question of Britain.* New York: Palgrave Macmillan, 2004.

Bronowski, Jacob. *The Ascent of Man*. London: British Broadcasting Corporation, 1973.

Brooke, Stephen. *Labour's War: The Labour Party during the Second World War*. Oxford: Clarendon Press, 1992.

Brown, Callum G. *The Death of Christian Britain: Understanding Secularisation, 1800–2000*. Second edition. London: Routledge, 2009.

Budd, Susan. *Varieties of Unbelief: Atheists and Agnostics in English Society, 1850–1960*. London: Heinemann, 1977.

Burrow, John. *Evolution and Society: A Study in Victorian Social Theory*. Cambridge: Cambridge University Press, 1966.

Burk, Kathleen. *The Troublemaker: The Life and History of A.J.P. Taylor*. New Haven and London: Yale University Press, 2000.

Butler, Samuel. *Ernest Pontifex, or, the Way of all Flesh*. London: Methuen, 1965.

Caine, Barbara. *English Feminism, 1780–1980*. New York: Oxford University Press, 1997.

Calder, Angus. *The People's War: Britain 1939–45*. London: Cape, 1969.

Callahan, Daniel, ed. *The Secular City Debate*. New York: The Macmillan Co., 1966.

Chadwick, Owen. *The Victorian Church*. Parts 1 and 2. London: A and C Black, 1966–70.

– *The Secularization of the European Mind in the Nineteenth Century*. Cambridge: Cambridge University Press, 1975.

Chambers, Robert J. *Vestiges of the Natural History of Creation*. London: John Churchill, 1844; fifth edition, 1846, eleventh edition, 1860.

Chapman, Alister. "Secularisation and the Ministry of John R.W. Stott at All Souls, Langham Place, 1950–1970." *Journal of Ecclesiastical History* 56, no. 3 (July 2007): 496–513.

Childs, David. *Britain since 1945: A Political History*. London and New York: Routledge, fifth edition, 2001.

Clark, C.H. Douglas. *The Scientist and the Supernatural: A Systematic Examination of the Relation between Christianity and Humanism, with Special Reference to the work Religion without Revelation, by J.S. Huxley and Other Agnostic Writings*. London: Epworth Press, 1966.

Clark, Ronald W. *Sir Julian Huxley, F.R.S.* London: Phoenix House, 1960.

– *The Huxleys*. London: Heinemann, 1968.

– *The Life of Bertrand Russell*. London: J. Cape, 1975.

Clarke, Peter. *Hope and Glory: Britain 1900–2000*. London: Penguin, second edition, 2004.

Cocks, Joan. *Passion and Paradox: Intellectuals Confront the National Question*. Princeton: Princeton University Press, 2002.

Cockshut, A.O.J. *The Unbelievers: English Agnostic Thought, 1840–1890*. London: Collins, 1964.

Collini, Stefan. *Absent Minds: Intellectuals in Britain*. Oxford: Oxford University Press, 2006.

Collini, Stefan, Richard Whatmore, and Brian Young, eds. *History, Religion and Culture: British Intellectual History, 1750–1950*. Cambridge: Cambridge University Press, 2000.

Collini, Stefan. *Public Moralists: Political Thought and Intellectual Life in Britain, 1850–1930*. Oxford: Clarendon Press, 1991.

Collins, Francis. *The Language of God: A Scientist Presents Evidence for Belief*. New York: Free Press, 2006.

Collins, L. John. *A Theology of Christian Action: The Lichfield Cathedral Divinity Lectures, 1948*. London: Hodder and Stoughton, 1949.

Cornwell, John. *Newman's Unquiet Grave: The Reluctant Saint*. London: Continuum, 2010.

Cowling, Maurice. *Religion and Public Doctrine in Modern England*. 3 volumes. Cambridge: Cambridge University Press, 1980–2001.

Cox, Harvey. *The Secular City: Secularization and Urbanization in Theological Perspective*. New York: Macmillan, 1965.

Cox, Jeffrey. *The English Churches in a Secular Society: Lambeth, 1870–1930*. Oxford and New York: Oxford University Press, 1982.

– "Master Narratives of Long-term Religious Change." In *The Decline of Christendom in Western Europe, 1750–2000*, edited by Hugh McLeod and Werner Ustof, 201–17. Cambridge: Cambridge University Press, 2003.

Currie, Robert, Alan D. Gilbert, and Lee S. Horsley. *Churches and Churchgoers: Patterns of Church Growth in the British Isles since 1700*. Oxford: Clarendon Press, 1977.

Dacey, Austin. *The Secular Conscience: Why Belief Belongs in Public Life*. Amherst: Prometheus Books, 2008.

Darwin, Charles Robert. *On the Origin of Species by Means of Natural Selection*. Cambridge: Harvard University Press, 1859, reprinted 1964.

– *The Descent of Man and Selection in Relation to Sex*. 2 volumes. London: John Murray, 1871, second edition, revised, 1885.

Davies, Alistair and Alan Sinfield, eds. *British Culture of the Postwar: An Introduction to Literature and Society 1945–1999*. London and New York: Routledge, 2000.

Davies, Christine. *Permissive Britain: Social Change in the Sixties and Seventies*. London: Pitman, 1975.

Davies, Norman. "The Decomposing of Britain." *Times Literary Supplement* (6 October 2000): 15–16.

Davis, R.W. and R.J. Helmstadter, eds. *Religion and Irreligon in Victorian Society: Essays in Honor of R.K. Webb*. London: Routledge, 1991.

Dawkins, Richard. *The Selfish Gene*. New York: Oxford University Press, 1976.

– *The God Delusion*. Boston: Houghton Mifflin, 2006.

Dawson, Christopher. *Progress and Religion: An Historical Enquiry*. London: Sheed and Ward, 1929.

– *Religion and the Rise of Western Culture*. London: Sheed and Ward, 1950.

Donnelly, Mark. *Sixties Britain: Culture, Society and Politics*. Harlow: Pearson Longman, 2005.

Donnery, Wendy. *The Liberal Self: John Stuart Mill's Moral and Political Philosophy*. Ithaca: Cornell University Press, 1991.

Dronamraju, Krishna R. *If I Am To Be Remembered: The Life and Work of Julian Huxley with Selected Correspondence*. Singapore and River Edge: World Scientific Publishing Co., 1993.

Durant, John R., ed. *Darwinism and Divinity: Essays on Evolution and Religious Belief*. Oxford: Basil Blackwell, 1985.

– "Evolution, Ideology and Worldview: Darwinian Religion in the Twentieth Century." In *History, Humanity and Evolution: Essays for John C. Greene*, edited by James R. Moore, 355–74. Cambridge: Cambridge University Press, 1989.

Eagleton, Terry. *Reason, Faith and Revolution: Reflections on the God Debate*. New Haven and London: Yale University Press, 2009.

Edwards, David L., ed. *The Honest to God Debate: Some Reactions to the Book "Honest to God."* London: SCM Press, 1963.

– *Leaders of the Church of England 1828–1944*. London: Oxford University Press, 1971.

Edwards, Ruth Dudley. *The Pursuit of Reason: The Economist 1843–1993*. London: Harnish Hamilton, 1993.

Eisenbuch, Eldon J., ed. *Mill and the Moral Character of Liberalism*. University Park: Pennsylvania State University Press, 1998.

Ellis, Ieuan. *Seven against Christ: A Study of "Essays and Reviews."* Lerden: E. J. Brill, 1980.

Esty, Jed. *A Shrinking Island: Modernism and National Culture in England*. Princeton: Princeton University Press, 2004.

Evans, Eric J. *Thatcher and Thatcherism*. London and New York: Routledge, second edition, 1997.

Fichman, Martin. *An Elusive Victorian: The Evolution of Alfred Russel Wallace*. Chicago: University of Chicago Press, 2004.

Frazer, J.G. *The Golden Bough: A Study in Magic and Religion*. London: Macmillan, second edition,1900.

Freeden, Michael. "Eugenics and Progressive Thought: A Study in Ideological Affinity." *Historical Journal* 22, no. 3 (September 1979), 645–71.

Frye, Northrop. *The Great Code: The Bible and Literature*. New York: Harcourt, Brace Jovanovich, 1981.

Fyvel, T.R. *Intellectuals Today: Problems in a Changing Society*. London: Chatto and Windus, 1968.

Galton, Francis. *Inquiries into Human Faculty and Its Development*. London: Dent, 1907.

Gilbert, Alan D. *Religion and Society in Industrial England: Church, Chapel and Social Change 1740–1914*. London: Longman, 1976.

– *The Making of Post-Christian Britain: A History of the Secularization of Modern Society*. London: Longman, 1980.

Gladish, Kenneth LeRoy. *Barbara Ward Jackson and the Postwar World: The Ethic of Interdependence*. PhD Thesis, Government and Foreign Affairs, University of Virginia, 1985.

Gore, Al. *An Inconvenient Truth: The Planetary Emergency of Global Warming and What We Can Do about It*. New York: Rodale Press, 2006.

Gorham, Deborah. *Vera Brittain: A Feminist Line*. Oxford: Blackwell Publishers, 1996.

Gosse, Edmund. *Father and Son: A Study of Two Temperaments*. London: Heinemann, 1907.

Graves, Robert and Alan Hodge. *The Long Week-End: A Social History of Great Britain 1918–1939*. New York: W. W. Norton and Co., 1940.

Grayling, A.C. *Russell*. Oxford: Oxford University Press, 1986.

Green, E.H.H. and D.M. Tanner, eds. *The Strange Survival of Liberal England*. Cambridge: Cambridge University Press, 2007.

Green, S.J.D. *Religion in the Age of Decline: Organisation and Experience in Industrial Yorkshire 1870–1920*. Cambridge: Cambridge University Press, 1996.

Greene, John C. "From Huxley to Huxley: Transformation in the Darwinian Credo." In *Science, Ideology, and World View: Essays in the History of Evolutionary Ideas*, 158–93. Berkeley, University of California Press, 1981.

Haldane, J.B.S. *Science and Life: Essays of a Rationalist*. London: Pemberton Publishing Co., 1968.

Harris, John. "Political Thought and the Welfare State 1870–1940: An Intellectual Framework for British Social Policy." *Past and Present* 135, no. 1 (1992): 116–41.

– *Enhancing Evolution: The Ethical Case for Making People Better.* Princeton: Princeton University Press, 2007.

Harris, Sam. *The End of Faith: Religion, Terror, and the Future of Reason.* New York: W.W. Norton and Co., 2004.

– *The Moral Landscape: How Science Can Determine Human Values.* New York: Free Press, 2010.

Harrison, Frederic. *The Positive Evolution of Religion: Its Moral and Social Reaction.* New York: Putnam and Sons, 1913.

Hastings, Adrian. *A History of English Christianity 1920–1985.* London: Fount Paperbacks, 1987.

– *The Construction of Nationhood: Ethnicity, Religion and Nationalism.* Cambridge: Cambridge University Press, 1997.

Hedges, Chris. *I Don't Believe in Atheists.* New York: Free Press, 2008.

Helmstadter, Richard, ed. *Freedom and Religion in the Nineteenth Century.* Stanford: Stanford University Press, 1997.

Helmstadter, Richard J. and Paul T. Phillips, eds. *Religion in Victorian Society: A Sourcebook of Documents.* Lanham and London: University Press of America, 1985.

Helmstadter, Richard J. and Bernard Lightman, eds. *Victorian Faith in Crisis: Essays on Continuity and Change in Nineteenth-Century Religious Belief.* Stanford: Stanford University Press, 1990.

Hewison, Robert. *In Anger: Culture in the Cold War 1945–60.* London: Weidenfeld and Nicolson, 1981.

Heyck, Thomas W. *The Transformation of Intellectual Life in Victorian England.* London: Croom Helm, 1982.

– "Myths and Meanings of Intellectuals in Twentieth century British National Identity." *Journal of British Studies* 37, no. 2 (April 1998): 192–221.

Hilliard, Christopher. *To Exercise Our Talents: The Democratization of Writing in Britain.* Cambridge: Harvard Historical Studies, Harvard University Press, 2006.

Himmelfarb, Gertrude. *Darwin and the Darwinian Revolution.* New York: Norton, 1959.

– *The De-Moralization of Society: From Victorian Virtues to Modern Values.* New York: Alfred A. Knopf, 1995.

Hitchens, Christopher. *God is Not Great: How Religion Poisons Everything.* Toronto: McClelland and Stewart, 2007.

Hoggart, Richard. *The Uses of Literacy: Aspects of Working-class Life with Special Reference to Publications and Entertainments*. Harmondsworth: Penguin Books, 1958.

Hoover, Kenneth R. "The Rise of Conservative Capitalism: Ideological Tensions within the Reagan and Thatcher Governments." *Comparative Studies in Society and History* 29, no. 2 (April 1987): 245–68.

Hughes, Hugh Price. *Ethical Christianity: A Series of Sermons*. London: Sampson Low, Marston, 1892.

Hunter, Ian. *Malcolm Muggeridge: A Life*. London: Collins, 1980.

– "Seeing Thru' the Eye: The Prophetic Legacy of Malcolm Muggeridge." *Touchstone: A Journal of Mere Christianity* 16, no. 10 (December 2003): 22–8.

Huxley, Aldous. *Brave New World*. London: Chatto and Windus, 1932.

Huxley, T.H. and Julian Huxley. *Evolution and Ethics, 1893–1943*. London: Pilot Press, 1947.

Huxley, T.H. *Man's Place in Nature*. London: Williams and Norgate, 1863.

Inglis, K.S. *Churches and the Working Classes in Victorian England*. London: Routledge and Kegan Paul, 1963.

Ingrams, Richard. *Muggeridge: The Biography*. New York: Harper Collins, 1995.

Ironside, Philip. *The Social and Political Thought of Bertrand Russell: The Development of an Aristocratic Liberalism*. New York: Cambridge University Press, 1996.

James, Eric. *A Life of Bishop John A.T. Robinson: Scholar, Pastor, Prophet*. London: William Collins Sons and Co., 1987.

Jenkins, Peter. *Mrs Thatcher's Revolution: The Ending of the Socialist Era*. Cambridge: Harvard University Press, 1988.

Joad, C.E.M. *The Recovery of Belief: A Restatement of Christian Philosophy*. London: Faber and Faber, 1952.

– *Returning to the Church*. Worthing: Churchman, 1984.

Jones, Greta. *Social Darwinism and English Thought: The Interaction between Biological and Social Theory*. Brighton: Harvester Press, 1980.

Kent, John. "The Victorian Resistance: Comments on Religious Life and Culture, 1840–80." *Victorian Studies* 12, no. 2 (December 1968): 145–54.

– *William Temple: Church, State and Society in Britain, 1880–1950*. Cambridge: Cambridge University Press, 1992.

Knight, Margaret, ed. *Humanist Anthology: From Confucius to Bertrand Russell*. London: Barrie and Rockliff, 1961.

Kumar, Krishan. *The Making of English National Identity*. Cambridge: Cambridge University Press, 2003.

Larsen, Timothy. *Crisis of Doubt: Honest Faith in Nineteenth-Century England*. Oxford: Oxford University Press, 2006.

Lawrence, D.H. *Lady Chatterley's Lover*. Harmondsworth: Penguin Classics, fiftieth anniversary edition, 2010.

Le Mathieu, D.L. *A Culture for Democracy: Mass Communication and the Cultivated Mind in Britain between the Wars*. Oxford: Clarendon Press, 1988.

Levy, Leonard W. *Blasphemy: Verbal Offense against the Sacred, From Moses to Salman Rushdie*. New York: Alfred A. Knopf, 1993.

Lewes, George Henry. *The History of Philosophy from Thales to Comte*. London: Longmans, Green, third edition, 2 volumes, 1867.

Lewis, C.S. *Mere Christianity*. San Francisco: Harper Collins, revised edition, 2001.

Lightman, Bernard. *The Origins of Agnosticism: Victorian Unbelief and the Limits of Knowledge*. Baltimore: Johns Hopkins University Press, 1987.

– *Victorian Popularizers of Science: Designing Nature for New Audiences*. Chicago: University of Chicago Press, 2007.

Lloyd, Roger. *The Church of England 1900–1965*. London: SCM Press, 1966.

Lloyd, T.O. *Empire, Welfare State, Europe: History of the United Kingdom, 1906–2001*. Oxford: Oxford University Press, fifth edition, 2002.

Machin, G.I.T. *Churches and Social Issues in Twentieth-Century Britain*. Oxford: Clarendon Press, 1998.

MacKillop, I.D. *The British Ethical Societies*. Cambridge: Cambridge University Press, 1986.

MacLeod, Roy. *The "Creed of Science" in Victorian England*. Aldershot: Ashgate Variorum, 2000.

Malvern, 1941: The Life of the Church and the Order of Society being the Proceedings of the Archbishop of York's Conference. London: Longmans, Green and Co., 1941.

Manwaring, Randle. *From Controversy to Coexistence: Evangelicals in the Church of England, 1914–1980*. Cambridge: Cambridge University Press, 1985.

Martin, David. *The Religious and the Secular: Studies in Secularization*. London: Routledge and Kegan Paul, 1969.

Marwick, Arthur. *Clifford Allen: The Open Conspirator*. Edinburgh and London: Oliver and Boyd, 1964.

– "Middle Opinion in the Thirties: Planning, Progress and Political 'Agreement.'" *English Historical Review* 79, no. 311 (April 1964): 285–98.

– *The Sixties: Cultural Revolution in Britain, France, Italy, and the United States, c. 1958–c. 1974*. Oxford: Oxford University Press, 1998.

Mayr, Ernest and William B. Provine, eds. *The Evolutionary Synthesis: Perspectives on the Unification of Biology*. Cambridge: Harvard University Press, 1980.

McClelland, Charles, E. *The German Historians and England: A Study in Nineteenth-Century Views*. Cambridge: Cambridge University Press, 1971.

McIntire, C.T. *Herbert Butterfield: Historian as Dissenter*. New Haven and London: Yale University Press, 2004.

McLaine, Ian. *Ministry of Morale: Home Front Morale and the Ministry of Information in World War II*. London: George Allen and Unwin, 1979.

McLeod, Hugh. *Class and Religion in the Late Victorian City*. Hamden: Archon Books, 1976.

– *The Religious Crisis of the 1960s*. Oxford: Oxford University Press, 2007.

McLuhan, Marshall. *The Gutenberg Galaxy: The Making of Typographic Man*. Toronto: University of Toronto Press, 1962.

– *Understanding Media: The Extensions of Man*. New York: McGraw-Hill, 1964.

McOuat, Gordon and Mary P. Winsor. "J.B.S. Haldane's Darwinism in its Religious Context." *British Journal for the History of Science* 28, no. 2 (June 1995): 227–31.

Mehta, Ved. *Fly and the Fly-Bottle: Encounters with British Intellectuals*. Boston: Little, Brown and Co., 1962.

Miles, Robert. *Racism*. London: Routledge, 1989.

Miller, David. *On Nationality*. Oxford: Clarendon Press, 1995.

Moloney, Thomas. *Westminster, Whitehall and the Vatican: The Role of Cardinal Hinsley, 1935–43*. Tunbridge Wells: Burns and Oates, 1985.

Monk, Ray. *Bertrand Russell, volume 1, 1872–1921: The Spirit of Solitude*. London: J. Cape, 1996.

– *Bertrand Russell, volume 2, 1921–70: The Ghost of Madness*. London: J. Cape, 2000.

Moore, James R. *The Post-Darwinian Controversies: A Study of the Protestant Struggle to Come to Terms with Darwin in Britain and America, 1870–1900*. Cambridge: Cambridge University Press, 1979.

Moorehead, Caroline. *Bertrand Russell: A Life*. London: Sinclair Stevenson, 1992.

Morley, John. *On Compromise*. London: Chapman and Hall, 1874.

Morris, Jeremy. "The Strange Death of Christian Britain: Another Look at the Secularization Debate." *Historical Journal* 46, no. 4 (2003): 963–70.

Murphy, Craig N. *The United Nations Development Programme: A Better Way?* Cambridge: Cambridge University Press, 2006.

Norman, Edward. *Church and Society in England, 1770–1970*. Oxford: Oxford University Press, 1976.

– *Christianity and the World Order*. Oxford: Oxford University Press, 1979.

– *The Victorian Christian Socialists*. Cambridge: Cambridge University Press, 1987.

Numbers, Ronald L. *The Creationists*. New York: Alfred Knopf, 1992.

Oldham, Joseph Houldsworth. *The Churches Survey their Task: The Report of the Conference at Oxford, July 1937, on Church, Community, and State*. London: G. Allen and Unwin, 1937.

Onfray, Michel. *In Defense of Atheism: A Case against Christianity, Judaism, and Islam*. Toronto: Viking Canada, 2007.

Oppenheim, Janet. *The Other World: Spiritualism and Psychic Research in England, 1850–1914*. Cambridge: Cambridge University Press, 1985.

Oppenheimer, J. Robert. *Science and the Common Understanding*. New York: Simon and Schuster, 1954.

Orwell, George. *Nineteen Eighty-Four: A Novel*. London: Secker and Warburg, 1949.

Parker, Christopher J.W. "The Failure of Liberal Racialism: The Racial Ideas of E.A. Freeman." *Historical Journal* 24, no. 4 (December 1981): 825–46.

– "English Historians and the Opposition to Positivism." *History and Theory* 22 (May 1983): 120–45.

Paul, Diane. "Eugenics and the Left." *Journal of the History of Ideas* 45, no. 4 (October–December 1984): 567–90.

Peel, J.D.Y. *Herbert Spencer: The Evolution of a Sociologist*. London: Heinemann, 1971.

Perkin, Harold. *The Rise of Professional Society: England Since 1880*. London: Routledge, 1989.

Phillips, Justin. *C.S. Lewis at the BBC: Messages of Hope in the Darkness of War*. London: Harper Collins Publishers, 2002.

Phillips, Paul T. *A Kingdom on Earth: Anglo-American Social Christianity, 1880–1940*. University Park: Pennsylvania State University Press, 1996.

– *The Controversialist: An Intellectual Life of Goldwin Smith*. Westport: Praeger, 2002.

– "One World, One Faith: The Quest for Unity in Julian Huxley's Religion of Evolutionary Humanism." *Journal of the History of Ideas* 68, no. 4 (2007): 613–33.

Pigden, Charles R. "Bertrand Russell: Moral Philosopher or Unphilosophical Moralist?" In *The Cambridge Companion to Bertrand Russell*, edited by Nicholas Griffin, 475–504. Cambridge: Cambridge University Press, 2003.

Posner, Richard A. *Public Intellectuals: A Study of Decline*. Cambridge: Harvard University Press, 2003.

Potter, Michael K. *Bertrand Russell's Ethics*. London: Continuum, 2006.

Price, R.G.G. *A History of Punch*. London: Collins, 1957.

Rambo, Lewis R. *Understanding Religious Conversion*. New Haven and London: Yale University Press, 1993.

Ramsey, A.M. *The Resurrection of Christ: A Study of the Event and Its Meaning for the Christian Faith*. London: Fontana Books, revised edition, 1961.

Robbins, Keith. *History, Religion and Identity in Modern Britain*. London: Hambledon Press, 1993.

– *England, Ireland, Scotland and Wales: The Christian Church 1900–2000*. Oxford and New York: Oxford University Press, 2008.

Robinson, John A.T. *Honest to God*. London: SCM Press, 1963.

Robinson, Marilynne. *Absence of Mind: The Dispelling of Inwardness from the Modern Myth of the Self*. New Haven: Yale University Press, 2010.

Roodhouse, Mark. "Lady Chatterley and the Monk: Anglican Radicals and the Lady Chatterley Trial of 1960." *Journal of Ecclesiastical History* 59, no. 3 (2008): 475–500.

Roughgarden, Joan. *The Genial Gene: Deconstructing Darwinian Selfishness*. Berkeley: University of California Press, 2009.

Royle, Edward. *Radical Politics 1790–1900: Religion and Unbelief*. London: Longman, 1971.

– "Freethought: The Religion of Irreligion." In *Nineteenth-Century English Religious Traditions: Retrospect and Prospect*, edited by D.G. Paz. Westport: Greenwood Press, 1995.

Ruse, Michael. *The Darwinian Revolution: Science Red in Tooth and Claw*. Chicago: University of Chicago Press, 1979.

– *Monad to Man: The Concept of Progress in Evolutionary Biology*. Cambridge: Harvard University Press, 1996.

– *Darwin and Design: Does Evolution Have a Purpose?* Cambridge: Harvard University Press, 2003.

Sagan, Carl. *The Varieties of Scientific Experience: A Personal View of the Search for God*. Edited by Ann Druyan. New York: The Penguin Press, 2006.

Schultz, Bart, ed. "The Social and Political Philosophy of Bertrand Russell, Parts I and II." *Philosophy of the Social Sciences* 27, no. 2 (1996): 157–256 and no. 3 (1996): 317–416.

Scott, Christiana. *A Historian and His World: A Life of Christopher Dawson, 1889–1970*. London: Sheed and Ward, 1984.

Secord, James A. *Victorian Sensation: The Extraordinary Publication, Reception, and Secret Authorship of Vestiges of the Natural History of Creation*. Chicago: University of Chicago Press, 2000.

Smith, David C. *H.G. Wells: Desperately Moral*. New Haven: Yale University Press, 1986.

Smith, F.B. "The Atheist Mission, 1840–1900." In *Ideas and Institutions of Victorian Britain*, edited by R. Robson, 205–35. London: G. Bell, 1967.

Smith, Malcolm. *Britain and 1940: History, Myth and Popular Memory*. London and New York: Routledge, 2000.

Smith, Roger. "Biology and Values in Interwar Britain: C.S. Sherrington, Julian Huxley and the Vision of Progress." *Past and Present* 178, no. 1 (February 2003): 210–42.

Smocovitis, Vassiliki Betty. *Unifying Biology: The Evolutionary Synthesis and Evolutionary Biology*. Princeton: Princeton University Press, 1996.

Snow, C.P. *The Two Cultures and a Second Look*. Cambridge: Cambridge University Press, 1969.

Soffer, Reba N. *Ethics and Society in England: The Revolution in Social Sciences, 1870–1914*. Berkeley: University of California Press, 1978.

Somerville, Margaret. *The Ethical Imagination: Journeys of the Human Spirit*. Toronto: House of Anansi Press, 2006.

Soper, Donald. *Calling for Action: An Autobiographical Enquiry*. London: Robson Books, 1984.

Spencer, Herbert. *The Principles of Sociology*. 3 volumes. London: William and Norgate, 1876–96.

Stanley, Matthew. *Practical Mystic: Religion, Science and A.S. Eddington*. Chicago: University of Chicago Press, 2007.

Stapleton, Julia. *Englishness and the Study of Politics: The Social and Political Thought of Ernest Barker*. Cambridge: Cambridge University Press, 1994.

– *Political Intellectuals and Public Identities in Britain since 1850*. Manchester: Manchester University Press, 2001.

Stenger, Victor J. *Quantum Gods: Creation, Chaos, and the Search for Cosmic Consciousness*. Amherst: Prometheus Books, 2009.

Stepan, Nancy. *The Idea of Race in Science: Great Britain, 1800–1960*. London: Macmillan, 1982.

Stevenson, Nick. *Culture, Ideology and Socialism: Raymond Williams and E.P. Thompson*. Aldershot: Avebury Ashgate Publishing Ltd., 1995.

Stott, John R. *Basic Christianity*. London: Inter-Varsity Fellowship, 1958.

Swetlitz, Marc. *Julian Huxley, George Gaylord Simpson and the Idea of Progress in Twentieth-Century Evolutionary Biology*. PhD Thesis, University of Chicago, 1991.

Sykes, Richard. "Popular Religion in Decline: A Study from the Black Country." *Journal of Ecclesiastical History* 56, no. 2 (April 2005): 287–307.

Symondson, Anthony, ed. *The Victorian Crisis of Faith*. London: Society for Promoting Christian Knowledge, 1970.

Taylor, Charles. *A Secular Age*. Cambridge: Belknap Press of Harvard University Press, 2007.

Temple, Frederick, et al. *Essays and Reviews*. London: John W. Parker, 1860.

Temple, William. *Christianity and Social Order*. London: Shepheard-Walwyn, reprint, 1987.

Thompson, E.P. *The Making of the English Working Class*. London: Gollancz, 1963.

– *The Poverty of Theory and Other Essays*. London: Merlin Press, 1978.

Tiger, Lionel and Michael McGuire. *God's Brain*. Amherst: Prometheus Books, 2010.

Tönnies, Ferdinand. *Tönnies: Community and Civil Society*. Edited by Jose Harris. Cambridge Texts in the History of Political Thought. Cambridge: Cambridge University Press, 2001.

Towler, Robert. *The Need for Certainty: A Sociological Study of Conventional Religion*. London: Routledge and Kegan Paul, 1984.

Tucker, Mary Evelyn. "The Ecological Spirituality of Pierre Teilhard de Chardin." *Spiritus: A Journal of Christian Spirituality* 7, no. 1 (Spring 2007): 1–19.

Turner, Frank M. *Between Science and Religion: The Reaction to Scientific Naturalism in Late Victorian England*. New Haven: Yale University Press, 1974.

– *John Henry Newman: The Challenge to Evangelical Religion*. New Haven and London: Yale University Press, 2002.

Viswanathan, Gauri. *Outside the Fold: Conversion, Modernity, and Belief*. Princeton: Princeton University Press, 1998.

Vogeler, Martha S. *Frederic Harrison: The Vocations of a Positivist*. Oxford: Clarendon Press, 1984.

Wallace, Alfred Russel. *The World of Life: A Manifestation of Creative Power, Directive Mind and Ultimate Purpose*. London: Chapman and Hall, 1910.

Ward, Mrs Humphry (Mary Augusta). *Robert Elsmere*. London: Smith, Elder and Co., 1888.

Ward, Paul. *Britishness since 1870*. London: Routledge, 2004.

Ward, W.R. *Religion and Society in England, 1790–1850*. London: Batsford, 1972.

Waters, C. Kenneth and Alvert Van Holden, eds. *Julian Huxley: Biologist and Statesman of Science: Proceedings of a Conference Held at Rice University, 25–27 September 1987*. Houston: Rice University Press, 1992.

Watts, Harold. *Aldous Huxley*. New York: Twayne Publishers, 1969.

Webb, Beatrice. *My Apprenticeship*. London: Longmans, Green, 1926.

Webster, Wendy. *Englishness and Empire, 1939–1965*. New York: Oxford University Press, 2005.

Weight, Richard. *Patriots: National Identity in Britain, 1940–2000*. London: Macmillan, 2002.

Wells, H.G. *The Outline of History: Being a Plain History of Life and Mankind*. 2 volumes. London: Cassell, 1923.

Wells, H.G., Julian S. Huxley, and G.P. Wells. *The Science of Life*. Garden City: Doubleday, Doran, 1931.

Weiner, Martin J. *English Culture and the Decline of the Industrial Spirit, 1850–1980*. Cambridge: Cambridge University Press, 1981.

Welsby, Paul A. *A History of the Church of England, 1945–1980*. London: Oxford University Press, 1984.

Wernick, Andrew. *Auguste Comte and the Religion of Humanity: The Post-Theistic Program of French Social Theory*. Cambridge: Cambridge University Press, 2001.

West, Rebecca. *McLuhan and the Future of Literature*. London: The English Association, 1969.

Wickham, E.R. *Church and People in an Industrial City*. London: Lutterworth Press, 1957.

Wiley, Basil. *More Nineteenth-Century Studies: A Group of Honest Doubters*. London: Chatto and Windus, 1956.

Williams, Raymond. *Culture and Society, 1780–1950*. London: Chatto and Windus, 1958.

– *The Long Revolution*. London: Chatto and Windus, 1961.

– *Television: Technology and Cultural Form*. London: Fontana, 1974.

Williams, S.C. *Religious Belief and Popular Culture in Southwark, 1880–1939.* Oxford: Oxford University Press, 1999.

Willmer, Haddon. "John Collins, Gadfly of the Resurrection." In *Modern Religious Rebels*, edited by Stuart Mews, 245–57. London: Epworth Press, 1993.

Wilson, Byran R. *Religion in Secular Society: A Sociological Comment.* London: Watts, 1966.

Wolfe, Gregory. *Malcolm Muggeridge: A Biography.* Grand Rapids: William B. Erdmans, 1997.

Wolffe, John. *God and Greater Britain: Religion and National Life in Britain and Ireland, 1843–1945.* London: Routledge, 1994.

Wood, Barbara. *E.F. Schumacher: His Life and Thought.* New York: Harper and Row, Publishers, 1984.

Worthen, John. *D.H. Lawrence: The Life of an Outsider.* London: Allen Lane, 2005.

Wright, Robert. *The Evolution of God.* New York: Little, Brown and Company, 2009.

Wright, T.R. *The Religion of Humanity: The Impact of Comtean Positivism on Victorian Britain.* Cambridge: Cambridge University Press, 1986.

Young, Robert M. *Darwin's Metaphor: Nature's Place in Victorian Culture.* Cambridge: Cambridge University Press, 1985.

Index